# KANSAS CITY

# KANSAS CITY

## The Spirit · The People · The Promise

**By Patricia Ewing Pace**

Corporate Profiles by Shifra Stein

PRODUCED IN COOPERATION WITH
THE CHAMBER OF COMMERCE
OF GREATER KANSAS CITY

KANSAS CITY CORPORATION
FOR INDUSTRIAL DEVELOPMENT

KANSAS CITY AREA
ECONOMIC DEVELOPMENT COUNCIL

CONVENTION AND VISITORS BUREAU
OF GREATER KANSAS CITY

WINDSOR PUBLICATIONS, INC.
NORTHRIDGE, CALIFORNIA

*Frontispiece: The Kansas City skyline is silhouetted against a midsummer sunset. Photo by Michael A. Mihalevich*

*Contents page: The central city rises from what was once America's frontier. Photo by Bob Barrett*

Windsor Publications, Inc.—Book Division
Publisher: Hal Silverman
Editorial Director: Teri Davis Greenberg
Design Director: Alexander D'Anca

Staff for *Kansas City: The Spirit, The People, The Promise*
Senior Editor: Pamela Schroeder
Director, Corporate Profiles: Karen Story
Assistant Director, Corporate Profiles: Phyllis Gray
Editor, Corporate Profiles: Judith Hunter
Editorial Assistants: Brenda Berryhill, Kathy M. Brown, Una FitzSimons, Susan
  Kanga, Pat Pittman
Proofreader: Susan J. Muhler
Designer, Layout Artist: Ellen Ifrah
Layout Artist, Corporate Biographies: Mari Catherine Preimesberger
Sales Representatives: Ron Sutton, Roger Johnson, Robert Berry


Library of Congress Cataloging in Publication Data

Pace, Patricia Ewing.
  Kansas City: the spirit, the people, the promise.

  Bibliography: p. 266
  Includes index.
  1. Kansas City (Mo.)—History. 2. Kansas City (Mo.)—Description. 3. Kansas
City (Mo.)—Industries.
  I. Title.
  F474.K257P33    1987         977.8'411         87-10536
  ISBN 0-89781-211-5

# CONTENTS

# PROLOGUE:
# A PROFILE OF
# KANSAS CITY

It's a city of surprises, starting with the name. Visitors are often surprised to discover that Kansas City isn't in Kansas. (There is a Kansas City in Kansas, just across the state line to the west, but it's a relatively new kid on the block—about sixty-five years younger than the fur-trading post that began it all back in 1821.)

The next surprise is the cows—there aren't any. Newcomers from the coasts, conditioned by too many late-night TV movies, sometimes expect to see cattle roaming the streets. People like Joel Garreau, author of *The Nine Nations of North America*, know otherwise. Garreau called Kansas City the capital of that sector of America that works best in the twentieth century, the "Breadbasket." But somehow that romantic image of a prairie home where the buffalo roam just sounds too good to give up—until you see the reality.

We call it "the heart of America." Kansas City, Missouri, is in the Central Standard Time Zone, located very nearly in the geographic center of the continental United States, near the northwestern corner of the Missouri "anvil." Right in the middle of the Temperate Zone, we get a few very hot days in late summer and a few very cold days in the winter. (And what Mark Twain said of Missouri weather is true: "If you don't like it just wait five minutes and it will change.") We also have gorgeous, balmy springs that sometimes spill right over into summer, and breathtakingly beautiful autumns that often linger until late November.

The metropolitan complex we call Greater Kansas City takes in seven counties, two of them in Kansas, and encompasses a land area of 3,341 square miles.

Within those miles you'll find everything from the tobacco fields of Platte County, Missouri, to the millionaires' mansions of Johnson County, Kansas. The northwest corner of Jackson County, bounded on the north by the Missouri River, is where the town began. To the north

The changing seasons lend rich variety to the Kansas City landscape. Oak, ash, maple, poplar, and sumac all burnish to brilliant golds and reds in the fall. Photo by Hank Young/Young Company

Opposite: Children harvest an autumn crop of pumpkins in a Lenexa, Kansas, field. Photo by Roy Inman

Daffodils bursting with spring color provide a striking foreground for this cottage in Liberty, Missouri. Photo by Bob Barrett

Inset, top: Monarch butter-flies on their annual mi-gration to Mexico pause each fall in east Kansas City. Photo by Hank Young/Young Company

Inset, above: The blos-soming crocus, one of the first signs of spring, is al-ways a welcome sight. Photo by William W. Westerman

Inset, above, left: Wild columbine blooms in Swope Park every spring. Photo by Michael A. Mihalevich

The beautiful residential
area of Mission Hills glows
with the vibrant colors
of autumn. Photo by
Michael A. Mihalevich

are Platte and Clay counties. Just west, across the Intercity Viaduct, is
the other Kansas City—in Wyandotte County, Kansas. Cass County,
to the south, and Ray County, in the northeast, complete the seven-county
complex.

There's something here for almost everyone, from the young upwardly
mobile folks restoring fine old historical houses in the center of the city
to the county-dwelling weekend farmer with a couple of horses grazing
in his front yard.

People keep discovering Kansas City. Among the latest are the market
surveyors who know that our town is like Main Street, USA—so typical
of the general American populace that it's one of the most popular national testing grounds for new products and ideas.

With a population of nearly 1.5 million, Greater Kansas City is growing fast (up from just under 900,000 a generation ago) but not too fast.
There's economic stability in the number and diversity of its major industries, a growing labor force of people who still believe in the old-fashioned
work ethic, a surge of construction that's creating more jobs and more
growth, and a quality of life that few cities anywhere can equal.

Kansas City has more miles of boulevards than Paris and more fountains than any other city in the world except Rome. It has more than
5,000 acres of parkland in its 100-plus parks, including the second largest

in the nation, 1,334-acre Swope Park. Swope Park is also home of the Kansas City Zoo and the acclaimed outdoor auditorium, Starlight Theater.

Our city is first nationally in greeting card publishing, thanks to the giant Hallmark company, which has its headquarters and many manufacturing facilities here. It's the center of the largest flour producing area in the nation, with a daily output sufficient to produce eight million loaves of bread. We're first in foreign trade zone space, which alone accounts for about 5,000 jobs and $500 million in investments here over the past ten years.

As you might expect in the middle of the nation's breadbasket, Kansas City is first in hard winter wheat marketing, frozen food storage and distribution, and farm equipment distribution. Our city also ranks first nationally in the occupance and use of underground limestone cavern space for manufacturing, storage and offices, and in the manufacture of aircraft instrument landing systems. Kansas City is near the top of the national list as a rail center, and in the manufacture and assembly of cars and trucks, for grain elevator storage capacity, and as a feeder cattle market.

The Nelson Museum in Kansas City houses one of the world's foremost collections of Oriental art, in addition to numerous world-famous sculptures, paintings, and the Burnap Pottery Collection, consulted by scholars the world over. The Linda Hall Library here is one of the largest technical reference libraries in the nation. The 1985 world champion Kansas City Royals baseball team is a source of pride, along with the Kansas City Chiefs football team and the Comets soccer club. We put our name on the things we love—like the Kansas City Symphony and Kansas City jazz. The Truman Library, Lyric Opera, Missouri Repertory Theater, American Royal Livestock and Horse Show, the Renaissance Festival, Worlds of Fun . . . the list of Kansas City attractions goes on and on.

After all's said and done, though, it's the people that make the city great, and our people are a cross-section of America. There are descendants of the old settler families, and descendants of the waves of immigrants that came later in the nineteenth century. We owe a part of today's agricultural progress to the German Mennonites who came here from Russia with their pockets full of hard red winter wheat seeds. The great Kansas City jazz tradition grew up in our black community. Our railroad tracks were laid by Cantonese and Irish railroad workers. The city has welcomed them all over the years: German artisans, Welsh miners, Swedes, Italians, Scots, Greeks, Serbians, Croatians, and the dozens of other nationalities that make up the city's rich cultural mix.

They're still coming, and in Kansas City, they find the place that feels like home to the heart.

"I love Kansas City," said Vera Fastovskaya-Fyalkova, who emigrated from Moscow a few years ago. "After leaving Russia, we lived in many other cities. Only in Kansas City do strangers smile at you and greet you on the street. The city . . . the people . . . they are so beautiful."

*Childhood memories are made of scenes such as this, as winter weaves its own magic spell in Kansas City's parks and recreational areas. Photo by Bob Barrett*

# THE RIVER CITY'S SPIRITED PAST

## 1

The first local boosters to entice tourists to this area seem to have been a group of Osage Indians. Their stories of the land beyond the Mississippi interested a young explorer, Etienne Veniard de Bourgmont, who was with the French garrison in Detroit.

After a few false starts (he took one unscheduled right turn and ended up in Nebraska) de Bourgmont reached the Missouri River in 1723 and by 1724 was on his way back home to France with a delegation of chiefs from half a dozen Missouri Indian tribes. The Indians and their entourages were enthusiastically received at the court of Louis XV, dining at Fontainebleau, dancing at the opera in Paris, and hunting with the royal party in the Bois de Boulogne. They had a great time and came home with loads of gifts and tall tales about all the wonders they had seen— and smelled. Their perfumed hosts, they reported, smelled just like alligators.

It's hard to imagine that the ground you're standing on in your Guccis was once the frontier of civilization, but it was—and less than 200 years ago, at that. By the time Missouri became a part of the United States through the 1803 Louisiana Purchase, Daniel Morgan Boone had already been here, trapping animals for fur. The following year, Meriwether Lewis, William Clark, and their guide, Sacajawea, came this way. Their campsite, on the bluff facing the mouth of the Kaw River, is now known as Lewis and Clark Point at 8th and Jefferson streets.

The two explorers returned a few years later and established Fort Osage, just east of what is now Kansas City. The garrison was meant to scare the Indians, intimidate the Spaniards still in the area, and keep the British from establishing colonies west of the Mississippi.

By 1819, an Army surveyor named Stephen H. Long had come through on a governmental folly known as the *Western Engineer*. A boat with a prow in the shape of a dragon's head, it flailed the water with its paddle wheel and belched steam and smoke. The *Western Engineer*

*Opposite: Thomas Hart Benton's famous mural, "Wagon Train," captures the robust spirit of the frontier outpost that was once Kansas City when it served as a jumping-off point for pioneers headed west. Courtesy, the River Club. Copy photography by Bruce Mathews*

*Next page: Fort Osage, site of the annual "River Days" festival, showcases its history as the first U.S. outpost in the vast territory obtained by the Louisiana Purchase. Built in 1808 by William Clark of the Lewis and Clark expedition, the fort is a popular destination for history buffs of all ages. Photo by Tony La Tona*

was intended to serve the dual purpose of intimidating the local Indians while providing an efficient means to obtain surveying information.

The boat scared the Indians, and the land scared Surveyor Long, who reported that it was "almost wholly unfit for cultivation and of course, uninhabitable by a people depending upon agriculture for their subsistence." Well, you can't be right all the time.

Missouri became the twenty-fourth state in the Union in 1821, and by that time Francois Chouteau had already dug in. Chouteau, a fur trader from St. Louis, set up a trading post at the bend of the Missouri River in what later became the northeast industrial district. The French weren't as interested in colonizing as they were in commerce, though a small settlement did grow up around the trading post.

In those days, local and regional news kept on the move with nomadic Indians. The adventurer Samuel Becknell, setting out to barter with Comanches, heard about the rich trade in an old Spanish town—Santa Fe de San Francisco—and took his goods southwest to New Mexico. His financial success influenced others to follow his lead, and the Santa Fe Trail was born. The famous trail would spur development in Independence, which thrived on outfitting the westward migrants.

By 1835, a new town was on the plat books, but it wasn't Kansas City. John C. McCoy filed a plat for the town of Westport. The "town" was little more than McCoy's general outfitting store, but he correctly reck-

oned that a travel-easing wagon track direct from the river to the trading post would lure boats to his landing. It did, and Westport soon shouldered aside Independence as the favored trailhead for westbound pioneers.

Westport got a three-year head start on Kansas City, which was still Gabriel Prudhomme's back pasture. When Prudhomme, a French fur trader and farmer, was killed in a brawl in 1838, a group of fourteen investors paid their respects to his widow and bought from the estate a river levee and 257 adjacent acres for $4,220.

The investors called themselves the Kansas Town Company. At a meeting in the riverside shack of a trader known as One-Eyed Ellis, they considered names for the new town. Suggestions ran all the way from Possum Trot to Port Fonda (suggested by a Mr. Fonda), but they finally settled on the tribal name of the indigenous Indians: Kansas. In 1850, the settlement was chartered as the Town of Kansas.

Ever since then, locals have had to spend a little time explaining why Kansas City isn't in Kansas. It's very simple, really. Kansas City started out in Louisiana (remember when Napoleon sold the United States all that land?) and since, at the time, Kansas was in Nebraska (a part of the Nebraska Territory and not yet a state), nobody over there even missed it. And those people who knew about it didn't really care. Stephen Long sounded as though he knew what he was talking about when he declared the land unfit for habitation, and nobody was in a big hurry

*Above: Lake Jacomo's Missouri Town re-creates pioneer life in the 1850s. Photo by Roy Inman*

*Opposite, top: The confluence of the Missouri and Kaw rivers is significant as the site of Kansas City's earliest development. Photo by Roy Inman*

*Opposite, bottom: Native Americans of the Kansas City area celebrate their heritage at regional tribal festivals. Photo by Roy Inman*

17

This re-creation of a pioneer Conestoga wagon stands in Kansas City's historic Westport, the place where weary settlers stopped to rest before heading out on prairie pathways leading west. Photo by Robert Stout

to come out and starve to death on what they called "the great American desert."

Even C.C. Spalding, one of the greatest boosters the area has ever known, painted a fairly alarming picture of his favorite part of the country. Spalding's *Annals of the City of Kansas,* published in 1858 in the hope of luring more travelers westward, details such attractions as "millions of nomadic Indians, millions of buffalo, innumerable carnivorous animals," and a few cholera epidemics.

The more adventurous came anyway, and among them was a young Quaker named Kersey Coates. (Yes, that's his hotel on Broadway.) As he took leave of his father in Pennsylvania, he said confidently that he expected to make a fortune of $50,000.

"Well, Kersey," said his father mildly, "I'll be satisfied if thee makes $10."

Father Coates must have been astounded when, before long, Kersey Coates had not only established the all-brick, multistoried luxury Coates House Hotel and Coates Opera House, but had gone on to lay out the city's first silk-stocking district, Quality Hill, on the bluffs where Lewis and Clark had made camp about fifty years earlier.

It was still hard for the general populace to get excited about Kansas City's future. In 1857 Colonel Thomas H. Swope (who later gave the city Swope Park) purchased a tract of land that quickly became, and has remained, prime downtown business property. But where Swope saw future growth, critics saw folly. A newspaper editorial in nearby Liberty jeered, "The fools are not all dead yet, as one has just paid $250 per acre for a corn field near Kansas City."

The doomsayers were wrong, and the city continued to grow, helped along by the increasing interest in trade and travel westward. By the early 1800s the firm of Russell, Majors & Waddell, with its large fleet of stagecoaches and overland freighters, was moving a steady stream of passengers and freight along the Santa Fe Trail. Until recently, the company was best remembered for its short-lived, romantic venture, the Pony Express, but it now has a lasting monument. In 1984, Alexander Majors' home at 83rd and State Line was restored and opened as a museum, thanks in large part to the single-handed effort of his granddaughter, Louisa Johnston. (Miss Johnston, on a schoolteacher's salary, bought and preserved the old family home and protected it against commercial development for more than thirty years. The house was made a museum after her death.)

The Church of Jesus Christ of Latter-day Saints (LDS) put down the first of its long roots in Missouri in 1831, when pioneering church members arrived in Independence. They were responding to the proclamation of their leader, Joseph Smith, that the New Jerusalem would be founded there, at the prairie's edge. Members of the church founded and operated the town's first newspaper, the *Morning and Evening Star.* The first settlement did not last long; the Mormon settlers, as they were called, left after a series of bitter disputes with their non-Mormon neighbors, and the religious community did not flourish again until after the turn of the

Penn Valley Park holds this thirteen-foot-high bronze statue of the "Pioneer Mother" representing the pioneer spirit of all women who made the arduous trek westward by covered wagon. Photo by Bruce Mathews

# REORGANIZED CHURCH OF JESUS CHRIST OF LATTER DAY SAINTS
## A Commitment to Peace and Goodwill

The Reorganized Church of Jesus Christ of Latter Day Saints, headquartered in Independence, Missouri, is a Christian denomination organized April 6, 1830, in Fayette, New York, under the leadership of Joseph Smith, Jr.

The church moved to Kirtland, Ohio, early in 1831 and sent a colonizing effort to Independence during the following summer. Subsequently, headquarters were established in Caldwell County, Missouri, in 1838 and in Nauvoo, Illinois, the following year. The death of Joseph Smith, Jr., in 1844 prompted a leadership crisis of several years, marked by the dispersion of the church into several widely scattered groups.

Joseph Smith III accepted the call to succeed his father and was ordained prophet-president of the Reorganized Church of Jesus Christ of Latter Day Saints on April 6, 1860. The current president is Dr. Wallace B. Smith, a grandson of Joseph Smith III. The church has had headquarters in Plano, Illinois (1866), Lamoni, Iowa (1881), and Independence, Missouri (since 1920).

The largest concentration of members is within a 500-mile radius of the Auditorium, the international headquarters building at River and Walnut in Independence. The church is established in 38 nations, with a worldwide membership in excess of 235,000 people.

The Auditorium, long recognized as a local landmark, is a beautifully appointed building that occupies 65,648 square feet and sits on a five-acre section of the temple lot that was dedicated by Joseph Smith, Jr., the church's founder, in 1831. Construction was begun in 1926, and by 1928 the huge steel skeleton of the dome could be seen for miles. Work ceased during the Great Depression of the 1930s. The copper dome was installed in the late 1940s, the organ in 1959. The formal dedication was held three years later.

Inside, a conference chamber seating nearly 6,000 people is the most strik-

*The unique lighting of the Auditorium makes this landmark visible by night as well as by day.*

ing feature and the chief reason for the building's existence. The room overflows every other year as representatives of church members throughout the world gather to discuss and set policy for the church.

A highlight of the chamber is the 110-rank Aeolian-Skinner organ, one of the largest free-standing pipe organs in the United States. The main organ with six divisions is at the front of the oval chamber, and the three-division antiphonal organ is in the opposite balcony. The more than 6,000 pipes have speaking lengths from a quarter-inch to 32 feet. Organ concerts are given at 3 p.m. daily from June through August and at 3 p.m. on Sundays from September through May. It has been identified with great organ literature and the best of radio programming for two decades. Dr. John Obetz has acted as performer and host for a weekly half-hour radio program, "The Auditorium Organ," since 1967. It is now broadcast via satellite across the nation.

Many thousands of people visit the Conference Chamber throughout the year for religious, cultural, and community-centered activities. Harry S. Truman spoke to a large gathering at the Auditorium when he was President. Many local high school and college commencement ceremonies are held in the chamber. The Auditorium is a cultural center and organ concerts featuring internationally prominent organists, symphony orchestra concerts, and an annual performance of Handel's "Messiah" are presented there.

The Auditorium is a place that represents people with a purpose. The activities at the Auditorium are symbolic of the beliefs of church members throughout the world. Basic principles include a testimony of Jesus Christ, stewardship of the environment and all resources, the equality of all persons, an open cannon of scripture, and efforts to establish the Kingdom of God on earth.

*Nearly 6,000 delegates and visitors assemble in the main chamber of the RLDS Auditorium for the church's biennial world conference.*

*The 110-rank Aeolian-Skinner organ was designed specifically for the Conference Chamber of the RLDS Church, and is one of the largest free-standing pipe organs in the United States.*

Church programs dealing with health, cultural awareness, financial management, and the development of underprivileged nations and peoples are extended to the community and around the world.

Offices of the divisions and commissions of the church are located in the east and west wings and in the corner areas surrounding the Conference Chamber. Historical reference materials, membership and financial data, curriculum research files, radio and television recording studios, repair and maintenance shops, and committee rooms are also located in the building.

Other areas of the facility have particular functions. The Laurel Club Dining Room, with a seating capacity of 600, uses the culinary skills of church members to serve large dinners and banquets on a regular basis. A chapel that seats 125 people is reserved for meditation and small worship groups. The Assembly Room has a stage and reception area with movable seating for 900. The library and church archives also are housed in the building. Historical items are displayed in a museum called Heritage Hall. Free guided tours of the building are offered Monday through Friday from 9 a.m. to 5 p.m., and on Sundays from 1 p.m. to 5 p.m.

The traditional seal of the church, found as a motif in the Auditorium, depicts the concept of peace and goodwill. These aims are being strengthened year by year throughout the world by church programs. As the Reorganized Church of Jesus Christ of Latter Day Saints works toward these high goals, the Auditorium remains a symbol of the church's organized effort and commitment, and it is the base of those efforts.

The RLDS Church has been a part of metropolitan Kansas City for more than a half-century. Employees of the church and its affiliated institutions in the metro area contribute more than 365,000 hours annually to community service. The members are concerned about the quality of life, as well as the growth and development of the Kansas City area. As a representative of the Christian community, the Reorganized Church of Jesus Christ of Latter Day Saints continues to offer its resources and services to a growing Kansas City metroplex.

*The exterior of the Alexander Majors home at 83rd and State Line reflects the grand elegance of early nineteenth-century architecture. Photo by Bob Barrett*

century.

The discovery of gold in California set off a rush of would-be mining millionaires and Kansas City began to boom. Throngs of guides, trappers, Indians, gamblers, farriers, wagonmakers, scouts, and pilgrims happily tracked through the muddy streets of the city, spending money and making money.

By the time Kansas City was twenty years old, as many as ten steamboats a day docked at the levee to discharge passengers and freight. An average of 1,000 wagons per month left here on the overland trek westward. The *Western Journal of Commerce,* a couple of years earlier, had described how money was being made in Kansas City: trade with Mexico and New Mexico over the Santa Fe Trail, with Indians, with soldiers from nearby garrisons, with emigrants on their way west, and money paid by contractors who transported the mail. The total came to $5,100,000 circulating annually in the city.

The coming of the iron horse made things even livelier. By 1860 the city was laying the foundation of its later fame as a national railroad center, with seven railroad companies organized and two already laying track.

Railroad construction ground to a halt in 1861 with the shocking news that the nation was at war with itself. Further development was virtually at a standstill until 1865 when the war finally ended.

The seeds of war had been sown in our state forty years before with the Missouri Compromise, which allowed Missouri to enter the Union

as a state half slave, half free. According to the terms of the compromise,
slaveholding was legal south of the 36-degree, 30-minute line. Above that
line, Missouri was a free state. Sympathies, however, were not so neatly
divided. Kansas City was a Union bastion uneasily situated in the middle
of the Bushwhackers (Confederate guerrillas) and sympathizers in
southeast Jackson County; the Confederate sympathizers in Platte and
Clay counties to the north; and, on the other side, the Kansas guerrillas,
known as Redlegs, raiding across the state line in the name of the Union.

Most notorious of all the Bushwhackers was the furious gang of gue-
rillas known as Quantrill's Raiders. Led by the former schoolmaster
William Clark Quantrill, the gang included a teenager named Jesse
Woodson James and his older brother Frank. (The Jesse James farm
in Clay County is now a museum, and a play, performed annually there,
re-creates some of the high spots in the life of this legendary bandit.)
Less well-known outside Missouri is "Bloody Bill" Anderson, a Quantrill
lieutenant, whose sister Josephine died in the collapse of a makeshift
Union jail where she was being detained on suspicion of smuggling provisions to the rebels. Anderson's vengeful rage at his young sister's death
led to the raid on Lawrence, Kansas, a Union stronghold. The city, now
a thriving university town, was left in smoking ashes. At least 183 inhabi-

tants were killed—shot down or burned to death—and hundreds of houses and businesses were incinerated.

The Lawrence massacre outraged Union supporters, who demanded that the government take effective action to end the guerilla raids. The result was Order No. 11, a Draconian measure which commanded all the rural dwellers of Jackson County to sign an oath of loyalty to the Union or move from their farms within fifteen days. The intent was to deprive the Bushwhackers of friendly outposts where they could find food, shelter, and ammunition. The consequence was the uprooting and ruination of many families, who saw their stock animals confiscated and their crops—and sometimes their houses—burned before their eyes.

Before the war was over, one of the bloodiest battles of that conflict was fought over land that now makes up the elegant Country Club Plaza and serenely beautiful Loose Park. They called it "the Gettysburg of the West," but you'll follow its route through town on tour markers titled "The Battle of Westport." About 27,000 men took part in the pitched battle that raged in the area between Brush Creek and the high ground a mile or so to the south. Elegant houses on a winding road now obscure the hidden ravine the Union forces used to mount a surprise attack that turned the tide in their favor.

With the end of the war came renewed interest in the railroads. Promoters vied with one another to develop the era's most modern transport for goods and passengers. The first to make a direct rail connection with the East was the Missouri Pacific, whose western terminus was Kansas City. An even more important line was the Kansas City, Galveston & Lake Superior Railroad, which provided rail linkage with major markets in the northeast. The factor that ensured this line's success was the construction, by Octave Chanute, of the flood-resistant bridge across the Missouri River. It was the first time the Mighty Mo had been spanned successfully.

While the trains were gaining momentum as an economic force in Kansas City's growth, the first seeds of its future fame as Cowtown were also being sown. A second city shaper named McCoy—Joseph McCoy— while trying to figure out how to boost his Illinois livestock shipping business, came west to see what could be done to ease the situation created by the popularity of barbed wire.

Farmers had a new option with "bobwire." Formerly, fields had been enclosed with bois d'arc hedgerows, split rail, or stone fences. All required time and labor. The new wire was cheap, quick and easy to make into fences, and efficient at containing livestock.

It was also good at keeping livestock out. The existence of so many fenced acres prevented Texas cattle raisers from driving their herds overland to the rail stations that served northeastern markets. McCoy saw a solution that would work: a gathering point where cattle from Texas could be herded over open territory and then shipped east by rail. With the backing of Kansas City stockmen, he bought the town site of Abilene, Kansas, for $5 an acre and built holding pens and a drovers' hotel, then blazed a thousand-mile trail to Texas that bypassed most of the newly fenced territory.

By 1871 McCoy had persuaded local investors that it made good sense to establish a Kansas City cattle shipping center for the great herds that were being routed this direction from Abilene. The Kansas City Stock Yards Company was established in 1875, and influenced the expansion of local industry. Every major packing company in the nation followed the lead of Plankinton & Armour and set up factories near the Kansas City rail yards.

The days of the great trail drives and the packing houses have since passed, giving way to more sophisticated agribusiness like gigantic agricultural cooperative industries and commodities trading, but the tradition lingers on. There's an annual influx of young farmers from all over the nation when the Future Farmers of America (FFA) convene here. They come in time to attend the American Royal Livestock and Horse Show, held here every year since 1899. So esteemed is this exhibition that one of the yearly debutante balls names its young ladies "BOTARs"—Belles of the American Royal.

The Kansas City agricultural tradition owes another part of its heritage to Russia. In the late nineteeth century, German Mennonites in the Crimea began to migrate to this country. Farmers, they brought with them seeds of "Turkey red," the hard red winter wheat they had been growing in Russia. This hardy grain revolutionized wheat growing in the area. A hardier variety than the Michigan soft wheat which was formerly grown in the region, Turkey red gradually supplanted corn as the major Kansas crop.

With that development, Kansas City became not only a milling hub but a trading center. The year of 1869 saw the start of the Commercial Exchange, the forerunner of the Board of Trade, which was organized ten years later. Each year thousands of visitors to our city include the Board of Trade on their list of "must see" places. This is one of the world's largest indoor wheat markets, where commodities and futures are traded daily by skilled traders in the organized chaos of the public outcry auction.

The idea of our town as a rough-hewn frontier outpost is an article of faith with many, but the fact is that as early as 1870, Kansas City was one of the places in the country to go for a vacation. Only San Francisco had more places of entertainment. There were two opera houses, numerous elegant restaurants, scores of gaming rooms, and plenty of those places euphemistically termed "resorts." Most famous among them were the lavish houses of Madame Lovejoy and her contemporary, Annie Chambers. No sordid cribs, these tasteful mansions near the riverfront were filled with French furniture, plate-glass mirrors, crystal chandeliers, fine food, imported wines, featherbeds, and fancy women.

Gambling was big business back then, and it was conducted in high style. Bob Potee's Number Three Faro Bank was one of the most famous gambling halls west of the Mississippi, and the gambler, Mr. Potee, was riding high. There came a night, though, when a lucky citizen broke Potee's bank. Potee, dressed in ruffled shirt, cutaway and tails, and

*The Nelson-Atkins Museum of Art is internationally known for its collection of Oriental art and artifacts. Photo by Roy Inman*

carrying a gold-headed cane, congratulated the winner, paid off, and strolled out of the hall, adjusting his top hat to a jaunty angle. After a brief stop at his hotel room, he walked down to the Missouri River . . . and kept on walking until his silk hat floated. They recovered his body downriver. In his room was the brief note he'd addressed to his fellow gambler, Charlie Bassett.

"Plant me decent," Potee had written. Bassett obliged, and, just as in the song, six tall gamblers carried Bob Potee's coffin to his grave.

During the boisterous 1880s, Jesse James died at the hands of his erstwhile comrade Robert Ford, back-shot at his home in St. Joseph, Missouri, where they knew him as "Mr. Howard." President Grover Cleveland and his young bride stopped off for a night at the Coates House Hotel. An arrival with longer lasting significance was that of a wealthy Hoosier from Ft. Wayne, Indiana, William Rockhill Nelson.

The autocratic Nelson, nicknamed "Baron Bill" by his critics, came here to start an afternoon newspaper. There were already several papers in operation—all publishing in the morning as tradition demanded—and most people laughed at Nelson's paper, *The Kansas City Star,* which came out in the evening. The other publishers, with their nickel-a-copy sheets, stopped laughing at what they called "The Twilight Twinkler" when the new paper's two-cent price lured away their readers. Eventually the *Star* vanquished all competitors; today Kansas City has two major daily newspapers. Both *The Kansas City Times* (morning) and *The Kansas City Star* (evening) are owned by the same company. Baron Bill had the last laugh, after all.

Nelson left his mark not only upon the news of the city but upon its streets—literally. He was the guiding force behind the boulevard-and-parks plan that help make Kansas City beautiful, and it was bequests of the Nelson family that eventually gave the city its public art museum. The William Rockhill Nelson Gallery of Art and Mary Atkins Museum, now known as the Nelson Museum, was built on the site of Nelson's mansion, Oak Hall. Nelson's will provided for a trust fund of $11 million for the purchase of art objects. (Nelson was obviously no friend of modern art. A condition of the Nelson legacy was the publisher's stipulation that his money be used to buy only the works of artists who had been dead for at least 30 years.) The wills of his wife, daughter, and son-in-law left bequests for a gallery to house the collection.

The genius of attorney Frank Rozzelle, who also willed money to the cause, is credited with the plan that finally got the museum off the drawing board by putting together the Nelson bequests and that of Mary McAfee Atkins, another wealthy Kansas Citian. In December 1936, the gallery was formally opened. It housed an outstanding collection of paintings and art objects, bought at Depression prices by the fortune Nelson had left to the city.

Not every leading civic light in that era was concerned with fine art. (In fact, one ward-heeler doubted the museum idea would catch on. He dismissed the whole notion with the pronouncement, "Art is on the bum in Kansas City.")

*One of the country's fore-
most galleries, the Nelson-
Atkins Museum of Art was
formally opened in 1936
and funded primarily with
bequests from publisher
William Rockhill Nelson
and city benefactor Mary
McAfee Atkins. Photo by
Bob Barrett*

One of the most powerful men of the day was "Boss" Tom Pendergast. His interest was the art of politics. His brother Jim was a saloon keeper in the old North End of the city who got into politics almost by accident when he casually requested that his loyal, blue-collar patrons vote for a friend, and they did—overwhelmingly. "Big Jim," respected for his fair treatment of the working man, was on his way to becoming an important element in the faction-ridden politics of the day.

Accused of stuffing ballot boxes and buying votes, Alderman Jim Pendergast responded mildly. "I never needed a crooked vote," he said. "All I want is a chance for my friends to get to the polls."

Before long, enough of his friends had got to the polls often enough for the genial saloon keeper to have become a major force on the Kansas City political scene in the first decades of the twentieth century.

It was Pendergast's younger brother Tom, however, who gained fame as boss of one of the wildest and wickedest cities in the nation. Commentator Edward R. Murrow wrote, "If you want to see some sin, forget about Paris and go to Kansas City."

The town was wide open in the late twenties and thirties, a haven that became a playground for some of the nation's most wanted gangsters. They came here, not to get a piece of the action, but to relax in an area recognized as a kind of truce zone by both sides of the law. In speakeasies like the Subway Club and the Yellow Front Saloon, they could check their pistols at the door and listen to music played by up-and-coming jazz stars like Bill (later "Count") Basie, Mary Lou Williams, Lester Young, Lips Page, and Charlie Parker.

Ironically, it was the prosperity engendered by a multimillion-dollar gambling and bootlegging economy that helped save jazz in the midst of the Depression years. Out-of-work musicians from all over the country flocked to Kansas City where work was plentiful. They played for the paying customers until late at night, and then saw in the dawn with the duels of musical improvisation that came to be called "cutting matches."

Reform in the forties and World War II changed the city's face to a soberer one. By that time the University of Kansas City (now a campus of the University of Missouri) was founded; a professional orchestra had taken shape; the art museum and Kansas City Art Institute were well established; the Country Club Plaza was already a favorite shopping place; the Kansas City Bolt and Nut Company had metamorphosed into Sheffield Steel; the Municipal (now Downtown) Airport had been dedicated; and a couple of small airline companies had merged to form Transcontinental and Western Air, or T&WA. Later known as Trans World Airlines, it was among the first local companies to put the city on the map.

In 1944 "the man from Missouri," Harry S. Truman, became vice-president as Franklin Delano Roosevelt was elected to his fourth term as President of the United States. A year later, Roosevelt was dead and Truman became President.

Independence, Missouri, enjoyed a new heyday as the home (and frequent summer residence) of "Give 'em hell Harry." Thousands of tour-

*This desk is part of the memorabilia saved from Harry S. Truman's days as presiding judge of the Jackson County Court. Truman's office, the courtroom, and a multi-media presentation about the former President are included in the display at the Jackson County Courthouse in Independence. Photo by Michael A. Mihalevich*

*Independence, Missouri, preserves the memory of its most famous resident, 33rd President of the United States, Harry S. Truman. Visitors are free to walk Truman's old neighborhood, now a National Landmark District, and visit the Truman Home at 219 Delaware, which is open to tour. Photo by Bruce Mathews*

ists each year visit the Harry S. Truman Library and Museum, and tour the Truman House.

Following the Truman years, peacetime brought continuing prosperity to Kansas City, and a continuation of the diversification of industry that has helped keep the city growing and its economy strong. Local industries offered exciting employment that attracted young people from smaller towns in Kansas, Missouri, Iowa, and Nebraska. To them, Kansas City was simply The City—the place to be where things were happening. They stayed, and they prospered. Their children and grandchildren, many of them, are here yet.

One writer called Kansas City "the crossroads of America." It's an apt title for a city that has served, successively, as the last outpost of the great westward migration, a center for river traffic, a hub of railroad transportation, and a nerve center of the aviation industry. As we approach the twenty-first century, our city once again steps out front and center as a major center for the service and information industries that now make up a preponderance of America's business.

And with it all, the little settlement that began as a trapping and trading post has grown beyond its founders' wildest dreams. Kansas City is a bustling town where yesterday's vision of commerce and industry keeps growing greater with today's realities. But it's something more, besides, and French philosopher Andre Maurois won Kansas City's affection when he described the place we call "The Heart of America": "Who in Europe, or in America for that matter, knows that Kansas City is one of the loveliest cities on earth? . . . Few cities have been built with so much regard for beauty."

# 2
# BOOM TOWN AT PRAIRIE'S EDGE

Kansas City is like the kid born with a silver spoon in its mouth. From the start, the town has had everything it needed to keep it growing and prosperous. And as times changed, the city's economy adapted to meet new conditions, often as the result of entrepreneurial daring.

It came into being as a trading and transport town, and the city has kept that tradition growing and evolving to suit the times. From riverboats to prairie schooners, from railroad lines to airlines, its central location in the nation has made Kansas City an advantageous location for the manufacture, storage, and transportation of goods. Even more important, the mix of business and industry here makes the city virtually recession-proof, with an unemployment rate consistently lower than the national average.

Agriculture-related industries have retained an important role in the city's economy—they account for 14 percent (over 90,000 persons) of our total employment and for $5 billion in the sale of products and services.

In industries apart from agriculture, over 14 percent of the labor force is employed by government; over 8 percent each in wholesale distribution and in transportation and utilities; and another 17 percent in retailing. Manufacturing accounts for nearly 18 percent of the area's employment; while service industries, including finance, insurance, and real estate, employ nearly 30 percent of the non-agricultural work force.

Kansas City has always had its share of entrepreneurs and idea men and women whose creativity has added new products and new opportunities to the local scene.

One of the city's most colorful entrepreneurs was the legendary railroad man, Arthur E. Stilwell. Almost forgotten today, Stilwell was

*Opposite: The "Muse of the Missouri," one of Kansas City's many lovely downtown fountains, stands watch over the city's past, present, and future. Photo by Bob Barrett*

*Next page: One of Kansas City's most beloved landmarks, Cyrus E. Dallin's statue of "The Scout" overlooks a sweeping panorama of Kansas City from a bluff in Penn Valley Park. Photo by Bruce Mathews*

famous enough at the turn of the century to merit his own six-part serialized autobiography in a national magazine, *The Saturday Evening Post.* He was flamboyant enough to name towns after himself (Stilwell, Kansas, and Port Arthur, Texas), and far-seeing enough to recognize that a belt railway around the city could be a moneymaker.

His Kansas City Suburban Belt Railroad, incorporated in 1887, began operations in 1870 and Stilwell pushed on to pursue his dream—a railway with a terminus at the Gulf of Mexico. The dream came true in 1900, and the terminus was named Port Arthur.

Shortly afterward, Stilwell's wheeling and dealing became unbearable to his more conservative partners and associates, and the magnate was divested of his position with the railway. He went back to his home state, New York, made a highly successful lecture tour, and settled down to write a best-seller with the unlikely title *Cannibals of Finance,* in which he lambasted his former associates.

In the meantime, under the guidance of William T. Kemper, the railroad became the Kansas City Southern Railway Company. Since 1962, the railway has been a subsidiary of Kansas City Southern Industries, Inc., a diversified holding company with major businesses in transportation, financial services, communications, real estate, natural resources, and manufacturing. Its major subsidiary companies, in addition to Kansas City Southern Railway Company, are Pioneer Western Corporation, an insurance securities and energy investment company; DST Systems, Inc., a financial record-keeping company; Janus Capital Corporation, a mutual fund management firm; LDX Group, Inc., a communications

*Below: This construction worker helps to weld Kansas City's future as the new boom town of America. Photo by Bruce Mathews*

*Opposite: It's thumbs-up from the doormen at the Hyatt Regency Hotel for a city on the move. Photo by Bruce Mathews*

# KANSAS CITY CORPORATION FOR INDUSTRIAL DEVELOPMENT

## Meeting the Needs of the Business Community

For Kansas City and the Kansas City Corporation for Industrial Development (KCCID) it's been an uphill pattern of growth since the not-for-profit organization was created in 1978 to meet the needs of the business community.

*Chris N. Vedros, president of the KCCID, addresses its board of directors.*

Housed in the same building as the Chamber of Commerce of Greater Kansas City, KCCID serves as the major economic development arm of the city, and offers a comprehensive range of services. In addition to the work of KCCID and its subsidiary, the KCCID-Charitable Fund, the organization provides staff support for the Industrial Development Authority of Kansas City, the Planned Industrial Expansion Authority of Kansas City, and the Port Authority of Kansas City.

KCCID's prime activity is the business and industry contact program that promotes Kansas City as a city that can meet the needs of growing firms. Assisting private developers in planning and implementing new investment projects involves the organization's cooperation with various economic development associations. Assistance ranges from working with individual companies to supporting groups of businesses interested in broader area improvements.

"Promoting Kansas City as a place for business expansion and new investment is an underlying objective of all of KCCID's activities," says Chris N. Vedros, president of KCCID. "Through direct mail, local media advertising, seminars, and group presentations, we circulate information about our services and the advantages of doing business in Kansas City. Our major efforts this year have resulted in greater cooperation among local organizations, the city, and the state of Missouri."

During 1985 investment and economic development in Kansas City increased significantly. More than $1.5 billion of new investments has resulted from the efforts of KCCID and its affiliates, creating and retaining more than 31,000 jobs.

Additional specific functions of KCCID's staff include contacting businesses regularly to promote available services and to identify potential problems. This ongoing assistance has proven most valuable, and during KCCID's first seven years more than 1,200 firms have received support. As an ombudsman for the Kansas City, Missouri, business community, KCCID acts as a liaison between businessmen and city hall.

More than $1.5 billion worth of land, building, and equipment investment in Kansas City has occurred as a result of KCCID's financial assistance programs. Through the KCCID-Charitable Fund, the 21-acre Paseo West Business Center was completed.

"I think we've demonstrated that Kansas City cares about its business and industry," says Mayor Richard Berkley. "The excitement generated here has been picked up by local and national media, and the story is one of individual successes and overall community growth."

*Paseo West Business Center, a 21-acre light industrial redevelopment at the southeast gate to Kansas City's central business center.*

company; and Southern Group, which includes manufacturing, coal and coke handling, a sawmill, a railroad crosstie treating facility, and a full-service leasing company.

The Kansas City Southern (KCS) rail system has 786 miles of track that run straight down to Port Arthur and Beaumont, Texas. The railway has a total of 1,618 miles of track. The main line of its largest subsidiary, the Louisiana & Arkansas, runs about 500 miles from New Orleans to Farmersville in Texas, with nearly forty more miles via Santa Fe trackage rights into Dallas.

KCS has not carried passengers since 1969, and currently is a major carrier of materials and products for the chemical plants and refineries near Port Arthur in Texas and Louisiana. Coal and lumber products are another important element in the railroad's current operations; in recent years the shipment of coal to utility companies has amounted to as much as 12.6 million tons, or over $80 million in revenue—quite a legacy for the visionary Stilwell.

Another of Kansas City's spirited entrepreneurs is Edward J. King, Jr., who didn't build a better mousetrap—he built a new and better radio.

In 1952, King, president of a highly successful electronics company, Communications Accessories Corporation, earned his license to pilot a private airplane. He liked flying, but he disliked the poor quality and high price of the aviation radios then available. The best selling unit on the market at the time offered only twenty-seven transmit channels and sold at well over $1,000—a hefty price tag in those days when a luxury automobile sold for around $6,000.

King knew he could build a better radio and sell it more cheaply, and in 1959 he left his old company and started a new one: King Radio Corporation.

The first King radio was a 90-channel crystal-controlled VHF transceiver. In his first year of operation, King hand built five of the sets he had designed, and sold them for $845 each, correctly reckoning that word of mouth would do the rest.

It did, and by 1960 King had thirty employees working in an old dairy farmhouse at I-435 and 75th Street. In 1961, the company moved its rapidly expanding operation to a plant in Olathe, Kansas, where the firm is now headquartered. King Radio currently also has plants in three Kansas towns—Lawrence, Paola, and Ottawa—as well as a facility at Johnson County Industrial Airport.

In 1982 the company formed its Mobile Communications Division to develop a product line for the land mobile radio field using microprocessor-based two-way radios. The facility is housed in a 76,000-square-foot plant on a 57-acre tract in Lawrence.

The following year, the company opened a 24,000-square-foot engineering and manufacturing facility in Singapore to produce marine radio equipment.

Since Ed King first decided there must be a better way to build radios, the company has chalked up a lot of firsts—including the first all solid-state transceiver for airline use, and the use of compact digital frequency

# COOK PAINT AND VARNISH COMPANY
## On the Leading Edge of High Technology

Although more than 70 years have passed since Charles R. Cook founded Cook Paint and Varnish Company, his philosophy still permeates the firm's endeavors. From the beginning Cook designated a significantly high percentage of sales dollars for research and development of new products—a philosophy that has enabled the firm to outpace many of its competitors. Today Cook Paint and Varnish Company continues its search for better performing products.

Cook began experimenting with newer-type finishes as early as 1920. That work led to the perfection of a semipaste house paint that was the whitest and most durable solid covering paint available on the market. Soon thereafter, Cook designed a revolutionary interior lining for food cans that remains a standard in the industry. In fact, one out of every three soup and vegetable cans manufactured in the United States is coated with a Cook product. Following one success with another, Cook developed durable nonfade colors for automobiles, as well as lead-free commercial coatings.

Today the family-owned business is located at 919 East 14th Avenue in North Kansas City, Missouri. It is run by Cook's grandson, D. Patrick Curran, chairman and president of Cook Paint and Varnish Company, who has equipped his business to serve its customers from strategically located manufacturing facilities throughout the country. The firm's research centers employ more than 100 professional and technical people, who, in turn, are supported by equally efficient quality-control departments and specialized development laboratories in Cleveland, Ohio, and Milpitas, California. Blending plants nationwide strengthen the company's position as one of the world's leading producers of gel coats for the fiberglass-reinforced plastics industry. The firm is also America's top supplier of internal coatings for natural gas pipelines.

Until 1980 Cook Paint and Varnish Company continued to include generic retail paint and decorating items in its product line. At that time the firm be-

D. Patrick Curran, chairman and president of Cook Paint and Varnish Company.

gan to concentrate exclusively on what challenged it most—and for which it was extraordinarily suited—serving the high-tech needs of industry. Today all of the company's energies are devoted to the creation and manufacture of top-quality polymers, plastics, and coatings designed for specific industrial applications.

From speedboats to pipelines, from croquet sets to vending machines and offshore oil rigs, the quality and reliability of Cook Paint and Varnish Company's products are such that foreign coatings manufacturers, through licensing arrangements, are offering Cook-formulated products to industrial customers in many countries. As a private corporation, sales information is not released, but in 1978, its last full year as a public company, sales were $132 million.

"We are not content simply to meet today's coating needs," says Curran. "Our job is to anticipate coming technological and environmental complexities and to research and devise new products to help keep our customers in the forefront of their respective industries."

synthesizers to replace bulky crystal banks in airplane radios.

King Radio Corporation currently employs nearly 3,000 persons and has annual sales of about $110 million. In 1984, it announced a merger with Bendix Aerospace Division of Allied Corporation as a wholly owned subsidiary of Allied Corporation/Bendix Aerospace.

Nearly half a century ago, World War II and the push for war matériel production boosted the city's economy out of the Depression. The Ford and General Motors plants, the largest automotive production centers outside Michigan, were converted to defense work. Giant facilities like Remington Arms, Bendix Aviation, and Sheffield (now Armco) Steel were going all-out for the war effort, and more and more workers flocked to Kansas City from the smaller, surrounding towns.

"If one member of the family did well at the plant, others were likely to come, too," said Alan H. McCoy of Armco, himself a second-generation employee.

"Early on, there was a company policy of hiring relatives of workers whenever possible. The reasoning was that people in the same family came from the same work ethic, and if a man did a good job, his son or brother probably would, too."

Randolph Hatfield was a young man from Ray County when he went to work at Sheffield in 1938. By the time he retired in 1969, all four of his sons, David, Donald, J.R., and Richard, were employees at the steel mill. The total of those five family members' working years at the plant comes to 144.

"I never thought of working any place else," said David Hatfield, who retired in 1982 after thirty-two years in the bar joist department. "We lived right close to the mill, our father and two of our uncles worked there, most of the neighbors did, too . . . it was pretty much like the mill was a part of your own family."

David Hatfield's son Mike carries on the family tradition; he is now in his thirteenth year with the company.

"I have a lot of good memories," said David Hatfield. "I'm not an educated man, but I was fortunate enough to make some darn good money in a good job where I had a position of responsibility.

"It always gave me a warm feeling to look up and see the smoke coming out of those old smokestacks," he said. "I hope it never quits."

Armco, known for years as Sheffield Steel, began as the Kansas City Bolt and Nut Company in 1888, when a Pennsylvania steelman, James H. Sternbergh, opened the operation here to take advantage of the increased market for steel that was created by the westward expansion of railroads. A small portion of the existing factory dates from that period, and a large part of Kansas City's growth can be traced in the Sheffield products that went into the city's structures.

Although recent soaring energy costs have hurt the plant, with its electrically-powered furnaces, Armco Steel currently employs close to 2,000 persons, with an annual payroll of around $100 million and annual sales of about $300 million. The only steel mill in the state of Missouri, the plant's smoky stacks have been visible on the Kansas City horizon

for a century.

Millions of tons of locally-manufactured steel have made their way into the nation's railroads in the form of track bolts and wrought-iron forgings. Millions of tons more of Sheffield steel were used in Kansas City's roads and buildings, particularly after World War I. Following "the war to end all wars," when bids for construction of the Liberty Memorial were being taken, Sheffield won the contract to produce steel reinforcing bars for concrete ("rebars") with a typically Kansas City-spirited ploy. The plant had no facility for fabricating the bars—so they built one. For the next half century, tons of steel from the Kansas City plant—in the form of paving mesh, rebars, steel joists, bolts, even nails—helped shape Kansas City's skyline and roadways.

Sited in the center of an outstandingly productive agricultural region, crisscrossed by railroads, with both heavy and light industry going full steam and service industries big and growing bigger, Kansas City has been like a mirror of the nation as a whole, blessed with a diversified economy in which almost anyone who wanted work could find it.

One of the most significant shapers of the city's future has been the automobile. By the time World War II had begun people had seen just

# STRATCO, INC.
## The Chemical Reaction Technology Firm

Stratco, a chemical reaction technology firm, began in Kansas City more than a half-century ago. Today it has become a world leader in alkylation and grease-manufacturing technologies.

From its base at 1010 West 39th Street, Stratco's process technology, equipment, and professional staff of consulting and design engineers have served the United States and over 25 other countries.

Stratco is active in research and development in many areas—from the pharmaceutical, food, and cosmetics industries to the petrochemical and refining industries.

In 1928 Kansas City was on its way to becoming the grease capital of the world. C.W. Stratford patented the design for a grease manufacturing reactor, which he called the Stratco Contactor. Then and today the Contactor is recognized as a quality product built for efficiency and durability. The first Stratco Contactor, installed in 1929 in Kansas City, is still operating today.

During World War II, when the country needed high-octane aviation

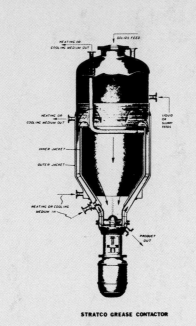

**STRATCO GREASE CONTACTOR**

*C.W. Stratford patented the design for a grease-manufacturing reactor, which he called the Stratco Contactor. The first Contactor, installed in 1929 in Kansas City, is still operating today.*

fuel, Stratford began supplying Contactors to refineries for their alkylation process to produce a high-octane component called alkylate for blending with gasoline. Today Stratco is the only supplier of both HF (hydrofluoric) and $H_2SO_4$ (sulfuric acid) alkylation technology and equipment.

In 1977 Ward Graham, executive vice-president and a chemical engineer with Stratford Engineering, bought the company. After his unexpected death less than two years later, his daughter, S. Diane Graham, became active in the management of the company, shortly becoming chairman and president. In 1984 the firm moved into its new corporate headquarters and was renamed Stratco, Inc., after its strong industry trademark. Graham now owns controlling interest in the company.

Stratco now offers a complete range of services for its customers, including process and design engineering, startup, national technical seminars, and replacement parts. The company was the first in the alkylation industry to offer a computer process simulator, which is being used by refineries and universities to train operators and students.

Two of Stratco's competitors are billion-dollar companies in the *Fortune* 200. The fact that a small company based in the heart of America can compete with such giants is, according to Diane Graham, the result of its employee "associates" resources.

"Our people are our greatest asset," she says. "Stratco employs a staff of 30 chemical, petroleum, and mechanical engineers and other professionals. Our associates are highly qualified in their areas of expertise and are used to wearing several hats."

The management (and marriage) team of Graham and Terry M. Robertson, an engineer and officer in the firm, provides an excellent blend of business, economics, and engineering experience.

"We believe in helping each team member become the best he or she can be," Graham relates. "Consequently, we get a lot in return. The synergism created by this kind of coordinated effort is incredible."

As for the future goals of Stratco, Graham and Robertson foresee a double sales volume by 1990. "Most of the added revenue will come from new markets for our reaction technology," she predicts. Adds Robertson, "Targeted areas for sustained growth are the food, drug, and cosmetic industries."

*A Stratco sulfuric alkylation unit recently installed in Japan.*

enough of this relatively new popular phenomenon to know that they liked cars   and, almost simultaneously, found they couldn't buy them.

In the shock that followed America's entry into the war in 1941, the government froze the retail sale of automobiles. Nobody knew how long the freeze might last, but one brash youngster successfully gambled that it wouldn't be long.

Berl Berry, one of the flashiest of a flamboyant breed, at that time had a Ford agency at 18th and Independence Avenue. He'd come here from Oklahoma just two years earlier, his stake of $5,000 pinned to his undershirt, safe from city sharpers.

When the freeze hit, most dealers were trying to figure out how to get out from under an inventory of cars they were not allowed to sell. Not Berry. Convinced the freeze would quickly thaw, he was trying to figure out how to buy up all the Fords in the Midwest.

"He darned near did it, too," recalled Bob Copenhaver, himself a veteran Kansas City car dealer. "Berl made a deal with the finance company—convinced them it made more sense to have all their financing under one roof. And then he went around all over the Midwest and bought up hundreds of cars—close to a thousand brand-new Fords—from dealers who didn't want to gamble on how long the freeze might go on."

The Oklahoma Sooner had called the shot correctly. Within a few months, the freeze was lifted and he was sitting pretty with a virtual Midwestern monopoly on new Fords. He eventually ran his string of dealerships up to a total of thirty-seven agencies nationwide from New York to Honolulu, bought a mansion on Ward Parkway, and was featured in a *Life* magazine article about Kansas City.

Berry, whom friends and admirers recall fondly as a man with a heart of gold, was also a man with class. In the late fifties he ran for mayor against an old-style orator who spent some time on the stump ridiculing the Berry family's opulent style of living.

It was a close race, and the orator won. No big deal for Berry, who had wheeled and dealed his way to success in one of the chanciest businesses around and learned that you win some, you lose some. As a matter of course and of good manners, he and his wife Alice strolled over to the winner's campaign headquarters on election night. The victor's staff and supporters, looking on with silent suspicion, burst into applause as the Berrys walked up to the platform, shook the surprised winner's hand and offered their congratulations.

In later years, a series of bad business calls virtually wiped Berry out and he retired to Springfield, Missouri, where he died in 1982.

"He was the Joe DiMaggio of the car business," said Copenhaver. "Berl Berry was a genius in his own way."

By the time cars had become a staple of the good life, car building had long been a part of Kansas City's manufacturing scene. Ford's Kansas City Assembly Plant, the first Ford plant outside the Detroit metropolitan area, opened in 1906 and just got bigger and bigger.

From a small operation at 318 East 11th Street, the Kansas City plant

# YELLOW FREIGHT SYSTEM, INC.
## Representing Safety, Quality, and Service Excellence

Overland Park, on the southern edge of metropolitan Kansas City, is the home office of Yellow Freight System, Inc. With nearly two billion dollars in revenues, Yellow ranks as one of Kansas City's top locally based companies. The firm employs nearly 2,000 people in the Kansas City area and approximately 25,000 nationwide.

Yellow is one of the three largest motor carriers in America, providing service throughout the United States. It also serves Canada and 25 foreign countries on five continents.

The Yellow system operates 21,000 tractors and trailers through 22 regional hubs and more than 600 terminals. It assigns over 6,000 drivers to daily schedules. It moves 2.4 million pieces of freight over 1.2 million miles of road to more than 30,000 destinations on any given day. This system is supported by the most up-to-date computer technology available.

The legacy of Yellow Freight began in Oklahoma City in the early 1920s. At that time A.J. Harrell pur-

*Yellow Freight's 1985 advertising campaign featured this photo of a twin-trailer combination taken in the Sand Hills of southeastern California.*

chased two 4-cylinder trucks and began a regional motor carrier service. He named his new business the Yellow Cab Transit Company.

From the beginning Harrell's concern for safety, integrity, and prompt service were the hallmarks of his operation. He chose, with the assistance of the Du Pont Company, the yellow-orange color still in use for greater truck visibility on the roads. He influenced Harvey Firestone to develop the manufacture

*The firm's general offices are located in Overland Park, Kansas, in south surburban Kansas City. Construction is underway on a new building to the north of this 10-story structure. The new four-story addition will be completed in late 1987.*

of safer tires. He was the first in the trucking industry to offer employee benefits. And he was the first to use the teletype to tie customer and motor carrier together.

In 1952 a group of businessmen from Kansas City purchased Yellow Transit and moved the headquarters to their hometown. The group was led by George E. Powell, Sr., a longtime Kansas City banker who had earned a reputation for integrity and know-how. His son, George E. Powell, Jr., became the company's controller and is now the chairman of the board.

The concept of safety, integrity, and a commitment to a high quality of service were adhered to by the new owners. The firm administers ongoing driver training and safety programs, and has rigid preventive maintenance and equipment inspection procedures. Yellow is actively involved in a nationwide campaign to promote highway safety through driver education programs and improved safety legislation.

Yellow's employees work closely with customers to meet their ever-changing freight transportation needs. The firm's management style is characterized as a team approach in which the opinions of customers and employees are involved. Yellow believes it is vitally important for all employees to be dedicated, inspired, and willing to go that extra mile with a very high level of concern for customers.

In keeping with A.J. Harrell's original philosophy on the importance of information, and because of dramatic improvements in information technology, customers are now supported by advanced electronic data interchange capabilities providing information on shipment locations, freight charges, and delivery times to customers 24 hours a day. In addition, the company offers electronic billing capabilities to reduce the time required by customers to process freight bills. And Yellow offers personal computer software packages to assist customers and their traffic functions in the retrieval of rates and the use of shipment and service information.

Such technological advancements complement the efforts of Yellow's employees to work closely with customers in meeting their needs and solving their problems—electronically, over the phone, and face to face.

These philosophies—safety, integrity, and service excellence—are the prime motivation behind the dramatic growth of Yellow Freight System, Inc., in the 1980s.

*Yellow Freight's huge break-bulk terminal in Kansas City, Missouri, is one of 22 such terminals in the United States. These terminals serve several hundred satellite terminals throughout the country and in parts of Canada. The satellites, in turn, serve even smaller locations known as substations.*

kept on growing and moving until it reached its present size and location—2.5 million square feet of factory and office space on a 155-acre site in Claycomo. The plant turns out 680 trucks and 1,060 passenger cars per day; both truck and car assembly lines are operated on two shifts. More than 4,480 persons are employed at the plant, which has an annual payroll of over $152 million.

The Kansas City Assembly Plant ships vehicles to all fifty states as well as Canada, Mexico, South America, and other overseas locations. The plant serves forty-five sales districts and about 7,000 dealers throughout the world.

The nation's continuing love affair with cars and—in those happy days before OPEC—gas that sometimes sold as low as 19 cents a gallon, made driving a popular entertainment. It also spurred improvement of existing highways and the building of new ones. Among the industries that took on new importance with this development was trucking.

Yellow Freight Systems is one of the "Big Three" nationally in over-the-road shipping. Headquartered in Kansas City, the company has 550 offices and 22,500 employees nationwide, including about 1,900 locally. Yellow Freight operates in all forty-eight continental states and in Hawaii. It's been a family-owned business since 1952, when George E. Powell, Sr., and his partners bought it.

"My father was a banker in Kansas City for thirty years before that," said Yellow Freight's chairman of the board George E. Powell, Jr. "When I got out of college in 1947, we decided we wanted to do something together."

The elder Powell accepted a five-year contract to manage another local trucking company, and his son joined the same firm as an accountant. When the term of the contract was up, the elder Powell and his partners bought a twenty-six-year-old, bankrupt trucking company headquartered in Oklahoma City and commenced business.

"We brought the company out of bankruptcy in six months," the younger Powell recalled. "Soon after that, we moved the headquarters here.

"There were several reasons for the move. We'd lived here for years—it's our home and we like it. Besides that, the central location is ideal for a transfer company. At that time, we had routes between Chicago and Detroit, Oklahoma and Texas. Now, of course, the company is nationwide, but the central location is still just as good for us, and the city is just as attractive as ever because of its cultural advantages, the parks, boulevards, sports, and all the things that make people want to live here."

One of those things, according to Powell, is the arts. Yellow Freight's corporate headquarters in Overland Park boasts several major works of art, including an Alexander Calder mobile sculpture and a piece by Duane Hanson, famed for his lifelike fiberglass sculptures of human figures. Fittingly enough, the corporation owns a figure called "Trucker."

The company, which contributes toward the support of the Nelson Museum, Kansas City Symphony, State Ballet of Missouri, Kansas City

Ford's Kansas City Assembly Plant ships vehicles to all fifty states as well as Canada, Mexico, South America, and other overseas locations. Photo by Hank Young/Young Company

Lyric Opera, Missouri Repertory Theater, and the Kansas City Art Institute, is one of a fairly select group called The 2 Percent Club. Begun by the Chamber of Commerce of Greater Kansas City, the club is made up of companies that pledge to donate 2 percent of their pre-tax earnings to the support of charitable organizations.

It's over four decades since the first computer, the thirty-ton, boxcar-sized ENIAC, started the communications revolution, which came of age with the transistor. Now, in Kansas City as elsewhere, the fastest-moving commodity in today's economy, information, moves electronically through modems, via satellites, and on microwaves. For the first time in its history, our nation is moving away from manufacturing and toward information- and service-oriented businesses, most of which rely upon various kinds of long-distance telecommunication.

Once again Kansas City is in the right place and at the right time. Businesses in this area have a natural geographic advantage because of our location in the Central Standard Time Zone. This enables them to extend the ordinary working day one hour in the morning for telecommunication with the East Coast, and two hours later to reach businesses on the West Coast during their regular working hours.

United Telecom is one of the communications giants in our city. Located a few blocks away from the Country Club Plaza, just across the

# STINSON, MAG & FIZZELL
## Successful in its Service to Clients

Stinson, Mag & Fizzell is Kansas City's largest law firm with more than 170 attorneys located in three offices in downtown Kansas City, Overland Park, Kansas, and Dallas, Texas.

The early principles expounded by the founders of the firm have influenced it throughout its history. Founder Frank Rozzelle was a city councilman and police commissioner, and was William Rockhill Nelson's personal lawyer. Rozzelle joined the law practice of Jesse J. Vineyard and John Hamilton Thacher. In 1920 Arthur Mag came aboard. Mag gained a national reputation for developing charitable trusts and supported many civic endeavors, including helping create the Kansas City Association of Trusts and Foundations.

Both Mag and Robert B. Fizzell, Sr., who joined the firm in 1944, were leaders in original efforts with the Citizens' Association to oust the Pendergast machine. Fizzell, the Midwest's foremost legal authority on municipal bonds, brought his municipal bond practice with him to the firm and, in 1948, chaired the commission that drafted the Jackson County Charter.

Today Stinson, Mag & Fizzell continues to be a business law firm, with the largest general corporate and banking

*Partners in the firm's Overland Park Office (Johnson County, Kansas) are represented by (from left) Michael Lerner and Roger Stanton, litigation; Stan Woodworth, corporate law; and Carl Circo, real estate development.*

law practice in the area geared to handle business and commercial matters for large and small clients. This capability includes mergers and acquisitions, registration of securities with the SEC, private placements of securities, leveraged buyouts, regulatory matters for financial institutions and broker-dealers, investment company work, bankruptcies, international business law, and hospital and health care law. The firm is also involved in mortgage banking, construction financing, real estate sales and leases, zoning and development, and historic preservation.

Corporate and financial institution law clients include the largest savings and loan association and two of the four largest bank holding companies in Kansas. In addition, Stinson, Mag & Fizzell is general counsel to the nation's largest farm supply cooperative.

The chairs of the firm's practice areas include James L. Viani, corporate, financial institutions, and real estate; John C. Noonan, litigation; Earl J. Engle, labor and administrative law; Morton Y. Rosenberg, taxation; John C. Davis, trusts and estates; and Jerry T. Powell, public finance.

The public finance department represents governmental entities, banks, investment banking firms, savings and loan institutions, private borrowers, and others in a wide variety of public finance matters. They include

municipal and industrial projects, public power, pollution control, health care, schools, and housing facilities.

According to Jerry T. Powell, who is also the chairman of the firm's managing committee, Stinson, Mag & Fizzell has represented many entrepreneurs from the early days of the founding of their businesses, helping make a difference in their success. "We have literally hundreds of clients relying on us for everything from the smallest legal matter to decisions of major importance to their businesses," he says.

Powell stated that the Stinson, Mag & Fizzell litigation practice is broad-based. The primary thrust of the practice is in the field of commercial litigation, including such areas as antitrust, securities, contract, professional malpractice, and environmental law. In addition, the firm defended Hallmark Cards, Inc., and Crown Center Redevelopment Corporation in cases resulting from the fall of the Hyatt Regency Hotel skywalks, and the firm is counsel for Goodyear Tire & Rubber Company and other companies with respect to product liability litigation. The firm has

*From left: John Noonan, commercial litigation; Ralph Wrobley, mergers and acquisitions; Mort Rosenberg, taxation; Jerry Powell (chairman of the managing committee), public finance; and Dick Nixon, securities and tender offers, comprise the firm's managing committee.*

fit financings, international transactions, and a wide range of employee benefit arrangements. They advise corporations, individuals, trusts and estates, cooperatives, and tax-exempt organizations on a variety of tax matters.

The firm has more than 4,000 estate planning clients, ranging from individuals with uncomplicated estates to complex estate problems requiring business planning, reorganizations, and recapitalizations.

Recently Stinson, Mag & Fizzell attorneys were instrumental in the effort to transfer President Harry S. Truman's home to the National Park Service. The firm's relationship with the Trumans goes back a long way. The firm represented both Harry and Bess Truman in the sale of the old Truman Farm, now Truman Corners Shopping Center, and also prepared their wills and various trusts.

Today the firm's attorneys continue to be active in civic affairs. Edward S. Biggar was recently president of the Kansas City Board of Police Commissioners. Donald H. Chisholm just completed a term as chairman of the Truman Medical Center's board of trustees. Michael Dorsey recently resigned from the partnership to serve as assistant secretary of the Department of Housing and Urban Development. James A. Heeter serves on the city council of Kansas City, Missouri. Annually the Stinson, Mag & Fizzell Foundation makes a substantial financial contribution to local causes.

Commenting on the firm's strengths, Powell says, "At Stinson, Mag & Fizzell, we devote all of our efforts to the practice of law and serving our clients, and we believe that doing this well will make our firm successful. There is a continuity here that is not often present in today's world. We have a singleness of purpose and feel that we are a part of—and have the responsibility to continue—an excellent legal tradition."

*A portion of the firm's extensive law library.*

successfully defended the suburban school districts in Kansas City's recent school desegregation case. Powell noted that "Today our litigation practice constitutes a larger percentage of our practice than at any time in the past."

In the area of labor and administrative law, Stinson, Mag & Fizzell represents management clients nationwide in all phases of labor and employment law, including labor contract negotiations, arbitration proceedings, and proceedings before the National Labor Relations Board. The firm's attorneys handle employment discrimination complaints, union organi-

zational efforts, and issues regarding the discipline and discharge of employees. They also assist clients in the development and administration of programs dealing with drug and alcohol abuse, affirmative action, sexual harassment, and other policies and plans dealing with employee relations.

Stinson, Mag & Fizzell's tax attorneys are involved in corporate reorganizations, acquisitions, liquidations, joint ventures, traditional and tax bene-

state line in Westwood, United Telecom has been headquartered in Kansas City since 1966. Founded in Abilene, Kansas, nearly ninety years ago as an independent telephone service, the company is ranked as the second largest independent telephone system in the nation. It currently serves 3,000 communities in nineteen states, and employs 27,000 persons nationwide, 2,700 of them in the Kansas City area. The company's newest venture is a nationwide fiber-optics telecommunications network which will use signals sent by lasers.

Do-it-yourselfers have been keeping the lumber business healthy in Kansas City as far back as 1858, when a Mr. Ranson was building up a section of the city. (Ranson's once-suburban addition is in Section 32, just east of the downtown business district. It's hilly now, and it was hilly then, but a contemporary writer made it sound good: "This Addition of Mr. Ranson's happens to be so located, and so laid out, that buyers can have property sloping or fronting in any direction . . .") The special appeal of Ranson's Addition was that prospective homeowners could get big bargains by using bricks from Ranson's brickyard and lumber from his sawmill nearby. Several substantial houses from the period still stand in Ranson's Addition, attesting to the appeal his innovative offer had for the hardy and handy homebuilder.

"Don't do it yourself without us," advises developer Ranson's spiritual successor, Payless Cashways, Inc., one of the city's biggest and fastest-growing industries. The company, with its headquarters at 23rd and Main, has over 160 stores in seventeen states and 14,000 employees nationwide. In Kansas City, the firm employs about 1,100 persons and

*Payless Cashways is one of Kansas City's fastest growing industries with over 160 stores in 17 states and 14,000 employees nationwide. Photo by Hank Young/ Young Company*

operates ten stores in the metropolitan area. In the last five years, the company has doubled its total facilities and tripled its sales—not a bad record for a Depression Baby.

Payless was founded in Pocahontas, Iowa, over half a century ago by an enterprising lumberman, Sam Furrow. Furrow was a man ahead of his time; his marketing concepts, one-stop shopping for building supplies, fair pricing, and extensive advertising are industry standards today.

The first years of Payless Cashways read like a Horatio Alger "luck and pluck" tale. The year of the Crash, 1929, when the country's economy was virtually going belly-up, was the time Furrow chose to go into business for himself. A bankrupt and heavily encumbered lumberyard was up for sale, an early victim of the Depression. Furrow and his two grown sons, Vern and Sanford, "did some tall scratching" to come up with the $10,000 needed to make the deal, and their business was launched.

The business grew and expanded steadily over the years as a privately-owned firm. In 1969, the company went public and its stock was traded for the first time on the New York Stock Exchange. In 1982, one year after moving its corporate headquarters to Kansas City, the company chalked up $500,000,000 in annual sales.

The usual meaning of the phrase "a house built of cards" suggests a very fleeting kind of fame, but not when it's applied to those cards you send "when you care enough to send the very best." They're the foundation of a $1.5 billion industry. Hallmark Cards, Inc., is a worldwide organization that has its international headquarters right here in Kansas

*Hallmark Cards, Inc., a worldwide organization, has its international headquarters in Kansas City. Photo by Michael A. Mihalevich*

# RUSSELL STOVER® CANDIES
## Only the Finest® Since 1923

Russell Stover Candies was born in the snow-capped mountain surroundings of Denver, Colorado, more than 60 years ago. In 1923 Clara and Russell Stover went to Colorado looking for success, and they found it with their first batch of home-fashioned candies.

The Stovers opened their first candy shop in Denver with a simple formula: provide the customer with quality, value, and service. This simple formula appealed to candy lovers throughout the region and set the stage for future growth. The fledgling business moved to Kansas City in 1928 to capitalize on middle America's love for its hand-dipped candies.

The company's move to Kansas City, Missouri, brought it to the attention of Louis Ward, a local box maker. Ward saw an opportunity to improve on the Stover success formula. He believed the formula was sound, but that it should be applied on a national basis in a variety of selling environments. So in 1960 he bought the interests held by the Stovers and their partners. The candy concern he bought was the fifth-largest candy company in the United States, with sales of approximately $18 million.

In the first 37 years of growth Russell Stover Candies derived the majority of its sales from company-owned candy shops. These shops were supported by candy kitchens that could barely keep pace with customer demand. Ward believed that if the firm was ever going to become a dominant force in the candy industry, it would have to expand its sales and manufac-

*The newly remodeled Russell Stover Ward Parkway store in Kansas City.*

turing capacity. Lacking the funds necessary to purchase the operation and provide for planned expansion, a public offering of the company's stock was made in 1960.

Armed with funds made available from the public offering, the firm set out to increase sales. Sales growth would be achieved in the 1960s and 1970s by opening company-owned candy shops and agency accounts throughout the United States. Company-owned candy shops were opened strategically to fulfill new sales opportunities and enhance consumer awareness. Agency accounts in department stores, drugstores, and card shops dramatically increased everyday impulse sales to consumers looking for convenience. The euphoria of record-breaking sales during the 1960s and 1970s was tempered by the inability of the small and outmoded candy kitchens to manufacture enough candy. The tremendous growth in selling outlets also strained the ability of the company to distribute candy on a timely

basis.

The 1970s and early 1980s were dedicated to building sufficient manufacturing and distribution capacity to fulfill ever-increasing sales growth. New candy kitchens were built in South Carolina (1967), Virginia (1968), Colorado (1973), and Tennessee (1979). These kitchens were designed to be the most efficient manufacturing facilities of their kind in the United States and the world. Distribution centers were built in Pennsylvania, Virginia, Georgia, Kansas, Texas, Colorado, Indiana, and California to efficiently deliver finished candy to all selling outlets.

The early 1980s saw Russell Stover Candies return to family ownership with a buy back of all public shares by the Ward family, as well as continued sales growth throughout the United States.

Today Russell Stover Candies approaches the end of the decade with sales of approximately $200 million and more than 22,000 agency accounts. The candy company that began more than 60 years ago has grown dramatically, but still adheres to the formula of providing the customer with "Only the Finest" of quality, value, and service.

*The Cookeville, Tennessee, candy factory is one of several designed to be the most efficient manufacturing facilities of their kind in the United States and the world.*

City. The company produces more than eleven million greeting cards per day, prints them in twenty languages, and distributes them in more than 100 countries.

It's a pretty staggering record for a product that began modestly. Greeting cards today are commonplace, but over seventy-five years ago, when Hallmark founder Joyce C. Hall produced the forerunners of today's ubiquitous Hallmark cards, the general public exchanged few cards, except for an occasional Valentine or Christmas greeting. Young Hall began by marketing picture postcards, a popular fad in 1910, but soon moved on to greeting cards.

Five years later, the young company was almost wiped out by a disastrous fire. One of the few things they salvaged was the sentiment on one of their early greetings: "When you get to the end of your rope, tie a knot and hang on."

They did. Today, Hallmark employs 20,400 full-time and 7,800 part-time employees nationwide, with about 6,000 employees in the Kansas City headquarters alone. Through the company's profit-sharing plan, Hallmark employees own about 33 percent of the company. *Fortune* magazine ranked Hallmark corporation number eleven in size in its most recent listing of privately held industrial companies.

The company occupies more than two million square feet of space in its own "city within a city," Crown Center. The 85-acre, $500-million development near the historic Union Station includes the 730-room Wes-

*Crown Center features the world-class Westin Crown Center Hotel (top) and Kaleidoscope, a hands-on art workshop for children (above). Photos by Michael A. Mihalevich*

53

# FAULTLESS STARCH/BON AMI COMPANY
## A Familiar Name to Generations of Consumers

For 100 years Kansas City's Faultless Starch/Bon Ami Company has proven its products to be reliable friends to generations of people across the country. Even the building that houses the firm's national headquarters is a century old—and is renowned in story and in song.

The historic New England Building was erected in 1887, the same year the Faultless Starch Company was founded. At that time the Massachusetts brownstone, Italian Renaissance-style structure was considered the most elegant office building in town. Newly renovated, the building has 16-foot ceilings, 57 fireplaces, and 2 walk-in safes on each floor. It is also considered one of the earliest examples of fireproof construction.

By 1968 the Faultless Starch/Bon Ami Company was beginning to outgrow the office space in its plant at 1025 West Eighth Street, where the firm had been located since 1903. Looking for just the right place to house his operation, Gordon T. Beaham III, company president, purchased the New England Building at 112 West Ninth Street and

*The century-old New England Building, home of the Faultless Starch/Bon Ami Company, was considered the most elegant building in Kansas City when it opened for occupancy. Listed on the National Register of Historic Places, it has been restored to its original grandeur.*

started renovating the structure, moving the firm's general offices into the top two floors.

Beaham was intrigued by the building, especially its place in history. According to legend, the body of outlaw Jesse James was stored in one of its vaults for several years, in order to keep it safe from grave robbers. Some say the seven-story building, the city's tallest prior to the turn of the century, is the same one referred to in the song from the musical *Oklahoma!* entitled "Everything's Up To Date In Kansas City."

Today the Faultless Starch/Bon Ami Company headquarters is very much up to date. Every floor of the building has been redone, and the structure is now listed on the National Register of Historic Places. It has a new elevator, and the heavy oak woodwork has been stripped of layers of paint to reveal its natural beauty. Tenants enjoy an exquisite, historically correct interior restoration, as well as excellent views of the Missouri River and North Kansas City.

The nineteenth-century structure, part of an up-and-coming business neighborhood, is included in an entire block that has been declared a historic district. Together the three entities—a magnificent historic building, a starch company, and a cleanser firm—are providing another century of fine service to new customers.

At the helm of the operation is Gordon T. Beaham III, the great-grandson of Major Thomas G. Beaham, founder of the original Faultless Starch Company in 1887. After moving to Kansas City where he bought a coffee, tea, and spice firm, Major Beaham met pharmacist Harvey Bosworth and purchased his formula for a dry white starch. Beaham eventually marketed the product that was soon to become a household word.

Faultless Starch was truly a convenience product of the time. In Faultless, housewives had a clothing starch they could use without boiling, a product to add an elegant finish to embroidery and lace, a treatment for skin irritations, and a baby powder.

Beginning in the 1890s, Faultless Starch books of fairy tales, activities, and household hints were distributed with boxes of the product in Texas, Indian Territory, and later in rural areas in the South. Popular for more than a quarter-century, the publications are credited with helping many children in isolated locations learn to read. The Faultless trademark, a red star of Texas, was granted to Major Beaham in 1902 and is still in use today.

Just a year before Faultless was founded, John T. Robertson had experimented with feldspar, a waste product produced in the manufacture of quartz soap. The soft mineral, when powdered and mixed with soap, created a less abrasive cleanser for polishing enamel and metal surfaces. According to legend, a local minister named the product Bon Ami, "good friend." It became one of the first all-purpose cleansers used on sinks, tubs, tiles, windows, pots, and pans. Today Bon Ami, with its 100-year-old trademark chick who "hasn't scratched yet," is recommended by many cookware and appliance manufacturers.

Faultless Starch grew through the 1960s with the addition of a unique high-quality aerosol starch and fabric finish to its product line. In 1962 Faultless Starch products were sold worldwide in U.S. military commissaries and exchanges, and by 1964 the firm marketed a line of bulk laundry starches to commercial laundries. Six years later Beaham acquired the Kleen King Company and its line of metal cleaning products for the home.

The corporation began to diversify as the market for starch and fabric finish began to decline between 1970 and 1976. With more and more permanent-press and synthetic fabrics being introduced, Beaham saw a new opportunity in acquiring the Bon Ami Company, a household products firm whose earnings had recently declined.

Beaham changed the name of his organization to Faultless Starch/Bon Ami Company in 1974 and reintroduced Bon Ami cleanser to the mass market with the slogan, "Never underestimate the cleaning power of a 94-

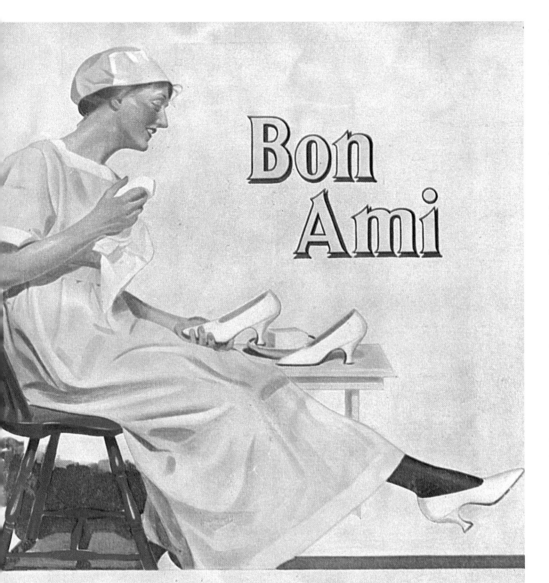

## Restores the "new" look to white shoes—

I used to paint right over the grime and stain with a shoe-whitener, and then, as soon as the whitener rubbed off, the stains would show again.

*Now* I scrub off the grass-stains and mud-stains with Bon Ami and uncover the original whiteness. That makes them look like new shoes again—none of that daubed-over, whitewashed appearance!

I won't need any shoe-whitener until the original whiteness is actually worn through. Then I shall still use Bon Ami to get a good clean basis for the whitener.

For canvas, cloth, and leathers, except white kid.

*"Hasn't scratched yet!"*

Made in both cake and powder form

*A* McCall's *magazine advertisement for June 1918.*

year-old chick with a French name." The product now has a 5-percent market share and is found in most of the nation's major supermarkets.

"Our strategy was to get to people who knew about Bon Ami and loved it," says Beaham. "We advertised in upscale magazines and on television, targeting people who were aware of the product but didn't know where to find it. We didn't change a thing about the odor-free, nonpolluting cleanser."

With the increased demand for cotton and other natural fibers in clothing, sales of Faultless Starch products also are on the upswing. And other well-known and new products have added to the growing corporation's successes. In 1976 Beaham acquired exclusive U.S. sales rights to Garden Weasel, a garden tilling tool that became a leading seller. Other product lines include Faultless Hot-Iron Cleaner and EZ-Off products, which remove melted fabric build-up and other matter from metal pressing surfaces; Touch-Up, an ironing aid for people who don't iron; and wrinkle-removing Valet in a Spray Clothes Freshener.

Beaham is especially proud of the fact that Faultless Starch/Bon Ami Company is manufacturing products that benefit people and won't harm the environment. "People believe in us because we believe in them," he says. "We won't put out a product unless it makes a real contribution to their lives."

*The Bon Ami chick who "hasn't scratched yet"® has been a company trademark for 100 years.*

tin Crown Center hotel and the 733-room Hyatt Regency Kansas City; a tri-level retail complex; Kaleidoscope, a creative art workshop for children five to twelve years old; several restaurants; a bank; movie theater; structured parking for 5,000 cars; apartment and condominium buildings; and a ten-acre central square.

"The Crown Center Redevelopment Corporation, a Hallmark subsidiary, was created to bring vitality to an aging area in which our corporate offices were located," said Donald Hall, chairman of the board of directors of Hallmark. "The result, after nearly two decades of construction, is a complex . . . of which all Kansas City can be proud. The entire project was designed to reflect the values of the community and to bring a human dimension to the relationships among corporation, employees, and city."

Hall called the city "less institutional and more human than many," with residents who share a sense of family and community that rests solidly on fundamental American values.

"Kansas City is an especially good place to live, to raise a family, and to conduct business," Hall said. "It is mainstream America, with a spirit and an ethic that live up to the 'heartland' image its location suggests. Its people possess a moral and spiritual fiber that give deep meaning to honesty, sincerity, and courage. And there is enough frontier spirit, reminiscent of the days of westward migration, to keep the city vibrant with new quests.

"Hallmark has been fortunate to sink its roots into this fertile soil. Our growth is a tribute to a city whose soul is a mix of fierce pride, pure Midwestern warmth and sound human virtues."

*Above: The Crown Center's retail shops provide endless opportunities for browsing, buying, and fun. Photo by Michael A. Mihalevich*

*Opposite: Crown Center's tri-level retail complex of boutiques, department stores, restaurants, and theaters attracts residents and visitors alike. Photo by William W. Westerman*

# 3
# BUILDING THE DREAM

Kansas City once boasted an upside-down house in what was, in the 1850s, the steep and hilly heart of the business district. Dr. Thomas B. Lester had a nice little office in the front room of his house on Main, between Second and Third streets, where the wagons sometimes had a hard pull up the steep slope.

The city fathers smoothed it out some, grading the street down a full ten feet—and leaving the physician's front door high and dry. No problem—Dr. Lester built a second story under the first and opened up to receive patients once more. A year or so later, here they came with the graders again, this time leaving the new front door twelve feet above street level. The good doctor built a third story—two floors down from the original ground floor—and carried on business as usual.

That dauntless attitude was typical of the city's earliest boom period. A reporter of the day described the city scene as one where "carts and horses wallowed in the mud of . . . excavations, and the houses stood trembling on the verge . . ." It was typical of the town in its early days— business people were eager to see Kansas City grow, and nobody thought much about a little inconvenience.

Those old-timers would feel right at home in the booming atmosphere of Kansas City today, with new construction, estimated at well over $1 billion annually since 1982, virtually on all sides. During 1984 and 1985, local developers have put more than $4.4 billion into new and renovated commercial projects. Commitments for future projects total another $2.25 billion.

A local wag commented that the crane ought to be the official city mascot—not the bird, but the machine. Throughout the metropolitan area, construction cranes jut against the horizon on all sides. Office towers, hotels, shopping centers, manufacturing plants, apartments, and single-family houses are rapidly filling in formerly vacant land.

After several years when very little happened after the "rebirth of

*Opposite: The setting sun highlights Kansas City's booming construction, estimated to be worth over $1 billion annually. Photo by Bob Barrett*

*Next page: Kansas City's central business district presents an ever-changing skyline, with more than a dozen new buildings undergoing construction or recently completed. Photo by Bruce Mathews*

Left: The new AT&T Town Pavilion complex has added 900,000 square feet of office space to Kansas City's downtown area. Photo by Bob Barrett

Opposite: Topping the United Missouri Bank building, shown here under construction in 1986, is the ubiquitous construction crane, a frequent sight in downtown Kansas City. The nearly completed Commerce Bank building towers to the right. Photo by Bruce Mathews

Next page: Barney Allis Plaza in the heart of the downtown area provides ample parking and a welcome respite for office workers and shoppers who come here to visit and sit in the sun during lunch hour. Photo by Michael A. Mihalevich

downtown" was heralded as imminent by hopeful new projects that died on the vine, the gridlock suddenly broke loose. With projects like the $64-million, 524-room Vista International Hotel, which opened late in 1984, and the redesign of Barney Allis Plaza as a park in the heart of downtown, things began to look more lively. But it was the sudden boom of business space construction that made things really take off.

In the downtown area alone, more than a dozen new buildings are in progress or recently completed, including the 1.2 million-square-foot AT&T Town Pavilion complex, which alone has 900,000 square feet of office space. There's also One Kansas City Place, Two Pershing Square, Commerce Bank Building, Mutual Benefit Life Insurance Company's Western Home Office, Twelve Wyandotte Plaza, United Missouri Bank Building, 2405 Grand on Crown Center Square, and Hallmark Technology and Innovation Center. Among them, they account for over four million square feet of new downtown office space.

In 1985 alone, more than 3.3 million square feet of new downtown office space were completed, followed by another three million square feet in 1986. In a single year, 1986, office expansions and new businesses attracted to Kansas City absorbed more than 2.5 million square feet of

Above: Downtown Kansas City is a blend of old and new architectural forms. Here the venerable Union Station (foreground) contrasts with the Pershing II building. Photo by Hank Young/Young Company

Left: Projects like the Vista International Hotel, seen at left, and Twelve Wyandotte Plaza, at right, have brought new business to the city center. Photo by Bruce Mathews

Opposite: Barney Allis Plaza is a picturesque place to pause on any tour of Kansas City's downtown area. Photo by Bruce Mathews

# THE ZIMMER COMPANIES
## Deep Roots Sow New Growth

For 40 years The Zimmer Companies have had a vital part in the building of Kansas City, with roots that have grown deep in the community and extend back until just after the turn of the century.

Hugh J. Curran came to Kansas City in 1907 on behalf of the Armour and Swift families to participate in the beginning of the development of the sprawling prairie on the north bank of the Missouri River that eventually became North Kansas City. For more than 30 years, as an officer of the North Kansas City Development Company, he helped build a city of industry that today employs 50,000 persons in a wide variety of business activities.

Curran's son-in-law, A.W. Zimmer, came to Kansas City in 1924 from Tampa, Florida, and worked for the North Kansas City Development Company until 1947, when he left to form A.W. Zimmer and Company, an industrial real estate brokerage firm. His son, Hugh J. Zimmer, joined the business in 1953 and has served as its president since A.W. Zimmer's death in 1957.

Gilbert Labar entered the industrial real estate brokerage business in

*The Zimmer Companies' commitment to the continued growth and development of the Kansas City area is evident in this new 45,000-square-foot headquarters building at 1220 Washington Street. This was one of the first new structures to be built in the Quality Hill district in an overall renaissance of this historic area.*

*Officers of the corporation are (left to right) Robert A. Beck, D. Michael Posten, Lewis L. Dail, Hugh J. Zimmer, A.W. Zimmer III, and Robert W. Steinbach. Each of the principals holds membership in The Society of Industrial and Office Realtors and other professional affiliations, as well as local real estate and civic organizations.*

1928, specializing in the vast industrial areas surrounding the Central Industrial District of Kansas City, Missouri, and Kansas City, Kansas. Robert W. Steinbach joined Labar in 1958, and eventually the firm became Steinbach Associates.

From the mid-1950s until the late 1970s A.W. Zimmer and Company and Steinbach Associates had major impact on the industrial development of greater Kansas City, locating and expanding much of the city's industrial base. In 1981 Zimmer and Steinbach merged their real estate brokerage op-

erations into Zimmer-Steinbach Brokerage Company, which, together with A.W. Zimmer and Company, Zimmer Development Company, and Zimmer Management Company, comprise the base of The Zimmer Companies today.

In addition to its position as one of the principal commercial and industrial brokerage firms in Kansas City, The Zimmer Companies are continuing their development of the city. Over 20 million square feet of office and industrial buildings have been constructed. Much of the development of the Paseo Industrial District of North Kansas City, the 330-acre AirWorld Center adjacent to Kansas City International Airport, and more than 1,000 acres in Lenexa, Kansas, are attributed to The Zimmer Companies.

Projects in the mid-1980s include continuing construction and improvement of AirWorld Center and the Lenexa Industrial Park; commencement of the 300-acre SOUTHLAKE project in Johnson County, Kansas; the Greenridge Office Park in Raytown, Missouri; and numerous other individual office and commercial projects throughout the city.

In addition to its brokerage and development activities throughout the metro area, The Zimmer Companies have developed commercial projects in 12 states across the country, comprising more than 4 million square feet of office and industrial buildings.

In 1984 the organization assembled a city block of land just west of the central business district of Kansas City, Missouri, on historic Quality Hill. Construction of a new 45,000-square-foot office building for The Zimmer Companies operations was completed in late 1985 and led to the rapid redevelopment of this historic area.

In the early 1980s the fourth generation of the Zimmer family joined the firm together with the second generation of the Steinbach family. Hugh Zimmer's children, David and Ellen, and Robert Steinbach's son, Brad, are carrying on traditions that will lead The Zimmer Companies into a second century of real estate activity in Kansas City.

*Office expansion and new business add to the phenomenal growth rate in Kansas City's commercial centers. Photo by Bob Barrett*

this space. Such a rate is little short of phenomenal—fully 38 percent above the previous year. Despite the exceptional amount of new available space, this influx kept the local office vacancy rate at 15 percent—a rate below the national norm. Although some doomsayers have viewed the boom with alarm—citing such Sunbelt cities as Dallas, Houston, and Oklahoma City while prophesying an office space glut—the demand for office space seems to be keeping pace with the growing supply.

Part of the secret of this success is no secret at all to Kansas Citians. Our town has long been hailed as "one of the few livable cities left," and the news keeps spreading.

In addition to all the new building going on, there are more than thirty downtown structures, totalling over two million square feet of space. This movement is playing a very important part in the long-awaited renascence of downtown. Buildings with a total of more than one million square feet of this renovated space arrived on the scene in a dead heat in 1985. The downtown profited in a sudden increase of new businesses locating there, and these new tenants benefited from the competition among developers to fill the new spaces.

Such major renovation projects have increased Kansas City's visibility on the national map of historic preservation. Some important, newly re-

stored Kansas City landmarks include the Coates House hotel, the Design Exchange, and Thayer Place, historic structures located in the heart of the city's old garment district. On the drawing board at Market Area Development Corporation are plans for a large-scale residential, commercial, and office project to revive the City Market area immediately south of the bend in the Missouri River—the city's original downtown.

One of the most exciting developments in historic preservation going on right now is the realization of a long-standing dream. In the late 1960s, Arnold Garfinkel, head of Quality Hill Redevelopment Corporation, started buying property in the area bounded by 10th and 14th, Washington and Jefferson streets: the historic Quality Hill area. The general view of many local real-estate promoters was that "Arnie must be nuts." All the movement was then away from the inner city—toward the suburbs. And Quality Hill's once-stately residential neighborhood of tree-lined avenues and prosperous nineteenth-century homes had long before declined to a shabby backwater of heartbreak hotels and derelict houses. It would take a loving eye to see much that was beautiful there, but Garfinkel had what it took.

"I fell for the history," he said, noting that some of the structures in the area dated from as early as 1856. "The architecture was swell, and the proximity to downtown was sensational, but it was the sense of history in the area that really got me."

*Opposite: The fountains of Barney Allis Plaza lend vitality and charm to a contemporary setting. Photo by Bruce Mathews*

*Below: Kansas City's demand for office space keeps pace with the growing supply as evidenced by the use of the new Twelve Wyandotte Plaza building in the downtown area. Photo by Bruce Mathews*

Above: Designed in 1900 by noted architect Louis Curtiss, the restored Folly Theater is the oldest and newest element of the Convention Center complex. Photo by Bob Barrett

Right: New residential construction in the Claymont Area north of the river reflects the overall boom in housing for Kansas City. Photo by Bruce Mathews

Opposite: The restored Bunker Building at 9th and Baltimore is one of several structures that formed part of the nineteenth-century financial district, an area now being revitalized. Photo by Michael A. Mihalevich

Next page: Downtown's Quality Hill, shown here during renovation, was a once-thriving nineteenth-century community. Upwardly mobile residents are moving back into the area now that it has been revitalized. Photo by Bruce Mathews

In 1983, Garfinkel's company teamed up with McCormack, Baron & Associates, a St. Louis developer, in a joint venture to begin renovation of the area. While modern buildings are a part of the plan—which feature office, retail, and residential spaces—between fifty and fifty-five historic structures and more than seven blocks of the district will have been rescued and reclaimed by the time the second phase of the $200-million project is completed. McCormack, Baron opened its first residential phase in 1986, a development consisting of 366 multifamily residential units. For the first time in decades there is a significant residential population in this area of the downtown. The first wave of returnees, eager for the charm and convenience of the new urban spaces, settled into apartments and renovated loft residences like SoHo West and Eighth Street Place—all carved out of former factories and warehouses.

At the other end of the metropolitan complex, in Overland Park, Kansas, is College Boulevard, the area's fastest growing business district. As recently as 1973, the street was a blacktop road cutting through prairie land. Now it's a divided four-lane thoroughfare so dense with business that it has its own weekly newspaper: *College Boulevard News* (circulation 22,000).

In this area, there are more than 100 office buildings, with a total of over five million square feet of office space—that's an average of a million square feet for each mile of the five-mile stretch known as the College Boulevard Business Corridor, which extends westward from Roe

*Above: Kansas City's new back-to-the-city movement has brought about a surge of urban renovation. Photo by Bruce Mathews*

*Opposite: Today large families are finding ample and gracious accommodations on the city's northeast side. Photo by Bob Barrett*

# BLACK & VEATCH
## Moving Ahead with Kansas City

Founded in 1915, Black & Veatch today ranks as Kansas City's largest engineering and architectural firm. Through the years it has grown along with the city, playing a key role in the expansion of local utility systems, industry, and government facilities.

Black & Veatch also is one of the leading design firms on a national scale. Its 3,000 employees provide services in every major field of engineering and architecture throughout the United States and in 40 countries overseas.

A comprehensive range of study and design services is provided by the firm's six major divisions: Civil-Environmental for water, wastewater, solid waste, hazardous waste, and transportation; Management Services for financial studies, regulatory assistance, and data-processing development; Power for electric power generation, transmission, and related electric system requirements; Industrial/Special Projects for plant, process, and systems design for industry and government; Architectural for total commercial, institutional, and industrial building design services; and International, which develops, contracts for, and manages the firm's overseas projects.

The firm also has expertise in such areas as dams, tunnels, storm drainage, flood control, urban and regional planning, resource recovery, energy management, and space and

*Black & Veatch occupies more than 500,000 square feet of office space located in several buildings throughout the Kansas City area.*

defense facilities. Through a wholly owned subsidiary, Black & Veatch offers specialized engineering services for the petroleum and petrochemical markets throughout the world.

Providing quality service means a commitment to give each project the full attention it deserves. That is the basis upon which Black & Veatch has built its reputation. Since its founding, the firm has been engaged in more than

*The firm's 3,000 employees provide services in every major field of engineering and architecture throughout the nation and in 40 countries overseas.*

13,000 projects for 3,000 clients with a high percentage of repeat commissions.

Black & Veatch can mark its progress by the projects it has completed. For example, the 14-mile Blue Valley and Gooseneck sewer trunk lines in Kansas City were designed by the firm in 1927 and are still in service. In 1946 the firm assisted the U.S. Government in converting its temporary facilities at Los Alamos, New Mexico, into a permanent research and development center for the Atomic Energy Commission.

More recently, Black & Veatch designed Trans World Airlines' air cargo facility and two-story reservations computer center at Kansas City International Airport. It also engineered the utility systems for the city's prestigious Crown Center commercial complex.

Significant projects to meet the growing environmental needs of the expanding metropolitan area include the Birmingham wastewater treatment facility and a major water system expansion program for the rapidly growing suburban areas in nearby Johnson County, Kansas.

In the architectural field, Black & Veatch lists among its recent work a Marriott Hotel and several major office buildings in suburban Overland Park, Kansas, as well as the renovation of Barney Allis Plaza, an urban park in the heart of downtown Kansas City.

Although its activities today reach throughout the globe, Black & Veatch has never outgrown the needs of its hometown and looks forward to being a part of Kansas City's exciting future.

*College Boulevard and Metcalf in Johnson County's Overland Park is part of Kansas City's fastest-growing business district. Photo by Roy Inman*

Boulevard on past Quivira Road.

More than 900 businesses have headquarters or branches on College Boulevard, including the establishment for which it's named, Johnson County Community College (JCCC). The largest community college and the fourth largest institution of higher education in Kansas, JCCC opened in 1972. Students, credit and non-credit, total close to 30,000 and the school employs nearly 1,500 full- and part-time personnel.

Black & Veatch Engineers-Architects has a branch on the boulevard where over 1,700 persons are employed, and Yellow Freight Systems, one of the nation's largest trucking firms, has its corporate headquarters on College Boulevard. Insurance service centers and telecommunications companies are big employers on the boulevard, where 51 percent of the labor force is female and the median salary is more than $25,000.

Over 60 percent of College Boulevard workers come from Johnson County, another 28 percent from counties across the State Line in Missouri, and 10 percent more come from other counties in Kansas. The 294-acre office complex, Corporate Woods Office Park, was the first significant commercial development along College Boulevard. It was developed as a joint venture of Metropolitan Life Insurance Company and Corporate Woods Associates, a partnership formed for the purpose.

*(continued on page 86)*

# HOWARD NEEDLES TAMMEN & BERGENDOFF
## Cloaked in History, HNTB Helps Shape the Future of Kansas City

Picture Kansas City without many of its corporate office buildings or bridges spanning the Missouri River. Visualize the metro area without a sports complex, international airport, the convention center, and a number of major freeways. That would be a picture of Kansas City if just some of the projects in which HNTB has been involved disappeared.

Howard Needles Tammen & Bergendoff (HNTB), architects, engineers, and planners, has participated in the growth of Kansas City in two ways. As a respected firm, HNTB has grown in stature and size to become one of the largest design firms in the country. And HNTB has literally helped shape Kansas City—its development, its transportation, its commerce, and its recreation. HNTB is proud of its involvement in Kansas City's past and of its continued role in the city's future.

Founded in 1914 in Kansas City, HNTB has become one of the nation's leading multidisciplinary design firms, with offices in 35 cities in the United States. HNTB provides comprehensive design services in architecture, engineering and planning.

HNTB's Kansas City and Overland Park offices represent nearly 350 architects, engineers, planners, and support personnel of the 2,000 employed by the firm. The firm has been involved in over 10,000 projects—at home and abroad—representing more than $100 billion in construction costs. HNTB has been consistently rated as one of the top 15 design firms in the country.

HNTB's influence on Kansas City's growth dates back to the firm's founders' design of the ASB bridge, spanning the Missouri River. With the opening of the bridge to traffic in 1911, the days of the ferry boat from Kansas City to north of the river were over. The young but rapidly growing firm went on to design 11 of the city's 15 Missouri River bridges as well as many of its freeways and traffic systems.

HNTB's projects have also contributed to Kansas City's reputation as "one of the country's best-kept secrets." In concert with the J.C. Nichols Company, HNTB designed the Alameda Plaza Hotel, Seville Square, and the Wornall Road Bridge—as the Country Club Plaza grew into one of the most famous shopping centers in America.

HNTB's mark on the city is also reflected in Kansas City International Airport, noted for its innovative gate system, and in the Harry S. Truman Sports Complex, the only individually designed and simultaneously constructed twin stadium facility in the country.

Important to Kansas City's economy are the HNTB-designed corporate offices of several national companies. The offices of United Telecommunications, Inc., Employers Reinsurance Corporation, and North Supply Company provide modern and efficient surroundings for Kansas City workers. North Supply's office building—the largest in Kansas—also serves as a gateway for Johnson County Industrial Airport, a growing suburban airport that HNTB helped design.

Working with national developers, HNTB has participated in a substantial way in the addition of office buildings that provide expansion space to draw new corporations to the greater metropolitan area. HNTB designed the Plaza West Office Complex, now US Sprint Plaza, as well as Copaken, White and Blitt's Renaissance Office Complex.

HNTB has also helped alter the Kansas City skyline. The 38-story AT&T Town Pavilion, already a landmark, takes its place among the older buildings downtown and beckons residents and visitors alike to a revitalized downtown. Its gleaming stainless-steel tower seems to reflect HNTB's rich history and the firm's impact on Kansas City's future growth.

The underlying theme to all the growth that HNTB has been involved in is summed up by Cary Goodman, a partner in the firm. "The projects we design, whether they're for a private entity or for the various cities that comprise the metropolitan area, ultimately affect the public," he says. "It is this public and the dreams they hold for their city's future that guide us in our creativity and final product."

HNTB's plan for restoration of the city's riverfront area takes into account people's age-old attraction to water and the once-important influence of the Missouri and Kansas rivers on Kansas City's own birth and development.

Situated at the foot of Grand Avenue and bounded by the Broadway

To reflect the vitality and history of a city, riverfront parks contain spaces for people to have fun, learn, or just gather.

Comprising three circular terminals for ease of circulation, the Kansas City International Airport displays a feeling of warmth to passengers.

*Although completed in 1972, the Alameda Plaza Hotel complements the character of the Country Club Plaza.*

*The United Telecommunications, Inc., corporate offices in Westwood, Kansas, creates flowing forms from the street, yet does not overpower the residential community it resides in.*

*This twin sports facility comprises a 78,000-seat football stadium for the Kansas City Chiefs and a 41,000-seat stadium for the Kansas City Royals baseball club.*

and exciting restaurants and shops overlooking the river would offer recreation as well as a scenic view to the throngs of visitors.

The riverfront plan includes riverside trails for hiking, bicycling, or horseback riding. Planned riverfront housing on scenic bluffs would attract a residential population, while an aquarium or a museum would interest both visitors and residents. This new-built environment would be designed to reflect the vision of vitality for Kansas City, a liveliness reminiscent of the era of Kansas City's birth along the rivers.

HNTB is also involved in a feasibility study for a new light rail system to provide more efficient transportation within the growing city. Cary Goodman believes that ". . . with more people using a transit system, traffic congestion downtown could be reduced, parking problems could be minimized, and our city's pollution would be improved. In addition, trolley cars add fun and excitement to any urban setting, thereby increasing the city's vibrance."

In keeping with the city's magnificent and visionary boulevard system planned by George Kessler at the turn of the century, HNTB's study and plan for Kansas City includes transforming the Grand Avenue/Main Street Corridor into a high-quality urban development. In addition to dotting the avenue and its environs with landscaping, sculptures, open spaces, and fountains, the plan entails tying the area from the riverfront to Crown Center into one contiguous business district—complete with retail shops, offices, hotels, and recreational and cultural activities.

Grand Avenue and Main Street are symbols of the city's past. As the spine of a growing city, this new Grand/Main corridor will give rise to Kansas City's future growth.

Bridge on the west and the Paseo Bridge on the east, a redeveloped riverfront would attract tourists and residents alike. Annual river festivals and outdoor musical performances would find ample space in a new public square or park. A marina and dock complex would provide visitors with easy access to explore the waterways. New hotels

*Offices, retail, and activity, and the restoration of two historic buildings, comprise the new AT&T Town Pavilion at 12th and Main streets—Kansas City's centerpiece for its downtown resurgence.*

# CLARKSON CONSTRUCTION COMPANY
## Part of Kansas City Progress

During the past decades and now in the 1980s the Midwest's urban areas have undergone a construction revolution. Enormous projects of great significance have literally changed the face and tempo of Kansas City, and the family-owned Clarkson Construction Company has played a role in virtually all of those projects.

Five generations of the Clarkson family have participated in the construction progress of Mid-America. The first generation got its start in the business over a century ago, when G.G. Clarkson and his two sons, Edwin F. and Ferd, hired out mule teams and buckboards, clearing and excavating landsites for residential areas. Clarkson Construction Company was formally established in 1880 and began to compete for road-grading contracts.

As the town prospered, so did the Clarksons. The firm's first office was at 3431 St. John, and in 1883 it landed one of its first projects: grading the roads of St. John from Belmont west to Cleveland Avenue, then the eastern edge of Kansas City.

As Kansas City grew, Edwin and Ferd Clarkson took the reins, building Kansas City's main arteries and excavating basements for the city's nation-

*Clarkson Construction performs the foundation excavation and shoring for many of the buildings that grace Kansas City's skyline.*

*Clarkson Construction work forces complete contracts on every major component of Kansas City's highway transportation system.*

ally famous residential areas. In the boom years between 1910 and 1930 Clarkson Construction was heavily involved in road and street excavation and building as Kansas City grew southward. When the automobile became available to average families, the Clarksons prepared for the work eagerly. But the Great Depression curtailed the majority of large construction projects, and Clarkson Construction, like other companies, suffered through the trying times. However, at the close of the 1930s and with the coming of World War II, a new era of construction was at hand.

Ed Clarkson, the third generation of his family to be involved in the business, saw the firm become heavily involved in the building of the Kansas highway system and flood protection dams prior to World War II.

During the war Clarkson Construction erected a number of air bases, among them facilities in Dodge City and Wichita, Kansas. The company also built Kansas City's Northeast Industrial Levee, which protected that vital area from the devastating flood of 1951. In addition, major earth-moving contracts for road construction were awarded to the firm. In 1954 Clarkson Construction cleared the site and built the dam for Lake Jacomo in Jackson County, Missouri, and also undertook major highway projects on the Kansas Turnpike.

As the company began to receive extensive regional recognition as a major heavy contractor, it began to diversify. When W.E. "Bill" Clarkson took over from his father, Ed, there were more changes as the firm became a premier highway contractor. Responsible for much of the construction of interstate highways I-70, I-29, I-35, I-435, I-470, and I-635, Clarkson Construction also built other midwestern pri-

*Superior Asphalt Company provides a complete reconstruction of the base for new playing fields for both Arrowhead and Royals stadiums at the Harry S. Truman Sports Complex.*

mary and secondary road systems.

The company expanded into concrete and asphalt paving work and construction material production involving crushed stone, sand, gravel, and ready-mix concrete. With its continuing capabilities in diversified drainage work and heavy structural concrete work, the firm was able to compete in almost every facet of heavy construction.

Today Clarkson Construction, located at 4133 Gardner, is at the forefront of the construction industry for Kansas City and the surrounding region. The fifth generation of the Clarkson family—D.J. "Don" Clarkson, vice-president of Clarkson

*Clarkson Construction Company provides major grading, structural concrete work, and surfacing at the Midwest's largest industrial and public works projects.*

Construction Company, and Bill Clarkson, Jr., president of Superior Asphalt Company—is involved with their father in every facet of the firm's operation.

As a transportation contractor, the company is heavily involved in new highway construction and in the extensive program for rebuilding and refurbishing aging and deteriorating highway, bridge, and street systems in greater Kansas City. The firm is also involved in air transportation with extensive work contributed to the building of airports such as Kansas City International. Superior Asphalt Company, a wholly owned subsidiary of Clarkson Construction Company, has successfully repaved both of the main runways at Kansas City International Airport.

As a site work contractor, Clarkson Construction has completed the excavation, grading, concrete and asphalt paving, drainage, and foundation concrete at such Kansas City landmarks as the General Motors' New Fairfax

Assembly Plant, Crown Center, City Center Square, the Hyatt Regency Hotel, and the Independence Shopping Center.

As water resource contractor, Clarkson Construction has built projects that provide flood control, water supply, and recreational lakes for such areas as Smithville Lake and Harry S. Truman Reservoir.

Related to the energy field, Clarkson Construction has completed the site preparation for a variety of energy-related installations, including the Jeffrey Energy Center and the Wolf Creek Nuclear Power Plant.

The firm prides itself on having the best equipment available and an excellent construction work force. The company's machine fleet is one of the largest in the Midwest. Bulldozers, scrapers, front-end loaders, ready-mix plants, asphalt plants, excavators, draglines, pumps, and bridge finishers are just a fraction of the inventory. Yet it is manpower, not machinery, that Don Clarkson believes is the company's most important asset.

Says Clarkson, "Without the right people, from the equipment operator through top management, no project can be performed properly and on schedule. Our construction, accounting, and engineering staffs provide expertise from project development, if desired, through construction completion, ensuring proper project control and coordination."

Equally important is the family's involvement in local civic and voluntary activities. Bill Clarkson, who served as a member of the Jackson County Sports Authority from 1967 to 1974, was chairman at the time the organization was coordinating the construction of the Harry S. Truman Sports Complex. He also served as chairman of the Convention and Visitors Bureau of Greater Kansas City from 1977 to 1979 and as chairman of the board of directors of Research Health Services.

Says Clarkson, "When opportunities arise to operate a business within the community, we feel an obligation to give something back to the community for that opportunity."

# BOYLAN & COMPANY
## Planning for the Future

Boylan & Company was founded July 1984 by Carroll J. Boylan, president and chairman of the board. A full-service commercial real estate company, the scope of its activities includes brokerage, leasing, development, and management of retail, office, warehouse, and apartment projects.

A team of approximately 40 licensed realtors specialize in each of the various fields. The highly qualified men and women of Boylan & Company are constantly improving their individual and collective knowledge of the real estate profession. By continuing to attend courses and seminars designed for their profession, Boylan realtors provide the best in a competitive and constantly changing field. The success of Boylan & Company lies in its ability to recognize the common goal of all real estate owners: to maximize the value of their assets.

The development division of Boylan & Company is currently constructing numerous shopping centers, office buildings, and mixed-use industrial parks for its clients, combined with its comprehensive services. The firm assists in in-depth design and construction, syndication, and property management. In addition, financing is available through the assistance of Mark Boylan.

*Boylan & Company—planning for the future. Courtesy, Bob Barrett*

The officers of the firm include Carroll J. Boylan, a licensed realtor since 1972 and a building contractor since 1962. Starting with a small firm in 1984, Boylan has built the business up to become one of the largest commercial real estate firms in the metropolitan Kansas City area by emphasizing top brokerage and leasing. Boylan, who is very active in the company's daily business, has been involved in the development of shopping centers, offices, and subdivisions for more than 20 years. She previously was licensed with another major developer as projects manager for several shopping centers.

Boylan was raised in real estate by her parents, Tom and Jeanette Jay, owners of Jay's Better Homes and Gardens Realtors, who also developed apartments, hotels, office buildings, and six residential subdivisions. Boylan says, "Without the loving support of my husband, Dr. Peter Boylan, and family, I could not have accomplished as much."

Mary K. Bishop, vice-president of Boylan & Company, holds a broker's license in Missouri and Kansas. She became sales manager of Boylan & Company in October 1984, after having been a successful brokerage agent for many years. Her experience includes the brokerage of office and retail buildings, apartment projects, and development tracts. In addition to her duties as sales manager, she manages development projects.

Brooke Management (named after Boylan's daughter, Amy Brooke Boylan), a division of Boylan & Company, was organized in 1985 to provide superior property management for all the company-related properties as well as provide the best management services available. Brooke presently has management contracts on several projects in Kansas City.

James L. Albertson II, director of office leasing, began his real estate career in 1978 as broker/manager for a national franchise residential/commercial brokerage firm. In 1982 he became executive vice-president of James M. Rodewald Company until 1984, when he started his own firm. Re-

*Boylan & Company performs on-site inspections. Courtesy, Bob Barrett*

cently his business was merged with Boylan & Company. Albertson has an extensive sales and leasing background and has been responsible for the marketing of significant mixed-use parks in the Kansas City area.

Jackson L. Burke, Jr., entered the commercial real estate business after completing his military service in 1978. He began in apartment management and development and soon moved into the retail division of a national building material retailer, where he completed more than 20 projects. As director of retail leasing for the firm, he supervises all retail leasing and has responsibility for the development of several retail projects.

Boylan & Company agents and their families are actively involved in the Kansas City community. Outside affiliations include membership on the boards of hospitals, banks, and area colleges. They also support the art gallery, symphony, and many other cultural projects. Boylan agents also belong to the various professional societies relating to their specialization. They also serve on many local government committees, boards, and political organizations.

In its earliest days Boylan & Company was referred to as a "new firm of experienced experts." Since its inception the firm attracted agents and brokers with prior successful careers in real estate. Every agent has additional special assets that combine to provide the best professional service possible for clients. Boylan & Company is recognized as a leader in the real estate community in Kansas City and as a fast-growing, energetic organization that is developing first-class projects throughout the metro area.

Boylan & Company strives today, tomorrow, and the next day to exemplify creativity and innovation for its clients.

*Weekly sales meetings are held to brainstorm as to logical buyers and the best way to market each product. Courtesy, Bob Barrett*

Above: A couple enjoys a stroll through Corporate Woods Office Park, a 294-acre complex that is an outstanding example of a planned environment that blends business with aesthetic pleasure. Photo by Roy Inman

Opposite: This office building is located on College Boulevard, a five-mile thoroughfare which has an average of a million square feet of office space for each mile. Photo by Bruce Mathews

Tom G. Congleton, managing partner of the office park, said he got the idea after developing Congleton Industrial Park in Lenexa, near the newly-improved Highway I-35.

"Rail traffic had given way to truck transport, and industry was beginning to move away from the railyards and closer to the highways," he recalled. "People were looking for a nice plant environment, and we tried to provide that in our industrial park. Back then, an industrial park was a new idea for this area."

Congleton said prospective tenants liked the look of the place and asked about office sites in the park. A few were added to the existing industrial park, but the idea gave rise to a bigger plan: the development of a complete business community.

Similar projects across the nation such as Atlanta's Perimeter Center and Las Colinas in Dallas were researched. The developers identified several factors all had in common: attractive executive housing close to the workplace; a belt highway system giving ready access to and from all parts of the metropolitan area; a large available labor pool; top quality buildings and maintenance; good security; and free parking for employees.

When Congleton first proposed the idea of Corporate Woods, backers urged him to consider a site farther east, near the state line and some of the city's most luxurious suburban housing. He held out for the more westward location near the U.S. Highway 69/I-435 cloverleaf interchange, correctly predicting that as traffic increased, ready highway access would prove an important attraction to future tenants. The Highway 69 Bypass links to Interstate Highway 35 near the office park providing quick communication with other commercial centers, and the fastest route to the airport from the southern part of the metropolitan area.

"Business transportation from all other eastward business locations has to pass us to get downtown or to the airport," Congleton said.

Close to 6,500 persons are employed by the more than 350 tenant firms in Corporate Woods. The office park has its own bank, a Doubletree Hotel, a park, a shopping center, and close to two million square feet of office space in twenty-two major buildings with seven more buildings on the drawing board.

"We didn't create the market for suburban office space, but we did build to accommodate it when we found out the market was there," Congleton said.

The success of Corporate Woods soon attracted other developers and other projects. The result was to turn College Boulevard into an important suburban business center in the metropolitan area. Major names in Kansas City real estate and development are prominent on the Boulevard—names like Executive Hills, Inc.; C.B. Self & Company; Copaken, White & Blitt; Property Company of America; Block & Company, Inc.; Leo Eisenberg Company; Trammell Crow; Varnum/Armstrong/Deeter; and R.H. Sailors Company.

Hop on I-35 and head north and you'll hit yet another of Greater Kansas City's new boom towns, "Northland." The area is in Platte and Clay

(continued on page 91)

# DOUBLETREE HOTEL
## Adding First-Class Luxury to the Community

The Doubletree Hotel in Kansas City opened in 1982 as part of an exciting, innovative new concept called Corporate Woods—an office building complex constructed in a scenic, park-like setting, complete with hotels and recreational and entertainment facilities.

When Doubletree was first conceptualized, the now-flourishing area stretching south and east along College Boulevard was just taking root. Since opening, the residential and business community has continued to mushroom.

Operated by Doubletree, Inc., of Phoenix, Arizona, the Doubletree was the premiere first-class luxury hotel to open in Overland Park and the Corporate Woods area. Today, with 357 rooms, it is the second-largest hotel in Overland Park. Other Doubletrees are located in Monterey, Seattle, Tucson, Dallas, Houston, Vail, Scottsdale, Denver, Tulsa, Orange County, Atlanta, Santa Clara, and Salt Lake City.

Due to its unique location, the Doubletree caters to a specialized segment of the business meeting market. As an executive conference hotel, it is equipped and designed to handle small corporate meetings of 50 to 75 people, and yet comfortably accommodate groups of 200 or more.

The Doubletree has 14,000 square feet of meeting space, including a 9,000-square-foot ballroom. It also is the only hotel in the area to offer a 50-seat tiered theater designed for sophisticated presentations. The Kansas City Theater is especially conducive for classroom or training meetings.

"Superior amenities and service are hallmarks of the Doubletree. The

*Located within wooded jogging trails, the Doubletree Hotel has such amenities as a whirlpool, sauna, and a glass-enclosed indoor pool, shown here.*

service-oriented staff begins with the top management and the employees go to extra lengths to provide what people really enjoy when they travel away from home," says Susan Blanco, director of human resources.

Eric Danziger, Doubletree's vice-president of operations, echoes her thoughts. "Our people," he says, "were the fundamental ingredient in our initial successes and are the driving force that moves us forward today."

*The Rotisserie Restaurant and Grill, located in the Doubletree Hotel, provides a comfortable yet sophisticated atmosphere to unwind and dine in after hours.*

Mary Mantle, director of marketing, adds that employees are specially trained to remember names and recognize repeat customers; they thank them for coming and ask them to return. "Whenever you walk in the door at the Doubletree, there is always a smiling face to greet you—someone to give you a helping hand and provide information or give directions."

The Doubletree is located in relaxed, comfortable surroundings retaining a cosmopolitan flair. All guest rooms are maintained to provide maximum comfort for the business executive as well as an attractive setting for a weekend retreat. The hotel, situated on nine miles of wooded jogging trails, features an indoor pool, whirlpool, and sauna. It is also the only hotel in the Kansas City area to offer two indoor racquetball courts. To unwind after hours, the Butterfly Club is an ideal place to enjoy dancing and cocktails before dining in the exclusive Rotisserie Restaurant and Grill.

The hotel's dedication to service has included community involvement. The Johnson County Cancer Society has been the prime recipient of that dedication. The Doubletree Hotel has also hosted the Ronald McDonald sports show, been involved in the Special Olympics, and sponsored a weekend for the Heartland School Riding Academy for handicapped children.

# GEORGE BUTLER ASSOCIATES, INC.
## Designing For Kansas City's Future

Since its founding in 1969, George Butler Associates, Inc., has provided engineering, architectural, landscape architectural, and planning services to clients throughout the Kansas City area and surrounding states. During that period the Kansas City-based company has grown dramatically in both size and scope. Today GBA is one of the largest and most prominent consulting firms in the area, with more than 200 professional, technical, and support personnel located in six offices in Missouri, Kansas, Iowa, and Oklahoma. The company's impact on the Kansas City community has been significant.

At the Harry S. Truman Sports Complex, home of Kansas City's championship professional baseball and football teams, GBA was responsible for the design and construction supervision of all site improvements, including grading, storm drainage, roadways and bridges, utilities, parking for 20,000 cars, and design of the vehicular circulation system.

At the University of Kansas Medical Center, GBA engineers and architects provided mechanical, electrical, architectural, and structural design for

*At Executive Park, a 1,200-acre commercial and industrial park in Kansas City, GBA provided a comprehensive range of services, including land planning and landscape architecture, civil engineering, and architectural and engineering services for approximately 1.46 million square feet of commercial and industrial space. Photography by Bob Barrett, ASMP*

an extensive addition to the Applegate Energy Center. The addition almost doubled refrigeration capacity while improving energy efficiency throughout the 45 buildings that make up the institution's 54-acre urban campus.

And at Executive Park, a 1,200-acre commercial and industrial park located in Kansas City's Northeast Industrial District, GBA provided a comprehensive range of services, including land planning and landscape architecture, civil engineering, and architectural and engineering services for approximately 1.46 million square feet of commercial and industrial space. Reynolds Metals Company selected GBA for the architectural and engineering design of its 350,000-square-

foot aluminum can manufacturing plant in Executive Park. Tnemec Company, Inc., Keebler Company, and the Midwest Terminal Warehouse Company also selected the firm to provide design services for structures in the park.

GBA's multidisciplinary staff of engineers and architects has played a significant role in much of the area's recent industrial, commercial, and residential development. The company provided planning and engineering services for area landmarks such as the award-winning AirWorld Center, a 320-acre business and industrial development located adjacent to Kansas City International Airport; SouthLake, a 310-acre business park in Lenexa, Kansas; Northgate, a 270-acre commercial, office, and residential development in Olathe, Kansas; and Hawthorne, a 200-acre planned community in Overland Park, Kansas.

In addition, GBA has worked closely with many area cities to accommodate growth and help improve the quality of life for residents. The firm has designed thoroughfares and bridges, water- and wastewater-treatment facilities, storm drainage systems, and parks and recreational facilities for a long list of cities, including Kansas City, Blue Springs, Gladstone, Independence, Lee's Summit, and Liberty in Missouri, and Kansas City, Fairway, Leawood, Lenexa, Olathe, Overland Park, and Prairie Village in Kansas.

As Kansas City and its neighboring communities continue to grow, George Butler Associates, Inc., intends to continue its participation in that growth, providing the most comprehensive, high-quality design services available.

*At the Harry S. Truman Sports Complex, home of Kansas City's championship professional baseball and football teams, GBA was responsible for the design and construction supervision of all site improvements, including grading, storm drainage, roadways and bridges, utilities, parking for 20,000 autos, and design of the vehicular circulation system. Photography by PHOTOTechnique*

# PATTY BERKEBILE NELSON IMMENSCHUH ARCHITECTS
## Providing Architectural Services for Downtown Revitalization

Patty Berkebile Nelson Immenschuh (PBNI) Architects was formed in 1970 by three men who wanted to go beyond the "traditional architectural services." The three founding PBNI architects— R. Bruce Patty, Robert J. Berkebile, and Thompson C. Nelson—were joined in 1972 by David Immenschuh, an interior designer who has since become a partner. Together they provide innovative architectural services, interior design, development planning, neighborhood conservation, landscaping, and graphics.

At PBNI the principals developed a corporate philosophy that reflects a team approach that includes the client. "Design at PBNI is not a mystical exercise, it is a rational process rooted in economic and functional logic," the firm's philosophy statement says. "The product is invariably better when the owner is involved in the process from beginning to end—when there is a give and take, review and criticism."

The firm is actively involved in the revitalization of Kansas City's central business district, having provided com-

*In the midst of downtown development, the rounded corner and faceted mass identifies 12 Wyandotte Plaza as a distinctive addition to the area.*

plete architectural design services for two major downtown buildings for Executive Hills, Inc.: the 18-story, mirrored-glass 12 Wyandotte Plaza Building, which now houses PBNI's offices, and One Kansas City Place, a 42-story office and retail complex that will be Missouri's tallest building. Other

downtown projects include the three-story Zimmer Building, designed to showcase the quality of brick detailing that was so evident in the history of Quality Hill.

Several projects have been designed on the Kansas side of the metro area, including the award-winning corporate headquarters of MAST Publishing Co., located near the College Boulevard corridor.

Space planning and interior design expertise also figure prominently in PBNI's accomplishments. These services, ranging from programming through selection of furnishings and fixtures, have been provided to a wide array of clients, including hotels, medical facilities, educational institutions, and governmental facilities. Their firm's experience with office space encompasses the design and planning of more than four million square feet of space for such clients as IBM, the Federal Reserve Bank, the American Red Cross, and Southwestern Bell.

PBNI's restoration of the Folly Theater is illustrative of its involvement with historic structures. In addition to design work, the principals served as fund raisers, historians, and construction managers. The project's result was a 1,000-seat performing arts center, for which PBNI received the Kansas City Chapter of the American Institute of Architects 1982 Design Award.

Recognized locally and nationally for their work, the four principals of PBNI Architects have contributed significantly to community development. R. Bruce Patty was the 1985 national president of the American Institute of Architects, a 50,000-member professional organization. Robert J. Berkebile, an AIA member, is the current president of the Folly Theater Performing Arts Foundation and a member of the State of Missouri Advisory Council on Historic Preservation. Thompson C. Nelson, an AIA member, is chairperson of the Kansas City, Missouri, City Planning Commission, a vital group in the planning of Kansas City's future. And David Immenschuh is the current national vice-president of the Institute of Business Designers.

*The capstone of current downtown development is One Kansas City Place. The 42-story structure, when completed, will be Missouri's tallest building, combining a form influenced by 1920s architecture with sheathed glass rising from a granite base.*

counties, north of the Missouri River bend. In an earlier day, it was best known for tobacco fields, apple orchards, and a rich vein of history—featuring our own American Robin Hood, Jesse James.

The interconnecting highways that make a fast-track loop around the city have helped to change all that. Together with the new bridges that carry traffic northward on two interstate highways and a much improved system of east-west streets in the Northland area, the road system now provides good access for commuting workers. The opening of the western leg of Interstate Highway 435, following hard on the heels of the eastern opening of the interstate, tying into Interstate 29 near Kansas City International Airport (KCI), has also influenced growth. It's estimated that by the year 2000, job opportunities in the Clay and Platte counties area will have grown to over 125,000.

Boosters point to the many advantages of Northland—an excellent school system, low taxes, a population shift that has increased the area's political clout, and a concerted effort by a diverse collection of development groups to publicize the charms of this part of the city, which has numerous residential and recreational lakes as well as a number of important industries.

# J.C. NICHOLS COMPANY
## Keeping an Eye to the Future

The vision of developer Jesse Clyde Nichols (1880-1950) is nowhere more keenly exemplified than in his Country Club Plaza, one of Kansas City's favorite tourist attractions and its premiere shopping district. Opened in 1922 in what once was home to shanties and muddy hog pens, the Country Club Plaza is remembered as the first shopping center designed to meet the demand of the emerging motoring public. Nichols also envisioned the Plaza as the gateway to his Country Club District, a residential development of neighborhoods to the south and west.

Today Christmas on the Plaza is a nationally known event as 155,000 brilliant lights and 47 miles of wiring colorfully outline the buildings. Nichols patterned the architecture after the classical charm of colonial Spain, and the entire area reflects that design. Moorish towers and brick-paved courtyards house shops and boutiques that, along with the lure of big names such as Saks and Bonwit Teller, have made the Country Club Plaza a shopper's fashion paradise.

The Country Club District's 60 neighborhoods reveal Nichols philosophy of real estate development in that he studied successful residential areas nationwide, analyzed neighborhood problems, and forged solutions. He also startled contemporaries, saying that it didn't have to cost any more to build a beautiful community than an ordinary one. He theorized that such an area would attract people inclined to maintain its nicer-place-to-live image.

Nichols introduced large-scale planning innovations, including land set aside for schools, churches, park facilities, and shopping centers. He advocated building codes to ensure appropriate land use for all time. He also encouraged city planners to adopt a street and boulevard system that took advantage of the area's rolling terrain. In addition, Nichols invested in Italian statuary and art objects to enhance the neighborhoods and shopping centers. He later was instrumental in organizing homes associations in order to assist home owners in the maintenance of their communities.

*Every year from Thanksgiving through December, thousands enjoy the magical splendor of Christmas, when the J.C. Nichols Company illuminates its Country Club Plaza with 155,000 brilliantly colored lights.*

Since 1905 the J.C. Nichols Company has created nearly 20,000 homes, as well as scores of apartment communities, office buildings, business parks, and shopping centers within more than 8,000 areas. Successors at the firm have carried on the founder's commitment to excellence and sense of civic responsibility, striving to ensure that the quality of life will continue from one generation to the next.

As for the future, the J.C. Nichols

*Contributing to the eternal appeal of the Country Club District—and a distinction that sets it apart from residential neighborhoods of other developers—is the J.C. Nichols Company's investment in statuary and art objects.*

Company will continue to invest in area development as it has in the past. The development of hotels represents an area of future growth for the corporation. First there was the Alameda Plaza Hotel in Kansas City. That was followed by the European-concept Raphael hotels in San Francisco, Chicago, and Kansas City. Recently the firm has embarked upon a joint venture with Marley Continental Homes of Kansas, Inc., in a modular home building plant, and has set up a marketing arm for the product.

Another major event in the history of the J.C. Nichols Company occurred in 1985 when it entered the Des Moines market. An office park, a large apartment complex, and an industrial park have proven profitable. That experience has encouraged the enterprising firm to seek opportunities in other U.S. markets.

Trans World Airlines is an important employer in the area, with a major aircraft overhaul base and reservation center near KCI. Years ago, Hugh Zimmer, a principal of the Zimmer Companies, saw the opportunity for development of the airport area as an office and distribution center. Today, companies large and small are beginning to jump on the bandwagon that started to roll with Zimmer's development of Airworld Center on Interstate Highway 29, just south of KCI.

One of the first developments to bring Northland into the news occurred in 1972, with the opening of the 150-acre theme park, Worlds of Fun. Street shows, international cafes, a railroad, a riverboat, and a host of exciting rides and roller coasters made it an instant favorite. Ten years later, the park's developer, Hunt Midwest Enterprises, Inc., followed with a second hit, the 60-acre Oceans of Fun—a particular boon for us landlocked residents of what Kansas City author Richard Rhodes called "The Inland Ground."

These leisure-oriented enterprises were the first projects of Hunt Midwest Enterprises in the area. Now the company is developing 2,500 acres in Clay County for limestone mining, commercial, and residential use. The company's recently opened Value World shopping mall has already become a hit with economy-minded consumers.

Further, Hunt Midwest leads the area's development of commercial and warehouse activity in underground space. Kansas City is a major storage and distribution point because of its man-made limestone caverns, the result of intensive quarrying in the area. The temperature-constant environment, dust-and vibration-free, is valuable not only for storage but for housing facilities that manufacture precision instruments so sensitive that, above ground, surface street vibration would be a problem. Dean's Fairmount Company is another leader in the development and innovative use of limestone cavern space. Its Downtown Underground Industrial Park at 31st and Mercier was one of the earliest, and in 1986, the firm announced plans for SolarGardens, an underground project at Interstate Highway 35 and 23rd Street in Jackson County.

Another early Northland booster is Ted Ehney, Jr. Ehney is chief executive officer of Executive Hills, Inc., whose projects include Executive Hills South, an office complex on College Boulevard; Executive Hills East, near I-435 and Holmes; the downtown office towers One Kansas City Place and Twelve Wyandotte Plaza; the Radisson Muehlebach Hotel renovation downtown; and development of a 4,000-acre tract near the airport, which Platte and Clay countians expect will materially advance the commercial and residential possibilities of the area.

The plan for the Northland development of Executive Hills North includes nine million square feet of office, warehouse, and retail space, plus hotels and motels. Approximately half of the 4,000-acre assemblage is slated for use as residential development; about 9,000 houses are expected to be built over the next ten years. An unusual feature of the planned roadway system for the area is one familiar to Cape Codders—the traffic "rotary," or circular intersection. Ehney has office buildings and retail shops open in the Northland project and additional office

(continued on page 101)

# BUCHER, WILLIS & RATLIFF
## Transforming Creative Ideas into Practical Solutions

The Bucher and Willis partnership was established in 1957 in Kansas City, Missouri, by civil engineer and city planner James D. Bucher and Shelby K. Willis, a structural engineer. In 1983 the firm merged with the Ratliff Company, an engineering firm headquartered in Texas, and changed its name to Bucher, Willis & Ratliff.

As a consultant, Bucher, Willis & Ratliff offers professional engineering, planning, and architectural services to commercial, industrial, and governmental clients. Fourteen partners now own the firm and guide an operating staff of more than 200 people, working in offices located in Missouri, Kansas, Texas, and Illinois.

The firm's formative years were spent producing street, highway, bridge, utility, and communications plans and specifications. Later an Environmental Division was established to design water, wastewater, and pollution-control facilities. The Planning Division was created in 1960 to as-

*The Salina Bicentennial Center represents one of the complex design projects handled by Bucher, Willis & Ratliff.*

sist cities with development control strategies, and was later followed by an architectural arm of the company in 1966.

"Through the 1960s and 1970s new areas of expertise were created in response to the changing needs of our clients," says Jon Meulengracht, a partner in the firm's Kansas City office. "As governmental entities and developers became more concerned with evaluating new technology, and the public became more concerned with the impact of these changes, our clients required more sophisticated services. In response, we added professional specialties."

Today Bucher, Willis & Ratliff specializes in total project design and approval, covering such areas as major flood-control and drainage analysis; airport and transportation planning; civil, traffic, structural, mechanical, electrical, and environmental engineering; urban development planning; architecture; landscape architecture; and communications.

In addition, each of Bucher, Willis & Ratliff's 14 partners are responsible for operating a small, independent divi-

*James Street Viaduct, Kansas City, Missouri. The firm handled the replacement of the viaduct.*

sion of the company. Each "small firm" is characterized by a specialized area of expertise. In this manner, each partner is given immediate access to all of the company's resources.

"For example," says Jimmy Lin, a Kansas City partner, "an architectural project usually requires input from civil, structural, mechanical, and electrical engineering. A planning project may require input from environmental and traffic engineering."

According to Lin, many of the firm's projects begin by working with various interest groups whose input usually carries a significant influence on the project design. The process is often the same for commercial, industrial, and governmental clients.

"We recently completed a preliminary study for the Kansas City Area Transportation Authority, which developed a general design and improvement concept for the proposed Country Club light-rail system from Westport Road to 85th Street," says Meulengracht. "We assembled concerns and opinions from home owners' and business associations, private developer groups, and local governmental departments."

The company also guided the efforts to bring a new metro area general aviation airport on-line in Harrisonville, Missouri. Other area projects include the Research Downtown

*The company's highway engineers have expertise in a wide variety of roadway projects such as U.S. 71 in Missouri.*

Health Care Center, improvements at Kansas City International Airport, Brush Creek flood-control analyses and repair management, and replacement of the James Street Bridge over the Kansas River, saving the substructure.

In addition, the firm completed a transportation improvement study for the entire Kansas City, Missouri, street network, as well as numerous intersection redesign projects, traffic corridor modeling of I-35, and various industrial, commercial, and residential subdivision projects.

With changes in Bucher, Willis & Ratliff's clientele came an increasing need for more sophisticated support facilities. Several years ago the company purchased a VAX 11/780 computer for computer-assisted design and drafting capabilities, and the ability to link each office together for rapid data transmission and access to a central software library.

"Aerial photography, land survey, and contour plotting equipment will soon be integrated with the central com-

*Bucher, Willis & Ratliff's extensive experience with building renovations includes the Sunflower Electric Cooperative, Inc., building in Hays, Kansas.*

puter system," says Lin. "These totally automated systems will allow faster service to meet more rigid time schedules for our clients."

By continuing to develop multi-discipline capabilities, the firm has been able to provide continuity from idea to implementation. Yet the real strength, according to the company's owners, comes from its people.

"The ability, dedication, and enthusiasm to transform creative ideas into practical solutions is the talent we search for and foster in all areas of our work," says Meulengracht. "We're for-

tunate to have a vast pool of dedicated, talented people in Kansas City, and this enables us to competitively offer our services throughout the United States."

Most of the firm's business comes from repeat clients, many of whom have worked with Bucher, Willis & Ratliff for decades. According to Lin, clients keep coming back because of the company's rigid quality-control standards. "Our clients know that a partner will be directly involved in every project, and they've come to expect that kind of direct communication and commitment from us."

# J.A. TOBIN CONSTRUCTION COMPANY
## A Commitment to Kansas City

For nearly 60 years three generations of the J.A. Tobin Construction Company have played a major part in the development and growth of Kansas City and surrounding areas.

As one of the nation's leading heavy-construction contractors, Tobin's wide range of projects includes railways, airports, bridges, viaduct construction and renovation, flood control, energy centers, sanitary and storm sewers, dams and reservoirs, pipelines, pile driving, and diversified heavy construction for major shopping centers and stadiums.

The firm's major work, however, has been highway and heavy construction. Innumerable miles of federal, state, county, and city roads and bridges stretching across the heartland are the work of the J.A. Tobin Construction Company. The firm is qualified in 12 states, all west of the Mississippi, as a

*Framing the Kansas City, Missouri, downtown skyline with completed bridges and paving in progress—Dillingham Freeway I-670.*

transportation contractor.

Tobin's services encompass a comprehensive range of field engineering, surveying, quality control, and field testing—including nuclear density testing. The company is also concerned for the environment as well as the practical business aspects of construction in its extensive site investigations. It accomplishes its projects through vigorous coordinated management, coupled with an impressive array of modern equipment and technology. Guiding the total operation is a versatile and experienced

engineering staff, backed by dedicated long-term employees.

Dotting the Kansas and Missouri landscapes, Tobin construction projects, like a family album, record the proud history of achievements for each of the generations that have been included in the business.

Today's diverse family-run business was formed in 1928 by Joseph A. Tobin. In his 23 years as a contractor, Tobin guided his expanding firm and built thousands of miles of roads under contracts that totalled over $100 million.

The first project he completed was the Seventh Street Trafficway, a durable brick road with a strong base. Later he extended his work to include sewers and viaducts.

Among the first-generation projects were the Turkey Creek and Grand Avenue viaducts, as well as many municipal parking lots. The firm was the contractor for the improvement of Reidy Road, the first link in the creation of U.S. Highway 40 as a super expressway out of Kansas City. J.A. Tobin, whose company completed the enormous project on schedule, was honored with a community celebration.

A next generation of projects fell under the guidance of Joseph E. Tobin, son of the founder. Among them were the site preparation for the Harry S. Truman Sports Complex, grading and paving major portions of Kansas and Missouri Interstates I-29, I-35, I-45, I-70, I-435, and runways for Kansas City International Airport, excavation and grading for the Hall's Plaza store, Great Midwest Corporation's headquarters, Kemper Arena, Worlds of Fun, and joint venture on Smithville Dam, the Oak Park, and Independence Center shopping malls.

The J.A. Tobin Construction Company is also responsible for bridges built in the areas of Russell Road, Parvin Road, and Greystone Heights, and the KCI access road bridges. Included are the original Lewis and Clark and Blue Ridge Boulevard viaducts, and the McGee Street Bridge.

Recreational areas and fishing grounds resulted from the company's

*Joseph A. Tobin, founder (1928) and first president.*

construction on the Harry S. Truman Reservoir Dam. Flood control was the outcome of its work on the Birmingham Levee, the Missouri River Levee, and the Hillsdale Dam in Paola, Kansas.

Quality accomplishments, completed on time, are the hallmarks of success that have won the firm recognition and awards. In 1956 the J.A. Tobin Construction Company received a commendation from the U.S. Army Corps of Engineers for work on the Whiteman Air Force Base runway and taxiway extension.

Three years later it became a member of the Mile-A-Day Concrete Paving Club. Following this the firm was acknowledged as a national leader for interstate highway miles completed in 1969-1971, and several subsequent years.

Randolph Bridge, the longest bridge in Kansas, achieved an AISC Award of Merit for the J.A. Tobin Construction Company. The firm also completed more of the Kansas Turnpike than any other contractor and was cited by the Kansas Turnpike Authority for completing its portion of work on the 18th Street Expressway far ahead of schedule.

In a 1984 anniversary issue of the

*CMI Corporation Magazine,* a lengthy article praised the J.A. Tobin Construction Company for finishing more than one million square yards of paving on schedule as promised, despite rains and flooding.

The following year the firm was presented a Contractor of the Year Award by the American Public Works Association in recognition of outstanding achievement in the successful completion of the McGee Street Viaduct in Kansas City, Missouri.

The company's ability to complete its scheduled goals on time is a result of a carefully orchestrated, fast, and smooth equipment and manpower operation that, through the coordinated efforts of each component, operates almost nonstop. In tight sequence the equipment is moved in constant succession under the direction of experienced Tobin supervisors. The net effect is a substantial savings on transportation expenses as well as time.

Because top condition equipment is a key element in Tobin Construction's total equipment operation, trained maintenance people in the firm give the inventory exceptional care. They lube virtually every day, with the obvious conviction that "grease never wore out a machine."

The third generation of the J.A. Tobin Construction Company is represented by grandson and chairman Shaun O'Rourke, who is committed to the same high standards of the founder. "This commitment is born from tradition and translates into a continued high-quality product that will serve and benefit everyone who lives in a city, county, or state," says O'Rourke.

Mr. O'Rourke's three brothers, Dary, Michael, and Conn, are also associated with the J.A. Tobin Construction Company along with their mother, Patricia Tobin O'Rourke, who serves as vice-chairman of the board.

Responsive to community and business needs, Patricia O'Rourke serves on the advisory board of Donnelly College. Shaun serves on the boards of the Kansas City Art Institute, Johnson County Community College, and the Kansas and Missouri Contractors Association.

# EXECUTIVE HILLS INC.
## Building a new Kansas City

The rapid development of Executive Hills Inc. has an aura of magic about it. In its first seven years the company developed a remarkable five million square feet of new space in Kansas City. Its expansive urban designs have not only changed skylines, but also have thrust the city into a competitive status as a major business and convention center.

The magic growth formula for Executive Hills Inc. comes from the development genius of its principals, Ted Ehney and Larry Bridges. Their formula is an admixture of single-focused vision, determination, aggressive action, and business know-how. They will attest, however, that it is hard work, not wand waving, that brings results. As Bridges has stated: "Development is performance-driven. If you perform, you succeed."

The formula has been good for Executive Hills and for Kansas City. It brings work and business to the people who live here. Local architects and engineers have been chosen to design the company's numerous buildings, and Kansas City-based construction firms complete the jobs. Hundreds of people

*Glenwood Place*

are employed to complete the work, and office buildings, retail shops, commercial businesses, and restaurants have opened as a result of the joint labors.

Under the restless force of its owners, Executive Hills' vast suburban holdings have exploded with new development. Commercial office parks, high-tech office warehouses, hotels, retail centers, town homes, and residential subdivisions have been built in continuous succession. At the same

time the company's high-rise office buildings have revitalized Kansas City's downtown. In 1986 Executive Hills will account for at least 66 buildings completed or under construction, and the firm is landlord to more than 530 businesses.

In a virtual building blitz, the corporation has developed land to the south, north, and east, as well as the heart of the central business district. To date, Executive Hills South in Overland Park has seen the completion of 50 multitenant office buildings. The tallest of those is a $35-million, 250,000-square-foot structure that houses commercial office space above and features a bank, restaurant, stock brokerage firm, and travel agency on the lower floors. A four-acre landscaped lake provides spectacular views for tenants of another 15-story building.

The development also includes the Kansas City Merchandise Mart and Overland Park Expo and Convention Center. The 605,000-square-foot facility is the new home for the Kansas City Gift Mart and its support services, as well as the convention and exhibition hall for Overland Park.

At Glenwood Place, located at 95th and Metcalf, the company has completed two office buildings, with a third 450,000-square-foot structure planned for 1987.

Executive Hills East, at I-435 and Holmes Road in Missouri, is also a master-planned office park. Among

*An artist's rendering of One Kansas City Place.*

the occupants of the five office buildings are the regional offices of several national corporations, including US Telecom, a wholly owned subsidiary of Kansas City-based United Telecommunications, Inc.

North of the river on I-29, 4,000 acres of land are well under way toward the development of a total community. Executive Hills North includes nine million square feet of planned development for residences, offices, retail centers, hotels, and high-tech warehouses. "We are, in a very real way, building a city," says Ehney.

The first hotel to be completed is on the west side of I-29 near Tiffany Springs Parkway. It features 112 units with 15 separate, garden-style structures. On the east side of the highway, multitenant office buildings circle a boulevard on which is centered a major fountain, one of several incorporated into the office park landscape.

Within the development are the Town and Country shops, a complex of retail and supportive services, and three residential subdivisions of town houses and single-family homes. With a total of 9,000 units, the residential developments include Thornhill, with 1,178 custom-built luxury homes sites; Post Hill town homes; and Thistle Hills. The Executive Hills Polo Club opened in 1985 and features guest rooms, equestrian trails, a polo field, practice field, and practice cages.

Executive Hills has not confined itself to creating new development environments on Kansas City's outer edges. It is also using its innovative urban design concepts in the heart of the city. The company's initial commitment to the downtown area began in 1983, when it started construction on the first new office building to be erected in the area in nine years. Twelve Wyandotte Plaza, a $35-million, 18-story office building, was completed in 1985.

One Kansas City Place, a $150-million project targeted for completion in 1987, is a 42-story structure and will be Missouri's tallest building when completed.

The company further expanded its opportunities by initiating a master

*Executive Hills East*

plan for a massive development that calls for an additional 19 buildings on 15 blocks in the downtown area. Appropriately named Kansas City Place, the proposal would represent about 10 percent of the area bounded by the freeway loop and would be about 1.5 million square feet shy of doubling the amount of commercial office space in that area. In addition to the new office buildings, a 400-room hotel and parking facility for nearly 13,000 cars are also being proposed.

The gigantic proposal demonstrates the firm's concept of urban design, which concentrates on clusters of buildings with mixed uses, assembling the parts to create a whole new environment. Kansas City Place will have a diversity of architecture, but common themes in streetscapes, lighting, and landscaping. The buildings will be connected by pedestrian bridges and tunnels. It is estimated that the projected 10-year development period will involve an investment of about one billion dollars.

With its succession of new growth, Executive Hills Inc. has emerged as the area's largest developer in recent Kansas City history. Its strategy of success, based on a can-do philosophy, demonstrates the realm of the possible. It also confirms a belief in Kansas City and its future as one of the top-ranking progressive cities in the nation.

*Executive Hills South*

buildings are under construction.

The Executive Hills developer has said that he expects to attract 80 percent of his tenants in the Northland project from firms not now operating in the Kansas City market.

The eastern side of the metropolitan area is also marked by residential and retail growth. Blue Springs, Lee's Summit, and Independence are bustling with new apartment and residential projects, being led by Farm & Home Savings Association; Weathersone Development Company; Mark Morgan; J.R. Stewart; and Kingston Construction Company, among others. This trend is expected to accelerate as plans progress for the proposed development of historic Longview Farm in Lee's Summit and the public opening of nearby Longview Lake.

A growing office and retail market is pushing the development of the city's midtown and southern sections. Office buildings have sprung up to encircle Kansas City's premier retail center, the Country Club Plaza, developed and owned by the J.C. Nichols Company. Nichols opened its new Board of Trade Center in 1986. Linclay Corporation's One Main Plaza now has a hotel next to the towering office building, just north of the plaza. Fountainview Office Complex, by Property Company of America, is nearing completion, and the George K. Baum Company has plans for a multi-use complex in the area. Irv Maizlish of Leo Eisenberg Company has plans for a midtown office tower, and the R.H. Sailors Company will build an office and residential complex on the east side of the Country Club Plaza. Even further to the east, along Troost Avenue and Brush Creek Boulevard, is the site of a planned office and research park to be developed by the University of Missouri-Kansas City.

Immediately north of the Plaza is Westport, the entertainment playground of the city. It's a complex and diverse area of shops, restaurants, and night spots overlaid on a vital old town that once competed with Kan-

*Above: Kansas City's colorful trolley cars take visitors back and forth between downtown and midtown. Photo by Bob Barrett*

*Opposite: Kansas City's premier retail center, the Country Club Plaza, is playing host to a growing number of new offices and shops. Photo by Michael A. Mihalevich*

Above: Trendy and attractive, Chili's Restaurant is a big draw for many Kansas Citians. Photo by Michael A. Mihalevich

Opposite: Stanford and Sons restaurant in Westport is one of many fine restaurants in the area that attracts throngs of people who come often to see and be seen. Photo by Michael A. Mihalevich

Above: Historic Westport celebrated its sesquicentennial in October 1983. More vital than ever, its many shops, restaurants, and night spots continue to attract locals as well as visitors to the midtown area. Photo by Bruce Mathews

Right: A Saturday excursion to Old Westport includes a stop at an old-time phone booth. Photo by Roy Inman

Opposite, top: The renovated Union Arts Building is an important addition to midtown development. Photo by Bruce Mathews

Old Westport, with its easy-going ambiance, is a popular spot for casual outdoor dining. Photo by Michael A. Mihalevich

Mario's in Old Westport is one of many restaurants that appeal to the trendy crowd that frequents this part of town. Photo by Michael A. Mihalevich

# BURNS & McDONNELL
## An Employee-Owned Success Story

They were seniors at Stanford when Clinton S. Burns and Robert E. McDonnell formulated the idea of a consulting engineering firm. It was 1897, and neither of them had the money to be out on their own. They decided to get jobs for a year and then start their own company.

Today Burns & McDonnell has grown from a one-room office in the New England Life Building at Ninth and Wyandotte streets to a full-service, employee-owned engineering and architectural consulting firm located at 4800 East 63rd Street.

"Burns & McDonnell now has more than 700 capable owners, each one of us dedicated to upholding our proud tradition of excellence," says Newton A. Campbell, chairman of the board. "These are strong shoulders to rely on, the same kind of foundation on which our firm was founded 88 years ago."

In the past decade Burns & McDonnell has worked on several international projects, including a stainless-steel rolling mill in the Republic of China, the planning and design of a $500-million airfield in Saudi Arabia, air base expansion projects in Egypt, water supply and wastewater projects in Indonesia and Guam, and

*The architectural design of this Federal Employees Credit Union main office building won Burns & McDonnell a 1985 Kansas City Corporation for Industrial Development (KCCID) Commitment to Kansas City Award.*

*Burns & McDonnell's master plan and design of Kansas City International Airport helped boost the city's reputation as one of America's fastest growing transportation hubs.*

a geothermal heating project in Iceland.

On December 31, 1985, Burns & McDonnell began a new chapter in its history by once again becoming employee owned. The three men who lead the company today are Newton A. Campbell, chairman of the board; Dave G. Ruf, Jr., president; and Darrell M. Hosler, executive vice-president. Its staff includes engineers of every discipline, architects, planners, economists, environmental scientists, and computer experts.

The company's major areas of expertise include industrial and commercial facilities, airports and aviation facilities, environmental systems, electric power generation and transmission, civil works, and chemical processing. A key subsidiary is the C.W. Nofsinger Company, which specializes in chemical process engineering.

The firm also offers expertise in site selection and planning, environmental impact assessment, economic and financial feasibility studies, assis-

tance with permits and code compliance, facility access design, and construction management.

Many of Burns & McDonnell's projects are award winners. Among its most prestigious was the master planning and engineering of Kansas City International Airport, which was completed in the early 1970s. The project was cited as one of 10 outstanding achievements in the United States in 1972 by the National Society of Professional Engineers. The company has earned many other awards for projects such as the Oceans of Fun and Worlds of Fun theme parks, the Federal Employees Credit Union facility, the Little Blue Valley Sewer District's Pilot Treatment Plant, and the TWA 747 airframe overhaul facility.

"The Burns & McDonnell vision is a bright one," says president Dave Ruf. "For 88 years, we've carried on a strong tradition of being responsive to our clients' needs—in fact our goal has always been to function as an extension of our clients' staff. Now, as employee owners, all of us—from our folks in the mailroom to our board of directors—realize that our practice is a service business, and we exist only to serve our clients. We intend to keep on helping our clients make Kansas City a better place to live."

Boutiques, shops, restaurants, and even hair salons add to the pleasing diversity of Old Westport. Photo by Roy Inman

sas City and finally became a part of it. Because of its rich layering of the old and the new, trendy and stable, business and fun, it's one of the most viable parts of the city. In recognition of Westport's many advantages, developers of hotels, offices, and new residential projects are planning yet more Westport projects, all of which will add to its diverse ambience.

Kansas City's southern bounds have always been its most natural area for growth. A century ago, the outskirts of town were the cornfields at 12th Street; now, nearly 100 blocks to the south, growth continues, with particular vigor around Ward Parkway, Holmes Road, and Interstate Highway 435.

Farther south, at Holmes Road and Interstate Highway 435, both Linclay Corporation and Executive Hills are developing major office parks, and Leo Eisenberg Company has also announced plans to enter the competition there.

Leawood, on the Kansas side of the state line, abuts much of this south Kansas City, Missouri development. This long-established community has always been noted for the high quality of its environment. Residential development continues marching southwest with the plans for a prestigious residential community on the site of the Hall family farm property—to the south of Interstate Highway 435 along State Line Road.

In recent years, the western edge of the metropolitan area has entered its own growth spurt. Kansas City, Kansas looks with pride to its 1985 coup in getting the General Motors Corporation to build a new automotive plant in its Fairfax Industrial District; however, many see most of

the city's future growth occurring along Interstate Highway 70 and the western loop of Interstate Highway 435. Similarly, Shawnee, in northern Johnson County, has a burgeoning area of growth in both commercial and residential properties which lie along Interstate Highway 435 in that sector.

Lenexa, Kansas, once a sleepy little town, was one of the early front-runners in expansion, and now more development is occurring along the new western Interstate Highway 435 loop, with office, warehouse, and light industrial business parks filling the land from 95th Street south, and apartments, houses, and offices spreading northward from there.

Home is where the heart is in Kansas City, and especially if it's a new house. In the Johnson County suburban communities alone, residential permits averaged nearly 6,000 per year in a three-year period. But it wasn't supposed to be that way. All the experts told us so.

As early as the 1960s, sociologists were predicting the demise of the suburbs within ten years. With them would go single-family housing, the pundits said. As the cost of living continued to rise, and particularly as energy costs soared, they predicted that people would no longer be able to afford the luxury of a nuclear-family home and instead would live in high-density cluster housing near the cities' centers.

It was a swell idea and a terrific theory, and the only thing it didn't take into account is that cluster housing is an idea whose time has not yet come. People in Kansas City like single-family dwellings—preferably in the suburbs. The fact that it's still possible here to drive your car without getting gridlocked in traffic—even at rush hours—makes that choice much easier. (Being able to find a place to park it—even downtown—also sweetens the situation.)

Left: Residential construction in Kansas City's suburbs continues to grow to meet the demand for single-family dwellings. Photo by Bruce Mathews

Opposite: This mansion is part of Mission Hills, Kansas City's dream bedroom community. Meandering partly into Kansas, the area boasts natural creeks nestling into hills and valleys that provide a perfect setting for opulent residences. Photo by Michael A. Mihalevich

Next page: Executive Hills South office park offers excellent workspace close to residential communities. Photo by Bruce Mathews

# LINSCOTT, HAYLETT, WIMMER & WHEAT, P.C.
## Creating Architecture that Stands the Test of Time

Architectural beauty and quality that stand the test of time are hallmarks of Linscott, Haylett, Wimmer & Wheat. The award-winning, multispecialty architectural planning and interior design firm was founded in 1951 by William M. Linscott. It is the oldest firm in Kansas City in which all of the partners, including Ward H. Haylett, Jr., Edward John Wimmer, and Richard A. Wheat, are actively involved in every project.

Linscott, Haylett, Wimmer & Wheat's existence spans the post-World War II era that coincides with the period of accelerated growth that has shaped much of present-day Kansas City. The partners are proud of the part the firm has played in making Kansas City one of the country's most beautiful cities. "As architects we have the greatest opportunity to touch and improve people's lives," states Haylett. "It's up to us to make the physical environment as pleasing as possible, and we take that responsibility seriously."

Linscott, Haylett, Wimmer & Wheat is one of the nation's larger architectural firms, with nearly 40 employees, including an eight-person

*The 4900 Main Building, adjacent to Kansas City's unique Country Club Plaza District, exemplifies the high quality of architecture practiced by Linscott, Haylett, Wimmer & Wheat, and expected by its client, the J.C. Nichols Company. Photo by Michael Mihalevich*

office in Fairway, Kansas. Although each partner has several specialties, in many ways the partners are truly generalists. "What we learn from one building type we apply to another," says Wimmer. "We know what it takes to make a structure sound, useful, beautiful, and economical."

Long-term repeat clients of the firm have provided the basis for its success. Typical of these are the J.C. Nichols Company, for whom recent projects in the Country Club Plaza include the 12-story 4900 Main Building; a building, tower, and parking garage; the Ponte d' Espagne; the Court of the Penguins Building; and the Aleman Court. Another local client is Hallmark Cards for whom the firm is currently designing the American Heartland Theater, and for whom past projects include the six-theater Crown Center Cinema Complex, the Streetcar Named Desire Restaurant, and the Crown Room Employee Cafeteria and Card Shop. Educational repeat clients include the underconstruction Longview and Maple Woods campuses for the Metropolitan Community Colleges; three major buildings for Missouri Southern State College in Joplin, Missouri; and eight projects for the Lee's Summit School District No. R-7.

Other prominent commissions of the firm are the H.D. Lee Building,

*The four principals, pictured at the recently completed United Missouri Bank Plaza facility in Kansas City, Missouri, bring a unique blend of talent and expertise to the design of both exterior and interior architecture. Photo by Michael Mihalevich*

which now houses the Marley Company; the feline and primate exhibits at the Kansas City Zoo; the Unity Village Auditorium; the Allstate Insurance Company regional headquarters; the Municipal Court Building; and the Georgetown Apartments.

Linscott, Haylett, Wimmer & Wheat contributed to Kansas City's restaurant renaissance with interiors for Plaza III, the Buttonwood Tree, the Alameda Plaza Hotel, and many others. The unusual interiors have won the firm national acclaim and restaurant commissions nationwide.

Linscott, Haylett, Wimmer & Wheat handles both small and large projects, among which are office buildings, warehouses, restaurants, government facilities, interior designs, theaters, churches, and schools. New business comes mainly through referral from satisfied clients.

In summing up his company's philosophy Wheat says, "As a firm we want to break some new ground in architecture while leaving behind landmarks for people to appreciate for years to come."

J.C. Nichols, father of the world's first shopping center, the renowned Country Club Plaza, is also known as one of the greatest pioneers in community planning.

Nichols and N.W. Dible, another early community builder, did much to influence the direction of Kansas City's residential bent. Virtually all of their subdivisions have retained their desirability, partly because of the developers' insistence on quality building, and partly because of their innovative use of legal covenants to set up mandatory memberships in homeowners' associations.

These homeowners' associations lie at the foundation of many of the strong neighborhood groups that work to protect and enrich the quality of life in their respective corners of the city.

Kansas Citians take pride in their homes and their communities; developers of commercial properties build to these high standards, too. The result is a well-located, model city for mid-America that offers a rare combination of stability and charm, rooted in history and ready for the future.

*Above: Leawood South, a new development, is known for the high quality of its environment. Photo by Michael A. Mihalevich*

*Next page: The lavender hues of dusk cast a mellow glow over the city in this view of Crown Center Square looking north along Grand Avenue. Photo by Michael A. Mihalevich*

Kansas City has been called "The City of Fountains," and indeed claims more fountains than any city in the world except Rome. Top, left: The Muse of The Missouri greets downtown visitors. Photo by Bruce Mathews. Bottom, left: A classic fountain graces Mission Hills. Photo by Roy Inman. Above: Night lighting enhances this Country Club Plaza display. Photo by Tony La Tona

From the weighty to the winsome, statues take many forms in the city French philosopher André Maurois termed "one of the loveliest on earth." Above: A robin alights on Auguste Rodin's "The Thinker," a reproduction of the famous statue at the Nelson Gallery. Photo by Michael A. Mihalevich

Sculpture on the Country Club Plaza is an endless source of delight for Kansas Citians. Photo, far right, top: Michael A. Mihalevich. Photos, right and far right, by Bruce Mathews

# 4
# THE NATION'S BREADBASKET

"The Breadbasket, of which Kansas City is indisputably the capital, is that North American nation most at peace with itself. It is the nation that works best. . . . Based on the most prodigiously successful agriculture the world has ever known, the Breadbasket has built an enviable, prosperous, renewable economy," wrote Joel Garreau in his 1981 bestseller *The Nine Nations of North America.*

Those are sweet words to a city that for years smarted under the disparaging appellation, Cowtown. "Everything's up-to-date in Kansas City . . . they've even got a building there that's seven stories tall" chorused the cowboys in "Oklahoma!"

We knew it didn't take much to impress those cowboys, and somehow we got accustomed to thinking we didn't have much in Kansas City. By the 1950s, it had become fashionable to be just a little bit apologetic about those grass roots of ours.

It took the Russians to change people's minds. In 1972, folks were calling it "the great grain robbery"—the huge imports of Midwestern grain that the Soviet Union had secretly contracted to purchase when their own crops failed. The first news medium to break the story, incidentally, was *Milling and Baking News,* a weekly trade journal published here in Kansas City.

It made people think. We knew other countries envied America's sleek technology and our slick consumer goods, but somehow, here in the heartland, we'd come to take our bountiful agricultural products pretty much for granted.

It's no wonder, really. Grain elevators are commonplace sights on our major streets and highways. Some of the nation's most fertile fields are virtually in our back yard. Thirty agricultural associations have their headquarters in Kansas City.

One of our most important agribusiness institutions has been with us for well over a century: The Board of Trade of Kansas City, Mo., Inc.

*Opposite: The Heartland's golden fields of grain are a favored subject of the region's photographers. Photo by Hank Young/ Young Company*

*Next page: Farms and rolling hills rich with wheat are responsible for Kansas City's claim as the agribusiness capital of the world. Photo by Bob Barrett*

Above: The annual wheat harvest puts Kansas City in the heart of the nation's breadbasket. Photo by Hank Young/Young Company

Opposite: Grain silos like this are a frequent sight in the Kansas City area. Photo by Bob Barrett

It's an association of over 200 members with an annual operating cost of over $1 million. Billions of bushels of grains of all kinds are traded there annually, but the star of the show is wheat—a modern cousin of the Turkey red wheat the nineteenth-century Mennonite immigrants carried with them to this area from Russia.

Commodities trading goes on continuously Monday through Friday from 9:30 a.m. to 1:15 p.m. On an average day, as many as sixty traders may be on the trading floor and in the pit.

Note pad in hand, pen at the ready, the traders in the pit are as tense as runners at the starting line. When the bell sounds to signal the beginning of the day's trading, they spring into action, shouting and waving, looking like nothing so much as a group of frenzied game-show contestants.

Except for those faces. They're intent.

"Deece . . . deece . . . quarter deece. . . ." One trader offers to buy, or another trader offers to sell, a contract for a quantity of wheat due to come onto the market in "Deece"—December.

Surrounded by the latest in technology that keeps them abreast of ongoing fluctuations in the world market, these superstars of the commodities trade participate in one of the oldest forms of selling known to civilization: the public outcry auction, conducted at a dizzying pace where millions in profit—or loss—may ride on a trader's judgment in a single call.

Value Line stock contracts are the newest introduction at the Board of Trade—they enable traders to deal in stocks just the way they deal

Above: This bronze statue of a rodeo rider highlights the entrance to the Kansas City Board of Trade Building at 49th and Main. Photo by Bruce Mathews

Right: Kansas City's Board of Trade oversees the annual trading of billions of bushels of grain. Photo by Tony La Tona

*The technology available for harvesting Midwestern grain has made Kansas City a fertile field for agribusiness. Photo by Bob Barrett*

in grains. A Value Line Futures contract is a commitment between the buyer and seller to make or take delivery of an amount of money at a specific time in the future. The Value Line Average Stock Index is a listing of an equally weighted, geometric average of the prices of 1,700 stocks.

And what of Cowtown?

"Cowtown is here to stay," said Ray Davis, president of the Kansas City Stockyards Company. "The only cowboys that are left are at the American Royal once a year, but Kansas City is still the same city it was, and back then, everybody that was proud of it called it Cowtown."

Davis said the new title, World Food Capital, is just an upscale way of saying the same thing.

"The last I heard, beef, pork, and mutton are food. Contrary to reports that would make you think it's all over, livestock trading is alive and well in Kansas City."

The emphasis may have shifted from the stockyards to the breadbasket, but livestock trading is still going on here to the tune of over $150 million in annual trade. Nine commission companies in the city draw

*Livestock trading is still a thriving venture at the Kansas City Stockyards auction center. Photo by Michael A. Mihalevich*

The buying and selling of livestock in Kansas City is still going on to the tune of over $150 million in annual trade. Photo by Hank Young/Young Company

from livestock growers in Missouri, Iowa, Nebraska, Kansas, and Arkansas, who ship their stock to market by truck.

The transition from rail to truck transport made for a fundamental change in livestock trading, enabling shippers to reach more and different markets faster than in the old days of the railroad when trains were the quickest and most dependable way to get stock to the market.

"We'll never get back to what the business was fifty years ago because it's not the same situation now," Davis said. "Just the same, livestock trading is here to stay."

Healthy livestock is the concern of Cooper's Animal Health, Inc., a company with a history of over 100 years in veterinary medicine. Originally known as Wellcome Animal Health, the company was later bought by Jensen-Salsbury Laboratories. Cooper's Kansas City, Kansas location is its North American headquarters; the firm also has Cooper's Agrifarm in Canada. More than 400 persons work at the Kansas City facility, which has developed such products as a unique parvo virus vaccine for dogs, and Nasalgen IP, an innovative immunization treatment for infectious bovine rhinotracheitis which is administered as nose drops rather than by injection.

Another long-familiar veterinary landmark in the metropolitan area is Veterinary Medicine Publishing Company in Lenexa, Kansas, one of the nation's largest and most respected publishers of reference works, textbooks, and technical information for veterinarians. The company's two monthly magazines, *Veterinary Medicine* and *Veterinary Economics,* are distributed nationwide to professionals.

The American Hereford Association (AHA) surely would call our city Cowtown. One of several registries for purebred stock located in Kansas City, the AHA proudly boasts a larger-than-life illuminable sculpture of a bull atop its former headquarters on Quality Hill. (Once in a while a tourist or two from one of the coasts may scoff at the naivete of such a forthright display, but we don't care. They're usually the same ones

The giant steer atop the former American Hereford Association building symbolizes Kansas City's rise to prominence as a livestock capital. Photo by Hank Young/Young Company

who thought we all went barefoot until the first cold snap, anyway.)

The AHA employs fifty people locally to record and register information on approximately nineteen million head of cattle throughout the nation. They provide data not only on an animal's antecedents, but on its development, so that breeders can select for qualities they want to perpetuate in a herd.

Dewey Rounds of the AHA said the organization has been headquartered in Kansas City for all but two years since it was founded in 1881.

"In the early 1900s, there was a movement on to centralize things in Chicago, and they offered the organization free rent," he said, "so the association took them up on the offer."

But as soon as the free ride was over, the AHA was back.

"There are a lot of reasons it returned," Rounds said. "This location in the central United States, is the best place for our members—it's easy to get to. Then, too, there's tradition. The Herefords started the American Royal with a cattle show in the stockyards in 1898. That's how the whole thing started, as a cattle exhibition."

He's right. The American Royal began with a National Hereford Show held in a tent in the Kansas City stockyards in 1899. Within a few years, the event had been expanded to include sheep, swine, poultry, and horses.

By 1922, the show had its own home on the site of the present exposition building. After the original structure was damaged by fire in 1925, it was rebuilt and enlarged.

Like many Kansas City institutions, the Royal went to war in 1940 when it was converted into a glider plant. (During that period, the show was held in pens in the stockyards nearby.)

The American Royal has a habit of overcoming hard times—the facility was devastated by the 1951 Kaw River flood, but came through smiling and the show went on as usual that fall.

As the exhibition has increased in popularity, more and more space has been needed to house it, including the 120,000-square-foot Governor's Building and the Crosby Kemper Memorial Arena. (Kemper Arena was also the site of the 1976 Republican National Convention.) There's something for everyone, beginning with the joyous parade of bands, drill teams, and horses, of course. Such famous folk as the Spanish artist Antoni Miralda have lent a special touch to the extravaganza in past years. Miralda, internationally known for his work with food as an art medium on a giant scale, constructed extravagant floats of native produce, and introduced borrowed, thrice-lifesize fiberglass cows as parade participants, drawn by Cadillac convertibles carrying Royal queen contestants. (Remember, the next time you see Zarda Dairy's serenely-gazing "Big Bossie"—she used to be in show business at the Royal!)

The crowd-pleasing Royal rodeo brings cowboys from all over the country to compete for over $100,000 in prize money for bull riding, bronc riding, and calf roping. And when you see them, don't forget to applaud the clowns—some of the toughest fellows you'll see at a rodeo wear red rubber noses, baggy pants, and squashed-in hats. You rarely see them in oversize shoes, though, since the dead serious business of these quick-footed clowns is to dash in and distract a bucking bull or bronc when a rider falls.

Not everything is rough and ready at the Royal. One of the highlights of the social season is the annual BOTAR Ball when a score or more young women—Belles of the American Royal—make their bows to society. There's an art show connected with the Royal, too, as well as concerts and the recently added barbecue cooking contest that draws hundreds of entrants, each with his own special best recipe.

American Royal Horse Show exhibitors come from more than thirty states and Canada. In recent years the show has attracted as many as 4,000 horse show entries and over 5,000 livestock entries, as well as visitors from fourteen foreign countries. Horses compete in a variety of competitions, including roadster and jumping contests, and exhibitions of manners, conformation, training, and equitation.

The Crosby Kemper Memorial Arena plays host each year to the renowned American Royal Livestock, Horse Show and Rodeo exhibition. Photo by Bob Barrett

Visitors to the city number in the tens of thousands during American Royal time. They're attracted by the show, by the opportunity to meet others in the agricultural industry, and by the chance to see and enjoy one of the nation's most diverse and interesting cities. It's estimated that direct expenditures by visitors at Royal time come close to $1 billion.

There are plenty of agriculture-related conventions in Kansas City, and a great many of them take place in the fall during the American Royal. One of the city's favorite convocations brings out close to 25,000 blue-jacketed youngsters so handsome and wholesome you can't see them without thinking, "Yes, this is what America is all about." They're the Future Farmers of America (FFA), and many are exhibitors at the Royal.

Because these young people really are working farmers, often with herds, flocks, or fields of their own, the town names embroidered on their blue corduroy club jackets are usually those of small places. In some, perhaps, a building "seven stories tall" might be a tall one, indeed. These kids—the fresh-faced ones in neatly pressed jeans and shiny black shoes with white socks—make you want to stop and hug them. Their delight in our city is so sincere, and they're so willing to be impressed and pleased. They remind us of ourselves at our best.

On every side there are indications of the new realities in agribusiness. Nowhere is that more evident than in the national headquarters of an organization whose 2,500 members represent a range of companies engaged in virtually every aspect of agriculture—from instantly recognized

Above: A joyous parade of bands, drill teams, and horses kicks off the annual American Royal Livestock, Horse Show and Rodeo event. Photo By Bob Barrett

Left: One of the highlights of Kansas City's social season is the BOTAR ball when the young "Belles of the American Royal" make their bows to society. Photo by Bruce Mathews

Next page: Corn is one of the staples that provides the backbone of the heartland's agribusiness industry. Photo by Michael A. Mihalevich

names like American Cyanamid and Ralston-Purina to lesser known organizations like Noble Bear and Squealer Feeds. The National Agri-Marketing Association (NAMA), headquartered in Overland Park, was organized in the early 1960s to promote a better understanding of agriculture's role in the American economy.

"Some of our members work directly for the farmer as commodities representatives," said Rex Parsons, executive director of the association, "and most agribusinesses have individuals with marketing responsibilities. All of these people benefit themselves and their organizations by banding together with other NAMA members to assist American agriculture."

# MOBAY CORPORATION
## Its Product Lines Give it the Winning Edge

The metropolitan Kansas City community has become an increasingly important center of activity for Mobay Corporation. The Pittsburgh-based subsidiary of Bayer AG, West Germany, through its Agricultural Chemicals Division in Kansas City, Missouri, and its Animal Health Division in nearby Johnson County, provides employment for about 1,400 area residents.

In 1956 the Agricultural Chemicals Division established its first manufacturing and research facility on a 25-acre tract of land in Kansas City. That site has grown to encompass 200 acres.

Mobay has one of the broadest product lines in the industry. Its products, manufactured primarily at the firm's Kansas City facility, range from broad-spectrum insecticides, herbicides, and fungicides for the commercial grower, to specific chemicals for insect, weed, and disease control for specialized markets such as home and garden.

A major expansion of the Kansas City complex took place in 1976 with the completion of a plant to produce Sencor ®, a broadleaf herbicide widely used on soybeans, potatoes, and wheat.

One of the division's newest prod-

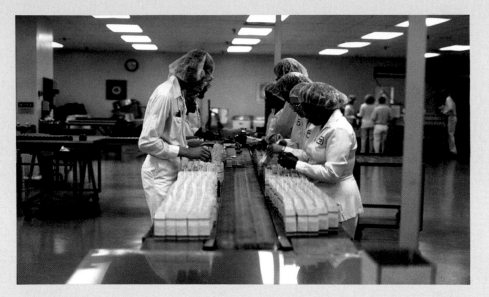

ucts is Bayleton ® Systemic Fungicide, the world's first triazole fungicide, offering both preventive and curative actions against plant diseases infecting cereal grains, tree fruits, turf, and ornamentals.

The Agricultural Chemicals Division has actively pursued its commitment to environmental quality by making investments in state-of-the-art,

*An aerial view of the Agricultural Chemicals Division complex of Mobay Corporation in Kansas City.*

*Pharmaceutical finishing line at the Shawnee production facility of Mobay Corporation's Animal Health Division, where products are labeled and packaged after quality-control tests are completed.*

waste-treatment facilities to assure that the plant operations meet or exceed all regulations governing environmental quality. The firm is also an active leader in the national movement to conserve this country's soil and water resources by endorsing the use of conservation tillage practices, chemical weed control in place of mechanical tillage, and other soil-saving techniques.

Mobay's Animal Health Division, a leader in the veterinary industry, manufactures and markets a complete line of animal health care products to the lay trade (feedlots, ranches, etc.) under the Cutter Animal Health trade name, and to veterinarians under the Haver label.

The Animal Health Division has a wide range of products. Its biggest seller is Droncit ®, a tapeworm control for dogs and cats used by licensed veterinarians. Some of the newest products are Pro-Spot ®, a convenient solution to flea control in dogs, and Hy-Guard ®, the first federally licensed biological product for preventing swine dysentery.

Mobay Corporation's Animal Health Division is geared to continued progress and industry leadership through the development of new products, market expansion, and the dedication of its employees.

Parsons said a part of the heavy weather agriculture is currently undergoing comes about as a result of its recent transition to a highly technologized industry.

NAMA annually makes an award to the Agri-Marketer of the Year. In 1985, for example, Dr. Kenneth Bader, chief executive officer of the American Soybean Association, was cited for his leadership in opening and developing international markets for American soybeans.

The group is also proud of its college program, which establishes chapters on campus for students interested in pursuing careers in agrimarketing. The University of Missouri-Columbia is among the colleges and universities nationwide which have NAMA chapters.

Like virtually everyone here in the nation's breadbasket, Parsons sees agriculture—and all of its related industries—as one of the most promising fields for young people.

"American agriculture will be an outstanding industry and an outstanding national resource for as far into the future as you can imagine," he said.

Looking at the Kansas City fall convention rolls gives you an entirely new way to look at agribusiness. Who knew there was a National Association of Farm Broadcasters? Who would expect to find several hundred of its members meeting here? There's also the Kansas City 4-H Conference, American Society of Farm Managers and Rural Appraisers, numerous breed association conventions, and another big one, second only to the FFA convention in size: Farmland Industries.

Farmland Industries, one of the largest agricultural cooperatives in the United States, has its headquarters in Kansas City. Begun during the Great Depression as a farmers' collective purchasing group, Farmland now operates in nineteen states. A federated cooperative made up of nearly 2,300 locals, it has hundreds of thousands of individual members.

Farmland's subsidiary, Farmland Foods, is a processor and marketer of pork and pork products. The co-op operates the nation's largest complex of farmer-owned manufacturing facilities, oil refineries, fertilizer plants, feed mills, and plants for the production of farm supplies such as agricultural chemicals, grease, batteries, paint, and steel structures. Farmland's sales in 1985 were over $3 billion.

Kansas City's agribusiness heritage comes to the fore again in the history of Butler Manufacturing Company. A major manufacturer of pre-engineered steel building systems, grain storage bins, farm buildings, and lines of agricultural equipment with customers worldwide, Butler's first product was a steel stock watering tank.

That was back in 1901, and prior to that time, most such tanks were made of wood. The new steel tanks, quicker to make, easier to install and longer lasting, were an instant success.

Werner Eugster, head of Butler's agriproducts division, said the company employs nearly 4,000 persons and had sales in 1985 of nearly $500 million.

"There are Butler buildings in Western Europe, the Middle East,

South America, Australia, Korea and many other parts of the Far East," he said. "They are sold through dealer organizations and we offer a complete service—product engineering, sales training, construction training, and preliminary layout and design assistance."

Eugster said Butler produces a complete grain handling system which is popular both for its efficiency and the speed with which it can be erected. Another popular product is the pre-engineered all steel building for the farm and rural market which can be constructed for uses as diverse as a peanut barn or dairy facility.

"Kansas City is an excellent base for our company," said Butler president Robert H. West. "It's a national and international center with a quality of life that makes it easy to attract the best people at all levels."

"International" is a word that crops up surprisingly often when you start talking about Kansas City. Mobay Corporation, a part of the giant international corporation, Bayer AG of Leverkusen, West Germany, has been an important part of the Kansas City agribusiness scene for more than a quarter of a century. The company has a huge Agricultural Chemicals Division on a 200-acre site in the northeast industrial district.

Mobay Agricultural Chemicals Division employs about 1,000 persons and manufactures a variety of insecticides, fungicides, and herbicides, one of the best-known of which is Sencor, an herbicide used to control

broadleaf weeds in crops such as soybeans, potatoes, and wheat.

At the consumer level, the pesticide industry accounts for over $4 billion in annual sales, and a spokesperson for the company said the Mobay facility here is among the top half-dozen in the industry nationwide. It is the only basic manufacturer of pesticides in the Kansas City area.

Dr. Robert C. Scott, Mobay divisional vice president of administration, was a member of the search team which originally selected Kansas City as the site for the plant.

"We chose this city for a number of reasons," he said. "We're in the agribusiness sector and Kansas City is right in the middle of agriculture. Kansas City understands agriculture. It has an excellent business climate for operations such as ours. It is centrally located, which is important to us since we ship our products to every part of the nation, and this can be done fast and economically from the center of the country."

Scott said the quality of life here was a factor, too, as well as the much-lauded Midwestern work ethic that is the envy of many other parts of the country.

"People here believe in giving an hour's work for an hour's pay," he said. "They're dedicated, enthusiastic . . . they want to be a part of the team. I believe our employees here at the Kansas City facility may well be the best work force in the United States."

# 5
# HUB OF THE HEARTLAND

"Reach out and touch someone," the television commercials advise us, and there's no place in the country where it's easier to do that than in Kansas City.

Some of the first commercial traffic in this region came by water on the Big Mo. The Missouri River, curving gracefully through the metropolis and across the state, has a nine-foot channel which carries 1,200-ton barges to its confluence with the Mississippi at St. Louis. Thence the barges travel south to New Orleans and back again. With containerized barges, goods can be shipped nonstop to all parts of the globe from Kansas City, the largest inland terminal in the country.

Next came the Iron Horse, and by the late nineteenth century Kansas City was already a railroad town. The majestic Union Station downtown is a monument to Kansas City's preeminence, a generation or so ago, as the crossroads of the nation. Currently, Kansas City is the third-largest rail center in the United States, and second in freight car handling. Twelve major railroads operate in the metropolitan area.

In the early days of the automobile, plucky touring drivers carried blueprints for the manufacture of spare automobile parts. When the flivver broke down, they headed for the nearest blacksmith or, if they were lucky, machine shop, and got the repairs done. Broken axles were frequent in those days until a campaign in the thirties urged "Lift Missouri out of the mud."

Today, three interstate highways and eight federal highways carry travelers through Kansas City to all parts of the country. Our city is the center of the crosshair formed by Interstate Highway 35, running north and south between Mexico and Canada, and Interstate Highway 70, which traverses the nation between California and New York. Going where the action is, more than 200 truck lines serve the city, which is the second largest trucking center in the United States.

When America took to the air, Kansas City's central location made

*Opposite: Kansas City is currently the third largest rail center in the country, and second in freight car handling. Photo by Michael A. Mihalevich*

*Next page: The "Hub of the Heartland" is dramatically lit at night. Photo by Bruce Mathews*

it a natural for air travel. Trans World Airlines is a name that has been familiar to the city for almost as long as there have been commercial flights. One of its forerunners, Western Air Express, was organized as a mail-and-passenger plane company in 1925. By 1930 the company had merged with its major competitor, Transcontinental Air Transport, to form Transcontinental and Western Air. It became Trans World Airlines in 1945.

The company's first coast-to-coast passenger service was inaugurated in 1930. (Back in those days, it took a day and a half to make the flight.)

In recent days, the Trans World Corporation has spread its wings ever wider. By 1982, it was the parent company not only of TWA, but also of Hilton International Company, Canteen Corporation, Century 21 Real Estate Corporation and Spartan Food Systems, Inc.

Kansas City International Airport (KCI) is the most advanced passenger and cargo facility of its kind in the world, and flights through here connect with virtually all points of the globe.

American hero Charles Lindbergh once flew the mail through here, landing at a barnstormer's field in eastern Jackson County that now is the site of a sedate subdivision. Mail is still a specialty in our town, with next-day air service to both coasts from the largest transit mail center in the nation. The international air mail exchange at KCI processes all the foreign mail for the states of Missouri, Kansas, Nebraska, and part of Illinois.

*Opposite: Kansas City's complex interstate system rings the city, making it relatively easy to get around, in, and out of town fast. Photo by Bruce Mathews*

*Below: The Missouri River carries barges to its confluence with the Mississippi at St. Louis. Photo by Bob Barrett*

143

Kansas City's first big airport, now Kansas City Downtown Airport, still serves as a receiving point for auto parts, private planes and, once in a while, the presidential jet. Photo, above, by Bob Barrett. Photo, right, by Hank Young/Young Company

One of the nation's bulk mail centers is located here, as well as an extensive Express Mail network center. About 80 percent of the letters going through the postal service here are electronically sorted, another boon for businesses where mail speed is essential.

The first big airport, downtown's Municipal Airport, is still the place the President's plane lands, but it now sees the most duty as a receiving point for auto parts shipped in for assembly at the General Motors Fairfax and Leeds plants, and at Ford's Claycomo facility. In addition to the big fields, several smaller fields handle charter and private flights.

The more time passes, the faster information flies. Where once it made its way in carefully-sealed envelopes aboard stagecoaches, now it flies by nearly instantaneous electronic communication, satellite transmission, and fiber optics.

Communications giants like Southwestern Bell, AT&T, and United Telecommunications, Inc., have major operations in the Kansas City area.

Perhaps the most familiar of these is Southwestern Bell, "the phone company" to generations of Kansas Citians. The company currently employs around 5,000 persons. Another 5,000 are employed by another part of the Bell System, Western Electric, which manufactures electronic integrated circuits and other telecommunications components.

AT&T Communications is the Midwestern regional headquarters of American Telephone & Telegraph. Its operations here include an AT&T telemarketing center and an AT&T Long Lines data center. One of the AT&T services here is private lines: dedicated circuits provided for the exclusive use of customers with a substantial number of transmissions to the same geographical area.

The company also offers Wide Area Telecommunications Service (WATS) for inward and outward calling in a calling area ranging between the United States, St. Croix, St. Thomas, St. John, and Puerto Rico. The company's other services include foreign exchange services

The advanced design of Kansas City International Airport, with its easy-access terminals and convenient baggage centers, adds to Kansas City's appeal as a Heartland hub. Photo by Bob Barrett

(FX), a long-distance calling alternative, and dataphone digital service for transmission of digital signals only.

Few people remember the days when telegraphic delivery meant a yellow envelope brought to your door—and perhaps sung—by a boy on a bicycle. Today Western Union Telegraph Company's messages come by voice, graphic, and alpha-numeric communication.

Services provided by the company include Info Master, which provides access to one of the world's largest commercial message-switching computer centers with automatic message-switching and storage; TelexI/II, which offers private print communication world- and nationwide; a radio beam network for telegraphic communication; money orders; Mailgrams; Easylink, a computerized message storage and forwarding service; and Westar, which transmits high-speed voice and data communication by satellite.

One of the most uncommon industries in the metropolitan area is the Greater Kansas City Foreign-Trade Zone, Inc., (FTZ). Currently there are four foreign-trade zone sites here: International Transit and Storage near KCI Airport; Midland International Corporation in North Topping; and two underground facilities, Hunt Midwest on Highway I-435 near Worlds of Fun, and Inland Storage and Distribution in Kansas City, Kansas.

These foreign-trade zones provide duty-free and quota-free entry of

(continued on page 151)

# UNITED TELECOMMUNICATIONS, INC.
## Bold Vision Leads Industry

"United Telecom's heart, as well as its headquarters, is located in Kansas City," says chairman Paul Henson.

Since he joined the corporation in 1959, Henson has built a reputation in the telecommunications industry as a visionary. The vision has paid off in spectacular growth. Assets have grown from $150 million in 1959 to $6.4 billion in 1986. Revenues have multiplied from $42 million to more than $3 billion.

The town of Abilene, Kansas, is not particularly well known as a telecommunications mecca. Yet it was there that United Telecom got its start.

"Actually, we trace our history to 1899, 23 years after Alexander Graham Bell took out patents on a gadget he called the telephone," says Henson. "That was the year Cleyson Leroy Brown began stringing iron wire for telephone service in Abilene. The Brown family's electric company already owned the poles. But Brown

didn't operate the only telephone company in town. There were competing companies that put up telephone poles on opposite sides of the street. Brown ran competitors out of business by charging less than they did, and he offered people a discount on their electric bills when they subscribed to Brown Telephone. Competition was benefiting the consumer even then."

Brown eventually controlled 84 telephone companies, including ones in Arkansas, Missouri, Indiana, Illinois, Ohio, Pennsylvania, and New Jersey. Following his death in 1935, the firm was hit hard by the Depression and went into receivership.

"We owe C.L. Brown quite a debt," says Henson. "He built the foundation for our very successful telephone business, and he created a com-

*United Telecom's block-long corporate offices are in Westwood, just west of the Country Club Plaza on Shawnee Mission Parkway.*

*US Sprint's network puts state-of-the-art, long-distance services at the fingertips of business and residential customers.*

pany work ethic that's been the envy of the industry. There's a lot to be said for being midwestern born and bred."

Some of Brown's companies were reorganized as United Utilities. "During World War II, when all resources went toward winning, United was a 'patch-and-pray' operation," adds Henson. "After the war United be-

came the first major telephone system to convert from operators to dialed connections."

With the 1960s came an ambitious acquisition program that quadrupled United's size. In 1964 the corporate offices were moved to Kansas City.

For United Telecom the 1970s were characterized by diversification within the telecommunications industry. The company was renamed to fit the vision: United Telecommunications, Inc. Anticipating the marriage of telephones and computers, United Telecom got into the data-transmission business and also experimented in a variety of telecommunications-related markets.

"Our philosophy has always been to test the marketplace," says Henson. "We aren't going to build a Bell Labs, so we take our experiments with the technology right to the customer. We've burnt our fingers many times, but we've learned a lot."

The 1980s brought diversification, technological advances, competition, and deregulation to the telecommunications industry. United Telecom saw the new opportunities and acted upon them. Says Henson, "We decided to tackle the long-distance market. It's the highest risk effort we've ever undertaken, and it has the potential for the highest returns. With 87 years' experience, we've got the expertise to be successful."

The proving ground for that expertise is the United Telephone System. Its companies provide local service in more

*Nearly 400 construction crews are building US Sprint's network across America—an effort that's been compared to crossing the continent with railroads 150 years ago.*

*Changes reshaping the telecommunications industry are having a direct impact on United Telephone System companies. The goal remains low-cost, high-quality service.*

than 3,000 medium-size cities, small towns, and suburbs in 19 states. The largest United Telephone operations are in central and southwestern Florida, and in eastern North Carolina. In partnership with Walt Disney Productions, Vista-United serves Walt Disney World and Epcot Center in suburban Orlando. Associated companies provide advanced mobile telephone service and yellow pages-type information, both in printed directories and over the telephone.

Entering the long-distance market, United Telecom's distinctive strategy for wresting market share from AT&T is to build the first nationwide, all-digital, fiber-optic integrated network. Fiber optics is the telecommunications technology of the future. Glass cable, the size of a human hair, carries 8,000 messages simultaneously. The messages have been digitized—translated into bits of light transmitted by lasers the size of a grain of salt.

The multibillion-dollar network will provide premium-quality transmission for data, voice, and video. "By the end of 1987 nearly all of the 23,000-mile backbone network will be completed,"

said Henson. "It will bring new communications capabilities and choice within reach of 90 percent of the country. Of America's *Fortune* 500 companies, 475 became customers even before the network was complete. They want the highest quality transmission."

A 50-50 partnership with GTE has blended United Telecom's long-distance and data-transmission companies with GTE Sprint and Telenet to create US Sprint, the nation's third-largest long-distance company.

From its modest beginnings on the Kansas prairie, United Telecom has become a large and prosperous corporate citizen in Kansas City and a major force in local and long-distance telecommunications both nationally and internationally. Henson is especially proud of the firm's 3,000 Kansas City employees and their participation in the civic and cultural life of the city.

An example of the extensive community involvement of United Telecom is its work with the University of Missouri-Kansas City to provide a graduate program in computer science and telecommunications. Says Henson, "This will, over the years, create a pool of well-trained people and should help attract other high-tech companies to the area. After all, Kansas City is our hometown now. We think it's a great place to live and work."

# MID-AMERICA CAR, INC.
## A Heartland Success Story

Mid-America Car, Inc., is in the business of maintaining, repairing, and modifying locomotives and railroad cars. C.D. Blanc, company founder and president, credits chamber of commerce leaders, the Mercantile Bank & Trust Company, and the Kansas City Corporation for Industrial Development for helping him launch Mid-America Car, a firm that has grown from an idea to a solid business in the past eight years.

Blanc started his venture in 1978 with a single contract to maintain 465 unit train coal cars for the Kansas City Power & Light Company. At that time the Power & Light Company wanted car maintenance done on its own property so that time would not be lost. The firm for which Blanc worked, which did the maintenance, was not interested, so Blanc himself participated in the bidding. He landed the account and pulled together six workers, renting enough tools to get the job done.

The contract, along with his resumé and a solid background in railroad car maintenance, enabled Blanc to secure a loan from the bank. The men who joined the entrepreneur in his new venture were former railroad associates

*Mid-America Car, Inc., is located in the industrial area of Kansas City east of the Paseo Bridge at 1523 North Monroe.*

*Curtis and Janice Blanc, president and vice-president, respectively, of Mid-America Car, Inc.*

respected by Blanc for their careful workmanship.

With the help of the Kansas City Corporation for Industrial Development and industrial revenue bonds, Mid-America Car expanded in 1981 to include locomotive repair and was able to enlarge its steel fabrication capabilities. In 1983, again with KCCID assistance and with industrial revenue bonds, the firm enlarged its freight car and locomotive repair services. Piece by piece, as the need arose, it added to its steel fabrication equipment.

Mid-America Car now operates in the industrial area east of the Paseo Bridge at 1523 North Monroe, utilizing the talents of nearly 60 employees. Railroad spurs run to the large shop

which is adjacent to a modest office. Nearby is a steel fabrication shop.

Blanc's wife, Janice, is vice-president and treasurer of the company. Both partners come from a railroad background, with Blanc gaining his experience working for the Rock Island Railroad Company where he eventually became a mechanic officer.

Today Mid-America Car services a wide variety of railroad equipment needs—from track maintenance and steel fabrication to locomotive repair. Blanc's Unit Train Maintenance Program includes the inspection and repair of locomotives on an annual schedule. Following inspection and routine maintenance, damaged or worn parts are replaced. The firm also provides scheduled inspection and maintenance or on-call repair and maintenance for road-beds within 100 miles of its Kansas City shop.

Crews from Mid-America Car can modify existing locomotives to meet the latest performance and fuel-conservation standards. They can also rebuild wrecks, update control and fuel systems, and totally rebuild a locomotive for about half the cost of a new one. (Total rebuilds are limited to four per year.)

In recent years mergers among railroad companies have increased, therefore influencing Mid-America Car's business. Frequently new owners in the mergers require a complete modification of existing locomotives. They also may need new color schemes and logos. Mid-America Car not only can make the mechanical design changes, it can also do the painting.

In order to meet the requirements of design change, the company opened its own steel fabrication shop. Equipped to custom fabricate almost any steel part necessary for rolling stock, including sheet, rolled, tube, and beams, the shop soon gained the reputation of being good at what it did. As a result, a new branch of the business was added that now does fabrication for other rail car maintenance companies in the area and for businesses outside the industry.

"Our business has expanded and our customer base has broadened

*The steel fabrication shop is equipped to custom fabricate almost any steel part necessary for rolling stock.*

throughout the years to include railroads and private car owners from 11 states," says Blanc. "Railroad maintenance business, however, is nourished through the umbilical cord of the rail industry. All of Kansas City, in fact, is impacted by the railroad economy because so much of the industry is concentrated here. Kansas City is now the second-largest rail center in the nation and will soon surpass Chicago to become the biggest."

Mid-America Car has developed working relationships with both large and small car owners to meet their needs. It is those relationships that have helped to develop the firm. It relies on its product quality and work integrity to attract and keep customers. "I feel fortunate to have employees who take pride in doing their jobs right," states Blanc. "They want the business to succeed as much as I do."

A community-oriented corporation, Mid-America Car supports Kansas City with sponsorships of the American Royal, the Kansas City Zoo, the Kansas City Chamber of Commerce, the Missouri Chamber of Commerce, and Little League baseball, soccer, and football.

Future plans include a larger yard and storage area for rail companies during slack time when the cars they pull off the lines can be stored and serviced at the firm's facilities.

Mid-America Car, Inc., exemplifies how it is possible to develop a business based on special skills and hard work. It is also proof that Kansas City institutions will aggressively lend support to small businesses when they see a good thing in the making. "There are not many cities that have institutions as responsive to the needs of small business as exist here in Kansas City," says Blanc. "Their support has enabled us to grow and expand."

*Railroad spurs bring rail cars and locomotives to Mid-America for repair, maintenance, or modification.*

foreign goods into specific areas under U.S. Customs supervision within the United States for an unlimited period of time. Goods brought into such a zone enjoy a duty-free status during which they may be stored, manipulated, mixed with other goods, used in a manufacturing process, or exhibited for sale. Any merchandise shipped out of the zone in United States Customs territory is subject to duty at that time; goods shipping to foreign nations are not subject to a customs levy.

The advantages to such an arrangement are considerable. Merchandise which is shipped into an FTZ may be stored indefinitely without duties being levied until the merchandise is sold and moved out. If the goods are transshipped to a foreign country, no United States duty is charged. The result is an increase in cash flow savings.

Getting better products to the customer at a cheaper price is another advantage for FTZ users. Foreign merchandise may be brought into a zone to be handled, sorted, manipulated, or processed before becoming subject to duty. Almost any kind of merchandise can use the concept

*Opposite: Kansas City's newly constructed AT&T Communications tower at 12th and Main is the Midwestern regional headquarters of American Telephone and Telegraph. Photo by Bob Barrett*

*Below: Kansas City's Foreign Trade Zone is a boon to international business. Photo by Bruce Mathews*

# CONSOLIDATED FREIGHTWAYS
## Continues a Tradition of Superior Service at Competitive Prices

When it comes to shipping freight, Consolidated Freightways—founded in 1929—helped write the book. An important chapter in that book is the company's 24-hour consolidation center in central Kansas City, where freight moving between 20 terminal cities in nearby parts of Kansas, Nebraska, Iowa, and Missouri on the one hand, and the rest of CF's nationwide system on the other, is reloaded for the most efficient possible movement in the company's vast freight-flow operation.

Serving all 50 states as well as eastern and western Canada, Puerto Rico, and islands in the Caribbean, Consolidated Freightways is headquartered in Menlo Park, California. The firm's Kansas City consolidation center is one of 33 such installations located throughout the country, and the big truck maintenance facility that it contains is one of 18 such shops with which CF keeps its equipment fleets in good running order.

The Kansas City area operation, which currently employs some 453 people, began in February 1959 with the CF acquisition of Knaus Trucking. The original Kansas City terminal handled both city pickup and delivery for the entire Kansas City area as well as a major breakbulk and relay operation. CF's Lenexa-Olathe terminal was opened in June 1978 as a consequence of the Kan-

*A superbly maintained and professionally operated fleet is not only vital to highway safety, but essential to a company miles ahead of its competition.*

sas City area's growth.

In June 1984 Consolidated Freightways added a fifth major operating area to the four in which its nationwide operations system had previously been divided. Designated the Midwest Area, it was headquartered in Kansas City, encompassing the states of Minnesota, North and South Dakota, Montana, Wyoming, Missouri, Kansas, Nebraska, Texas, Oklahoma, and parts of Arkansas and Iowa, as well

*Consolidated Freightways prides itself on its (clockwise from upper right) customer service and tracing, professional freight handling, maintenance of equipment, courteous drivers, (center) superior service, and on-time, claim-free delivery.*

as some operations in Canada and Mexico. Nearly 4,000 people are now employed in CF's Midwest Area.

In December 1984 CF terminals in Grandview, Platte City, and Independence were opened to better serve Kansas City. At the same time the facility on Gardner Lane became solely a breakbulk consolidation center, with other CF terminals handling the city pickup and delivery operations. When, in March 1986, CF growth in Kansas and Missouri necessitated a new division, the Kansas City Division was created, encompassing CF's operations in Kansas, Nebraska, and parts of Missouri and Iowa.

The growth of Consolidated Freightways in the Midwest reflects the operational philosophy of the company's founder, Leland James, whose personal vision led to the firm's early successes. He had organized the company in Portland, Oregon, in the year the Great Depression began. James, who served as the firm's president from 1929 to 1955, said he wanted to create an institution that would provide jobs for the greatest number of people, rendering the best possible service to the public, under the best possible working conditions, for the best possible wages.

By 1939 CF's routes had expanded eightfold, and annual revenues had reached $3.5 million. By 1985 Consolidated Freightways—now headed by Raymond F. O'Brien, chairman of the board and chief executive officer—had revenues of $1.8 billion.

Today's Consolidated Freightways is comprised of CF Motor Freight, the company's largest component, which provides interstate trucking service throughout North America. CF Air Freight serves most of the world's major market centers. Other CF companies offer regional motor carrier and specialized truckload services, customhouse brokerage, ocean freight forwarding, nonvessel operating common carriage, container handling, and a host of related services. All together the companies' 22,200 employees operate nearly 850 terminals, serving millions of people in more than 60,000 cities and towns.

to advantage since duty is levied only on articles actually entering into customs territory. For example, electronic and camera equipment can be unpacked, inspected, tested, repaired if necessary, or shipped back to the factory, all without duty charged until the merchandise leaves the FTZ for sale.

Because of the "upside down" schedule of duty on products, which is often less than that levied on individual parts, companies can keep costs down by using the FTZ for factory and assembly space. Since the FTZ is legally outside the U.S. Customs territory, it's possible to bring in parts, assemble a machine, and ship it at a lower rate of duty than the combined total duties that would have been levied on the individual, unassembled parts.

It's estimated that the Foreign Trade Zone is responsible for creating or maintaining about 5,000 jobs in the Kansas City area over the past decade, and for directly and indirectly related investments in the same period of about $500 million.

When you talk about communications in Kansas City, sooner or later you're going to be talking about *The Kansas City Star and Times*, the oldest surviving mass communications medium in town. *The Star*, derided at its founding as "The Twilight Twinkler" by the morning papers it eventually eclipsed, was founded a century ago by Indianan William Rockhill Nelson. An employee-owned newspaper in its later years, the company was recently purchased by Capital Cities Communications.

In the thirties the newspaper was a crusading political-machine buster; a veteran *Star* reporter, William Reddig, chronicled the decline of the Pendergast Machine and his newspaper's part in bringing down Boss Tom Pendergast in the 1947 book, *Tom's Town*. Undoubtedly, however, the newspaper's most famous alumni were William Allen White, who joined the staff as a cub in 1891, and Ernest Hemingway, who once allowed that his laconic style resulted from a stint in the *Star's* newsroom during a period when purple prose and editorializing were frowned upon.

The newspaper company, with a total circulation approaching 300,000, publishes six morning and six evening newspapers per week, and a Sunday edition which includes the locally written and edited weekly magazine, *Star*. The company employs 1,650 persons, and its main offices occupy a full block between 17th and 18th streets from McGee to Grand.

A relative newcomer on the scene is the *Kansas City Business Journal,* a weekly business paper with total circulation of over 15,000 that is perhaps the most widely read business publication in Kansas City. Founded in 1982 by local businessmen Mike Russell and Bill Worley, the paper became a success and its parent company, American City Business Journals, quickly expanded into other metropolitan markets across the country. In 1986 the company purchased the monthly magazine, *Corporate Report/Kansas City* from the Minnesota-based Dorn Communications Corporation.

Perhaps the newest and most surprising kid on the block is *College Boulevard News,* founded in 1984 by Steve Rose, president of Sun Publications, and edited since its inception by Steve Hale. A free tabloid publication distributed every week along the four-mile College Boulevard business corridor, the newspaper deals only with news "on the boulevard," and is one of the most popular print advertising media for merchandisers hoping to catch the eye of the well- heeled business population in that area.

Sun Publications, an old established suburban newspaper group, publishes a total of seventeen newspapers in the Johnson County area. Combined total circulation for the Sun papers is close to 75,000.

"All the Sun Publications share one feature," Rose said. "We serve one of the finest communities in America . . . I'm bullish on the Kansas City area, and Johnson County in particular."

*The Kansas City Call* is the city's old established black newspaper; *The Independent Magazine* carries news of high society; *Helicon Nine* is a widely respected journal of women's art; *Dos Mundos* is the Spanish/ English biweekly news publication; Squire Publications publishes the sprightly free tabloid *The Other Paper* and Kansas City's oldest city magazine, *Town Squire*. A host of other daily and weekly newspapers carry news of special interest to the communities they serve.

Although there are many fine video training grounds in local colleges and the university, few graduates can hope to start out on the small screen in our own home town, for Kansas City is a major media market.

The city has six commercial television stations, and a PBS channel, KCPT (Channel 19).

WDAF (Channel 4) is the local NBC affiliate. Originally owned by *The Kansas City Star,* along with radio station WDAF, Channel 4 is now a part of the Taft Broadcasting System.

WDAF-TV was the city's first television station when it began broadcasting in October of 1949. In those days, diehard TV-watchers would turn on the set in the morning and stare at the test pattern, featuring the dour profile of an Indian chief, satisfied with this evidence of new technological wonders. Only three or four hours each day in mid-afternoon carried programming: some locally-produced children's shows and newscasts, and kinescope recordings in the prime-time slots.

One of the station's earliest stars was Randall Jessee, a nationally-recognized newsman who gained fame as a political reporter. (President Harry S. Truman once remarked that there were only three political reporters he ever completely trusted. One of the three was Jessee.)

A familiar face at the station since those early days is that of Dan Henry, who joined the station in 1959. A former science teacher, Henry has been the news weatherman at Channel 4 for many years.

News anchor spots at Channel 4 are currently filled by Cynthia Smith and her co-anchorperson, Phil Witt. Smith has been with WDAF since 1977, and is perhaps best known for her program, "Thursday's Child," a weekly series which helps find permanent placement for homeless children. Out of this program, she developed the TV 4 Love Fund for medical and educational services for foster children in Kansas City. She also hosts the annual Easter Seals telethon and is active in various community services relating to the needs of children.

Phil Witt has been with the station since 1979. An all-rounder, Witt worked in broadcast journalism as a reporter- cameraman, weatherman, and promotion manager before becoming an anchorman. He was credited with the success of WDAF-TV's "Job Fair" telethon in 1983, which helped nearly 2,000 unemployed Kansas Citians find new jobs.

The station has put together the largest regional baseball network in the country with Royals Baseball. It also stresses community service through such programs as its Youthwatch fingerprinting sessions and reports; its campaign against drunk driving; and support of the Easter Seal, March of Dimes, and Children's Miracle network telethons, among others.

From its first small facility at 31st and Summit serving no more than 8,000 television set owners in the area, WDAF-TV has grown along with the city. Its broadcasting complex, Signal Hill, is located on Southwest Trafficway at 3030 Summit. Its 1,164-foot antenna is nearly twice as high as its original tower and its programming goes on nineteen hours a day and is seen by a large percentage of the two million Kansas City households with television sets.

KCTV (Channel 5) is Kansas City's CBS affiliate. On the air since 1953, the station is a favorite for its news coverage with longtime anchorpersons Wendall Anschutz and Anne Peterson. Anschutz, who started as a reporter with the TV station almost twenty years ago, also hosts a popular local features program called "In Your Neighborhood," and occasionally presents another locally-oriented show called "Place to Place," similar in format to Charles Kuralt's "On The Road."

A unique public service feature of KCTV is the Phone Friend program for children of working parents. By telephoning 722-KCTV, so-called "latchkey children" who are at home alone after school can talk to a trained volunteer to receive advice on where to call in an emergency, or just to hear a friendly voice.

Coverage of the annual American Royal parade is another popular item at Channel 5, and the station's ultramodern satellite news-gathering truck is equipped for live transmission of stories from anywhere in the nation. In the springtime, "anywhere" means Florida for close-up reporting of the Kansas City Royals baseball team at their training camp.

"Minority Matters," a Sunday morning feature on KCTV, brings a variety of minority interests to the TV audience in talk show form.

The tall tower near 31st and Main in Kansas City, Missouri, for years was the home of KCTV, then known as KCMO-TV. The station is now located in Fairway, Kansas, in the ultramodern Broadcast Center on Johnson Drive.

A native son, Larry Moore, is the longtime familiar face at KMBC-TV Channel 9, the local ABC network affiliate. Moore and Laurie Everett are the station's anchorpersons while Len Dawson, famous former Kansas City Chiefs quarterback, covers sports there.

TV 9 was the first local station to cover the news with a meteorologist on the air. Weatherman Dave Dusik, who holds a degree in meteorologi-

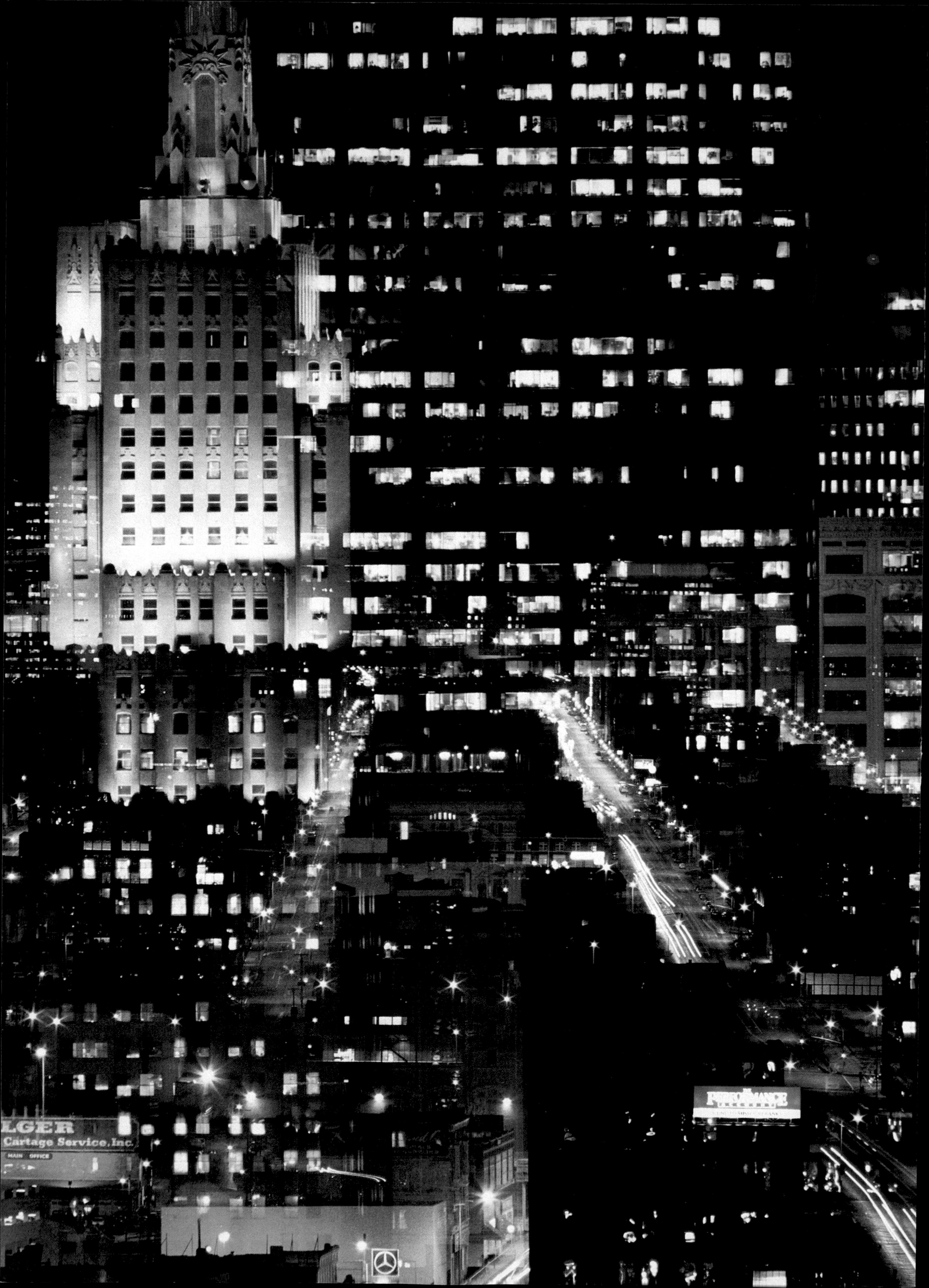
LGER
Cartage Service, Inc.
MAIN OFFICE

cal sciences from St. Louis University, has been with the station for a decade.

The station is proud of its News Star mobile unit which is equipped to travel nationwide for news coverage and for live transmission by satellite. Every year Channel 9 presents the Variety Club telethon over the Memorial Day weekend; proceeds of the fund-raising drive are used to benefit charities for Kansas City children. The station also broadcasts the Muscular Dystrophy Association telethon over the Labor Day weekend each year.

Kansas City conversation about people and events comes to Channel 9 viewers with "Good Morning," hosted by Olivia Dorsey, and a Sunday evening talk show centered on issues and presented by Peggy Breit.

The newest television station in the Kansas City area is KZKC-TV, Channel 62, which began broadcasting here in 1984. The station, owned by Media Central, bills itself as "Kansas City's movie station," and in addition offers such old network series favorites as "Gunsmoke" and "The Honeymooners," as well as the five top cartoon series nationwide.

KSHB-TV 41, formerly KBMA-TV, has been on the air in Kansas City since 1960. Formerly located in the BMA Tower on Southwest Trafficway, the station recently moved to an ultramodern facility at 4720 Oak near the Country Club Plaza. Community involvement is a strong suit of the station, which recently cooperated in the production of a widely-circulated audiovisual presentation of the Kansas City of the future as conceived by the Kansas City Think Tank, an ad hoc gathering of local creative lights.

KYFC-TV, Channel 50, is owned by the Kansas City Youth For Christ church. Located in the Youth for Christ building at 4715 Rainbow in Kansas City, Kansas, since 1978, the station has broadcast nationally syndicated Christian programming as well as locally produced religiously-oriented shows, including the weekly "Celebration," a taped presentation of the organization's Saturday night religious rallies.

KCPT-Channel 19 is the local PBS station, located at 125 East 31st Street, the former broadcasting facility of Channel 5. Channel 19 is noted for its public affairs orientation, and humor lovers tune in for favorites like "Wodehouse Playhouse" and "The Monty Python Flying Circus." An annual feature of this publicly-supported channel is its on-air fundraiser and auction.

KCUR-FM is the local National Public Radio Network station and is a part of the University of Missouri-Kansas City system. It features locally-produced in-depth news coverage, extended live coverage of national events, and the award-winning NPR network programs, "Morning Edition" and "All Things Considered."

All across the dial there's music and news on the commercial stations to fit every taste. Bible study, country/western, hard rock, classical music, easy listening, all-news, golden oldies—it's all here, with dozens of stations vying for a lion's share of the ratings. Kansas City is the twenty-ninth largest media market nationwide, and local radio time is one of advertisers' best buys.

Opposite: The central city, hub of a Midwest communications and commercial network, glitters in this nighttime double exposure. Photo by Roy Inman

# 6
# NEW FRONTIERS FOR ENTERPRISE

On a hill in Union Cemetery there are a dozen or so small grave markers. When the sun hits them just right, you can still see the names. You can see them, but the likelihood is small that you can read them. They're in Chinese, and they're all that remains of the Cantonese railroad laborers who came here more than a century ago and formed a small community known as "Hong Kong." That little neighborhood is long gone, and although no new Chinatown has risen up, Kansas City once again has a considerable Oriental population.

Jimmy and Alice Hung are typical of this new wave—Chinese born on the mainland, displaced by the political upheavals of the last decades, hoping for something better and starting all over again. They came here as young adults, worked together in the kitchens of others, saved their money, and finally opened their own highly successful business, the popular Magic Wok restaurant—appropriately enough, in Independence.

The Hung household is very like those of their young, upwardly-mobile neighbors, but with a significant difference. They and their all-American brood of jeans-clad youngsters live Chinese style, in an elegant house in a new Independence subdivision, with Jimmy's parents and Alice's widowed mother.

The grandmothers' tiny feet, bound in youth, and their grandchildren's sturdy, sneaker-shod strides speak volumes about the distances in history that the family has traveled together.

"Our parents had some very hard times in China when we were growing up," Jimmy Hung said. "I just feel very fortunate that we had the chance to make a good life here for our kids and for our folks, too."

Kansas City has always attracted heroes, and some of the most impressive are the quiet ones.

The late Andre Bollier arrived in Kansas City in 1955, when many Midwesterners still considered beer and barbecue topped off with a Twinkie to be cuisine as haute as they wanted to tackle. (In those days,

*Opposite: Alive with the sights and sounds of enterprise, the Country Club Plaza is one of the most frequented retail centers in the city. Photo by Roy Inman*

*Next page: The spectacle of the nationally-renowned Country Club Plaza Christmas lights draws visitors from around the country who come to see the hundreds of thousands of colorful bulbs which highlight the shopping district during the holiday season. Photo by Roy Inman*

*Above: Andre's Swiss Pastry Shop and Tea Room, with its delectable treats, sells about fifty tons of chocolates a year. Photo by Bob Barrett*

*Opposite: The late Andre Bollier, photographed here in 1980, guided his small patisserie into a successful venture. Photo by Roy Inman*

sour cream marked the outer limits of culinary daring, and cheesecake was still an exotic foreign dainty.)

Into this atmosphere came Andre and Elsbeth Bollier, determined to start a patisserie. A what? Hardly anybody around here knew what Swiss pastry was, and the fifties were not the decade of adventurous eating. Andre's Swiss Pastry Shop and Tea Room got off to a very slow start.

"If my parents did $100 worth of business in a day back then, they felt very fortunate," said Marcel Bollier, now president of the family firm.

Andre Bollier, who died in 1985, lived to see his dreams come true. He never had any doubts about success, and he was right. Under his guidance the little shop grew to a multimillion-dollar operation with franchises in several states. With mail-order customers in all fifty states and several foreign countries, the Kansas City Andre's alone sells about fifty tons of chocolates a year.

In an era when a six-month trial run is a long time, the courage, faith, and tenacity that went into building the Bolliers' American dream shows clearly in Marcel's comment.

"The first fifteen years were extremely difficult."

Entrepreneurs have always found a fertile field in Kansas City since the days when canny merchants stayed at home and sold equipment and provisions to westward-bound miners, trappers, and settlers. The next

# KANSAS CITY AREA ECONOMIC DEVELOPMENT COUNCIL
## In the Prime Time of its Life

The Prime Time News Bureau works with national editors to place stories about the Kansas City metropolitan area on television and in newspapers and magazines.

Founded in 1976, the Kansas City Area Economic Development Council (KCAEDC) has worked to bring more than 200 companies to the seven-county, bi-state Kansas City metropolitan area. The result has been the creation of more than 20,000 jobs and an annual payroll that has an economic impact of $1.3 billion on the area's economy each year.

In 1972 some aggressive businessmen, including Donald Hall, chairman of the board of Hallmark Cards; Dr. Charles Kimball, president emeritus of Midwest Research Institute; and Charles Wheeler, former mayor of Kansas City launched a national awareness program on the metropolitan area called the "Prime Time."

Then and now Prime Time takes a journalistic approach to spread the

Excellent transportation systems, including a first-class airport, help the Kansas City Area Economic Development Council promote the Kansas City metropolitan area to corporate decision-makers.

word on metropolitan Kansas City by writing, placing, and suggesting stories for publication and broadcast in the national media. These stories, which appear in such publications and broadcasts as *The New York Times, The Wall Street Journal, NBC News,* and others, tell of the new buildings going up, the arts, business, and the quality of life in Kansas City. Because these stories, aimed at a national audience, are geared toward corporate decision-makers, Prime Time's mission works effectively with that of KCAEDC.

Stories generated by the Prime Time News Bureau dovetail with KCAEDC's efforts, and the message to the national media is that Kansas City is a good place to live and do business.

"The council, which is an affiliate of the Chamber of Commerce of Greater Kansas City, works to attract both national and international business to the entire metropolitan area," says Jim Monroe, president of KCAEDC since the beginning.

Monroe and his 12-member staff

use direct mail, telemarketing, trade show exhibitions, and other methods to reach executives who may want to build or relocate businesses in the Kansas City area.

The membership of the KCAEDC is made up of 70 chief executives or senior officers of major Kansas City companies, along with the mayors of Kansas City, Missouri; Kansas City, Kansas; Overland Park; Lenexa; Olathe; Lee's Summit; Oak Grove; Independence; and the Jackson County executive. Other members are representatives of organizations that provide financial support.

Financial support is provided by corporate members; the Chamber of Commerce of Greater Kansas City; the City of Kansas City, Missouri; the City of Kansas City, Kansas; the City and chamber of Overland Park; and the Overland Park Economic Development Council; the City and chamber of Lenexa; and the Lenexa Economic Development Council; the City of Oak Grove; the City of Olathe; the Lee's Summit Economic Development Council; the Independence Economic Development Council; Jackson County; the Convention and Visitors Bureau of Greater Kansas City; the Civic Council of Greater Kansas City; the local chapter of the Society of Industrial Realtors; and several contractor associations.

The diversity of the membership and the strengths and assets of the entire metropolitan area are key factors to the success of bringing new business to Kansas City.

"We aren't tied to one kind of business, and we can weather the ups and downs of the economy," says Monroe. "Although the Kansas City area is in an expansion mode, care will be exercised to assure orderly growth."

generations saw the rise of manufacturing, and the current transition sees continuing growth in service industries, and once again, the atmosphere in Kansas City is right for growth and entrepreneurial courage.

Black & Veatch Engineers-Architects is a world-famous firm that began as a small Kansas City company in 1915. By the 1920s, the young company, growing with the city, had engineered the sewer trunk lines which still service Kansas City today, and had branched out to design water, sewage, and electric light projects for clients throughout the Midwest. Currently, its services encompass every major field of engineering with a clientele that spans the globe. One of its most recent projects is the Kansas City Power & Light Company's Iatan electric generating station which, it is anticipated, will help meet the metro area's power needs for years to come.

Black & Veatch Engineers-Architects has become a world leader in the design of power plants. The largest design firm in Kansas City, it's one of the ten largest in the United States, with a staff of 3,000 engineers, architects, planners, scientists, lawyers, technicians, economic and financial specialists, and administrative support personnel. It ranks as one of the top twenty-five employers in the city, and is among the ten largest privately owned businesses headquartered in the metropolitan area. Its Kansas City headquarters occupy more than 500,000 square feet of office space divided among several buildings.

In the energy field, Black & Veatch is known worldwide as a leading designer of power plants. The majority of these projects are designed to burn coal; others are fueled by gas, oil, and hydroelectric energy sources. Its Advanced Technology Group has been instrumental in the development of solar thermal energy, photovoltaics, synthetic fuels, fluidized bed combustion, and coal gasification.

The Pritchard Corporation, a wholly owned subsidiary of Black & Veatch, specializes in petrochemicals. From its Kansas City headquarters, Pritchard also services clients throughout the world on such projects as petroleum refineries, sulfur recovery and air pollution control, gas processing, lead phasedown, and tertiary oil recovery.

A leader in civil and environmental engineering, Black & Veatch also is known for its work in water supply development and treatment, hazardous waste management, wastewater treatment and re-use, air pollution control, and resource recovering.

J.H. Robinson, managing partner of the company, said Kansas City offers several advantages which have helped it develop into one of the largest centers in the nation for engineering firms.

"A central geographic location and good air service enable Black & Veatch and other Kansas City firms to service clients on a nationwide and worldwide basis," he said. "Proximity to the Big Eight Universities and their excellent colleges of engineering also contribute to the city's engineering growth."

Kansas City surely is the place where dreams can come true. Sometimes it's the dream of a single family, sometimes it's a big one that grows into a giant over decades. Once in a while it's an idea that takes off like

*(continued on page 176)*

# BAIRD, KURTZ & DOBSON
## Providing More Than a Half-Century of Service and Solutions

A part of the Kansas City business community for more than 60 years, Baird, Kurtz & Dobson was founded in 1923, when three accountants with the CPA firm of Clinton H. Montgomery & Co. formed a partnership with offices in Kansas City and Joplin. For the next 30 years William Baird, one of the founding partners, managed BKD's Kansas City office. Today Baird, Kurtz & Dobson is the largest regional CPA firm in the city, and ranks among the 20 largest CPA firms in the nation.

The Kansas City office, the largest of BKD's more than 20 locations, serves a diverse clientele that includes multimillion-dollar companies as well as smaller, family-owned businesses representing many different industries.

During the 1950s BKD employed only seven people. Accelerated growth in the 1970s and 1980s swelled its ranks to 100 employees, who now work in the firm's downtown office in the Bryant Building at 1102 Grand and in a suburban office in Liberty that serves the Northland area of Kansas City.

BKD has expanded its traditional tax, accounting, and auditing practice to include business and health care consulting departments. As advisers, BKD's professionals help clients solve problems, plan for the future, improve operating efficiencies, and explore those windows of opportunity that can lead to growth.

As a large, regional company, BKD has the resources and range of services of much larger firms, while at the same time there is the emphasis on service typical of a smaller firm. The result is a timely, personalized response to many diverse client needs.

"Our professionals are Kansas City people who know the city's business cli-

*The personal commitment of its professionals is a key factor in Baird, Kurtz & Dobson's success story, which spans more than 60 years. Representing the staff of nearly 100 are (left to right) Bob Pearson, Jim Martin, Chuck Wells, Bill Sinderson, Ed Crumm, Larry Fogel, and Kathy Laursen. Courtesy, Bob Barrett*

mate and their clients' needs. Clients stay with us because they want to maintain that personal, long-standing relationship with their BKD contact," says Jim Martin, partner-in-charge of the Kansas City office.

The firm's low staff-partner ratio also contributes to the personal involvement of partners with clients and allows partners to work closely with staff members of the client service team. Every BKD client benefits from the pooled knowledge and expertise of a team of advisers that may include an industry specialist as well as tax, accounting, audit, management, and computer advisers.

At BKD quality is always a priority. The firm's internal quality control program, coupled with its interoffice review procedure and its successful peer review record, ensure that quality always comes first.

"Personalized, timely assistance, reasonable fees, and a full complement of services are what people can expect from Baird, Kurtz & Dobson," says Martin. "These are the characteristics that have distinguished our company in the past and what we will continue to emphasize in the future."

# FLEMING COMPANIES, INC.
## Continues to Seek New Ways to Serve Retailers and Consumers

Established in Topeka, Kansas, in 1915, Fleming Companies, Inc., has grown to become the nation's second-largest food wholesaler.

In 1927 Fleming pioneered the voluntary group concept, whereby the company joined independent retailers in order to build their buying power and to advertise as a group, thus lowering expenses. In addition to the cost savings that enabled independent grocers to compete on an even basis with their chain competitors, Fleming also offered support services to its members. Today the firm is continuing this tradition by providing low-price merchandise and services to its affiliates.

Fleming entered the Kansas City market when it purchased the Ryley-Wilson Grocery Company in 1949. Ryley-Wilson was typical of old-line wholesalers whose inefficiencies hindered the ability of independent grocers to compete in the marketplace. As a result, supermarket chain stores dominated the market.

Fleming's Kansas City division is headquartered in North Kansas City, Missouri, and serves 80 member stores in the Kansas City metropolitan area and throughout western Missouri. The

*A produce-buying office in California's Salinas Valley helps retailers served by Fleming provide their customers with fresh fruits and vegetables year round.*

---

affiliated retailers operate under a wide variety of store formats and names, including United Super, Green Hills, Pak 'N' Save, Nowell's, and Food-4-Less.®

The Kansas City division is one of 34 Fleming operating centers that service nearly 4,000 retail stores in 33 states. It maintains complete inventories of virtually every national-brand product sold in supermarkets, together with a number of high-volume, private-label items. In addition, the branch provides full lines of perishables, including meats, dairy products, frozen foods, and fresh produce.

Fleming Companies, Inc., is recognized as an industry leader in both the development and use of high-technology systems to increase productivity at the wholesale and retail levels. It provides this support to affiliated retailers, who communicate inventory requirements through electronic order entry. These devices link the stores directly with the distribution center, where associates use advanced technology systems to assure rapid product delivery. A high-volume, efficient warehouse and transportation system enables Fleming to maintain a cost-effective distribution and service operation.

The firm offers a complete range of support services that provide an opportunity for its affiliated retailers to compete effectively in their markets. Among these services are store planning and development; financial support, including loan placement assistance, merchandising, advertising, and consumer services; retail counseling and training; electronic systems support; and a comprehensive insurance program.

"Providing these services along with low-cost merchandise is essential to the success of our affiliated retailers," says Matthew G. Jonas, Kansas City division president of Fleming Companies, Inc. "Their success is what builds our business, and we intend to continue to seek new ways to serve not only our retailers, but also their customers—the consumers."

---

*A familiar sight in Missouri and Kansas, this tractor-trailer is part of an efficient distribution system that helps Fleming-Kansas City keep expenses down and the cost of produce for its retailers low.*

# SAFEWAY STORES, INCORPORATED/
# SUPER FOOD BARN
## A Commitment to Quality Endures

A willingness to change and a zeal for giving customers solid value have kept the Kansas City-area Safeway stores in the forefront of grocery retailing for decades. The corporation got its start in 1915 in American Falls, Idaho, when its enterprising founder, M.B. Skaggs, opened an 18-foot by 32-foot grocery and revolutionized the distribution of foodstuffs.

Skaggs had come west as a homesteader with his wife and three small children, living on his homestead some 40 miles across the desert from his little store, and keeping shop from Monday until late Saturday night. Although much of the time he dreamed about new ways to sell groceries, every weekend he was preoccupied with weather conditions on the prairie as he headed back to be with his family on Sunday. If he was lucky, all he had to do was get on his horse and ride through the night. A few hours' sleep snatched on any haystack along the way would help, along with the light of a friendly moon.

Skaggs sought ways to reduce waste and expenses while buying in volume. He then passed the savings on to his customers. His ideas eventually led to a change in the field of food merchandising in all of southern Idaho, and soon

*A typical Super Food Barn has all the special departments to satisfy today's customers' needs. They can choose from fresh seafood, salad and soup bars, bakeries, Teleflorist flowers and plants, delis, bulk foods, and more.*

Skaggs no longer slept in haystacks or rode a horse across the plains.

His single grocery store in American Falls has grown into a large group of stores, and the new ideas that he conceived revolutionized the distribution of foodstuffs not only in southern Idaho but throughout the world.

In the beginning the new ideas that Skaggs espoused met with opposition from wholesalers who didn't see the merits of Skaggs' methods of operation. Skaggs believed wholesaling costs were far too high. He wanted a lower price on

quantity buys on behalf of his customers, and also because it would cost the wholesaler less to sell him a given volume than to sell the same volume in small orders.

To his consternation Skaggs discovered that the Idaho wholesalers had agreed not to sell him anything at a lower price than other retailers paid. Undaunted, he took a train to Portland and met with wholesalers there, finding them willing to sell to him at a lower price. Skaggs then opened stores in Oregon, and his business grew quickly.

Between 1921 and 1926 the stores increased in number to more than 350. Today the Safeway organization is a large-scale business and a natural outgrowth of the ideas of the young storekeeper. The foundation on which Safeway was built is just as sound today as it ever was, and consumers are still profiting from the application of the essential belief that is the company's creed and slogan: "Distribution Without Waste."

In Kansas City alone, there are 40 stores that are carrying on Skaggs' tradition of savings and quality. They are part of a division that covers 72 outlets in western Missouri and eastern Kansas. The division is part of a network of 2,343 Safeway stores worldwide. The organization's Kansas City headquarters, at 624 Westport Road, employs 3,800 people. It also includes a distribution center at 1243 Argentine in Kansas City, Kansas.

*In today's Safeway Super Store, you could place 100 stores the size of M.B. Skaggs' 1915 model. To stock a supermarket, it takes more than 20,000 items compared to 700 sixty years ago.*

*Congresswoman Jan Meyers presents R.F. Wilson, vice-president and division manager, and Gary Espy, human resources and public relations manager, with the "C" flag, which represents President Ronald Reagan's recognition of Safeway Stores, Incorporated's, dedicated involvement in the community. The "C" stands for commitment. Only 500 businesses in the nation have been honored with this achievement.*

The Kansas City stores met one of their biggest challenges beginning in 1980. As shoppers pressed increasingly for lower prices with no sacrifice in quality, 21 of the area stores began a dramatic conversion.

Changing their names to Food Barn and Super Food Barn, those stores installed warehouse shelving and elec-tronic scanning cash registers and elim-inated price marks on individual items. In addition, the stores undertook more aggressive volume buying and other streamlining measures. Eighteen Super Food Barns went even further by in-stalling a variety of specialty depart-ments.

According to Gary Spence, man-ager of retail operations, the undertak-ing was the most extensive expansion and remodeling program in the Kansas City Division's history. "Super Food Barn now leads the metropolitan area food industry in special departments such as fresh seafood, salad and soup bars, Teleflorist departments, in-store bakeries, delis, and bulk food," he says.

"The basic premise behind the Food Barn concept and Safeway as a whole is to provide for our customers the best-quality merchandise at the best-possible price," says Gary L. Espy, manager of human resources and public affairs.

While changing and enduring, the division has established an exemplary record of community service. It has been one of the key forces behind food banks in Missouri and Kansas—organi-zations that collect and donate food. In addition, the firm has provided support to various other groups that serve the disadvantaged.

During and immediately prior to the 1985 Easter Seals Telethon on WDAF-TV, Safeway employees raised $50,000 for the charity, much of it through garage and bake sales and chili suppers conducted on the workers' own time. The company also was a major sponsor of the 1985 National Figure Skating Championships held in Kansas City, as well as the 1984 Reagan-Mondale presidential debate.

In February 1985 division man-ager Richard F. Wilson accepted a new "C" Flag authorized by President Ronald Reagan in recognition of se-lected corporations' commitment to vol-unteerism, philanthropy, and social responsibility.

That would have made M.B. Skaggs proud.

*Safeway/Food Barn stores offer a wide variety of fresh fruits and vegetables from around the world.*

# PEAT MARWICK MAIN & CO.
## Building its Practice One Client at a Time

When James Marwick and Alexander Mitchell formed their accounting partnership in New York in 1897, they started a firm that is now recognized as a leader in the accounting field. Current partners number more than 2,500 in 360 offices nationwide, with 21,000 professional employees. Building its practice one client at a time, the company's total emphasis has been to fully serve each client's need.

That same philosophy was brought home to the heartland in 1908, when Peat Marwick Main & Co. opened the firm, providing it with many clients.

Since its founding Peat Marwick-Kansas industry have created a vibrant market for the firm, providing it with many clients.

Since its founding Peat Marwick-Kansas City has thrived and now serves more than 1,500 clients. During the past five years the firm's practice has moved ahead substantially. Now one of the largest of the more than 100 Peat Marwick offices in the United States, the Kansas City office has 165 employees and 15 partners. The firm prides itself on providing sound business guidance to clients ranging from small, one-owner shops to large entities with international focus.

Peat Marwick-Kansas City offers expertise in four areas: audit, tax, management consulting, and private business advisory services. One of the key elements in the firm's success has been the constant interaction of those functional areas. Through its continuing communication, the firm has been able to offer a collective approach that provides the best-possible service to its clientele.

The audit professionals serve a wide variety of businesses, including commercial and specialized industries. The firm has made strides in developing sophisticated auditing tools and techniques, and in creating a systems evaluation approach designed to facilitate analyzing complex accounting and management information.

The rapid growth of the tax service area of Peat Marwick's practice has come about as a result of the firm's ability to respond to changes in the tax environment for all businesses. Tax professionals work closely with the other functional areas to achieve the best-possible tax posture and to assure full accountability for all tax implications.

"We guide our clients in choosing the most effective tax accounting methods and periods," says James B. Judd,

*The Kansas City office partners (from left) are George Drakey, Craig Peterson, Stephen Clark, Richard Love, Jack Newman, Bud Vick, Charles Peffer, Robert Spence, Robert Lindner, James Judd, Jeffrey Green, Richard Toftness, Theodore Hempy, and David Winetroub. Not pictured, Cecil Miller.*

the managing partner. "In addition to our local tax professionals, we have a network of highly trained people who solve tax problems in specialized areas. For example, our Washington national tax office monitors current developments in Congress, the Treasury Department, and the courts. In addition, our international tax division offers a breadth of expertise that can solve problems clients may have in the area of foreign taxation."

Management consulting is the ultimate extension of Peat Marwick's philosophy of providing full service to each client. Highly specialized consulting services include computer systems design, cost accounting and budgeting, human resource planning, organization and operation reviews, health care consulting, and management information systems. The firm's large staff, educated in virtually every management and technical discipline, reviews and evaluates clients' operations and develops effective, practical recommendations.

Through its Private Business Advisory Service department (PBAS), Peat Marwick-Kansas City helps clients plan for growth with long- and short-term business strategies, and provides guidance for systems to manage them. The firm also identifies and evaluates alternative sources of financing and prepares pertinent financial informa-

NEW FRONTIERS FOR ENTERPRISE

tion. Because staff members from other functional areas assist in the strategies, PBAS is a strong, unified effort.

Peat Marwick also conducts continuing education courses for its clients that are designed to develop the practical skills of managers, financial executives, accountants, and internal auditors. Held several times a year, the courses are available nationwide.

An ongoing working rapport with clients is established by service teams headed by a partner who is responsible for coordinating a service plan. The team also includes professionals who direct the day-to-day performance of the plan and supervise the staff members needed to carry it out.

"In the accounting profession, the difference between one firm and another is its people," Judd states. "In our office we believe that it's our people that set us apart. Their most important attribute is the ability to combine a practical as well as technical approach to client needs. They're able to put things in a proper perspective that enables effective two-way communication to solve and prevent problems. To this end we emphasize the continuing education

of our own staff because it's absolutely vital to us to be aware of changes and their implications."

As an example of the kind of individual employed by the firm, Judd points with pride to Peat Marwick-Kansas City partner Bud Vick, one of the company's most vocal advocates of and friend to small business owners.

Says Judd, "Vick currently heads our PBAS department. He was named

co-winner of the 1986 Missouri Accounting Advocate Award by the U.S. Small Business Administration, and he shared the honor with Lawrence LeGrand of the Peat Marwick-St. Louis office."

In addition to its competent personnel, Peat Marwick-Kansas City has also paid attention to its surroundings. In July 1986 the firm moved its offices to the Commerce Bank Building at 10th and Walnut, in the heart of the downtown area.

The firm's growth seems dependent on its major objectives, which include the complete computerization of its operations to improve productivity. In addition, its forward movement has enabled Peat Marwick-Kansas City to invest personally in the civic and cultural life of the city.

"It's a very high priority of the partnership that we give back to the community," says Judd. "Our high standards include quality involvement as residents and neighbors."

By meeting specific needs of Kansas Citians with professional expertise, Peat Marwick Main & Co. is destined to bound ahead in the coming decades.

# BLACKWELL SANDERS MATHENY WEARY AND LOMBARDI
## An Asset to Kansas City's Business Community

For more than 70 years the firm of Blackwell Sanders Matheny Weary and Lombardi has had a reputation for developing highly competent attorneys, coupled with a history of involvement in civic and community affairs.

Since its founding as an outgrowth of the firm of McCune, Harding, Brown and Murphy in 1916, Blackwell Sanders has produced three federal judges and several of its partners are listed in *Who's Who in America*. In addition, recognition has been given in *The Best Lawyers in America* to William H. Sanders and Larry L. McMullen for work in litigation, to Daniel C. Weary for corporate and tax law, to John P. Williams for employee benefits law, and to David L. West for trust and estates practice. Others have distinguished themselves in such diversified fields as probate, education, hospital, securities, corporate, and utility law.

"In my view, what has set our firm apart since its inception has been a striving for excellence by those who, from time to time, constituted the firm—not only excellence in performance, but excellence in results for our clients," says senior partner Menefee D. Blackwell.

Blackwell Sanders' original offices were in the Land Bank Building at 15 West 10th Street, now known as the Hanover Building. The firm moved to the old Fidelity Bank Building at 911 Walnut in the 1930s, followed in succession by offices in the Federal Reserve Bank Building and, currently, 2480 Pershing Road in Crown Center. The firm is about to move into recently completed Two Pershing Square. Thirteen lawyers now occupy the firm's Corporate Woods office, located at 9401 Indian Creek Parkway in Overland Park, Kansas.

Since its founding Blackwell Sanders has served as legal counsel for the Kansas City, Missouri, School District. Through the years the firm's clientele has grown to include many of the area's largest businesses and institutions. Among them are Commerce Bancshares, UtiliCorp United, Kansas City

*Judge Henry L. McCune, founder.*

Power & Light Co., Black & Veatch, Employers Reinsurance Corporation, St. Luke's Hospital, and the University of Missouri.

To manage its diversified practice,

*Robert B. Caldwell, former managing partner, served as chairman of the district's Federal Reserve Board.*

Blackwell Sanders has a staff of some 70 attorneys, which ranks it among the city's top 10 law firms.

The firm's growth results from the increasing complexity and size of Kansas City business, and the volume and scope of the litigation handled by the trial department. The practice, which is varied and fairly balanced between litigation and nonlitigation, reflects a considerable degree of specialization.

Some of the attorneys limit their practices to specific areas of litigation. Others have expertise in corporate specialties such as securities law, labor, banking and finance, and commercial transactions. Blackwell Sanders partners also have special skills in probate and trust law, estate planning, and pension and profit sharing. Sophisticated tax planning is a specialty within the firm, as are the fields of antitrust, bankruptcy, and health care law.

The litigation segment of the practice has rapidly expanded during the past 15 years. Currently the firm is defense oriented and is experienced in business litigation and defending professional liability (malpractice) actions against physicians, lawyers, accountants, and engineers. It also offers professional expertise in litigation pertaining to product liability, commercial banking, securities, antitrust, construction, taxation, and insurance.

Despite the trend toward specialization, the philosophy of the firm has been to offer young attorneys an opportunity to gain a broad base of experience prior to developing particular areas of expertise.

Blackwell Sanders takes pride in its progressive approach to the practice of law, using the most modern resources available. It was one of the first firms in the nation to use computer support in litigation. Today the computer serves a variety of client needs, including sophisticated tax and financial planning, legal research, estate planning, and labor arbitration award cataloging.

Blackwell Sanders has also received national recognition for its videotaping department, initiated in the

*The present executive committee of the law firm consists of (seated) W.H. Sanders and (standing, from left) Edward T. Matheny, Jr., and Daniel C. Weary.*

early 1970s with a black-and-white system. In-house video facilities now include multiple color capabilities in stationary and mobile units and sophisticated editing and reproduction equipment. The video system is used to record meetings and depositions, assist in various types of discovery and investigation, and for the production of firm seminars.

Technology and paralegals have dramatically changed the practice of law in the past decade. However, the executive committee of William H. Sanders, Edward T. Matheny, Jr., and Daniel C. Weary have resisted change that would disrupt the small-firm atmosphere that is valued by attorneys and support staff alike. In this environment, associates and senior attorneys are readily accessible to each other for consultation and exchange of views and ideas.

The firm's interest and concern have extended also to community affairs. Founder Judge McCune, a school

*Members of the firm (left to right), Cornelius E. Lombardi, Larry L. McMullen, and Menefee D. Blackwell.*

board member and prominent citizen, began a legacy of civic involvement that has continued with succeeding partners. The list of their past and present activities covers a broad spectrum of interests. Former managing partner Robert B. Caldwell served as chairman of the district's Federal Reserve Board; Menefee D. Blackwell is a university trustee of the Nelson-Atkins Museum of Art; Edward T. Matheny, Jr., is

president of St. Luke's Hospital and chairman of the St. Luke's Hospital Foundation; and Cornelius E. Lombardi has served as president of the Kansas City Museum.

With legal expertise and civic involvement as common threads through the years, Blackwell Sanders Matheny Weary & Lombardi has been an enduring asset to Kansas City's business community.

# EMPLOYERS REINSURANCE CORPORATION
## Finding a Niche in Kansas City

One of the oldest and largest professional reinsurers in the nation, Employers Reinsurance Corporation is also the only major domestic property and casualty reinsurer that has chosen the Midwest rather than the shores of either coast for its operations.

Edward G. Trimble, Sr., the company's founder, fortuitously selected Kansas City for his insurance business in 1911 because of its central location. From that vantage point, the Employers Indemnity Exchange, as it was called then, soon expanded its business to other states. By 1926 the firm had become largely reinsurance oriented. Today Employers Reinsurance clients are in every state and province on the North American continent. In addition, the corporation has become a significant factor in the international market, with its treaty facilities extending worldwide through a network of branch offices and affiliated companies.

Employers Reinsurance Corporation has benefited Kansas City in many ways. With its international market, it has brought a dimension of distinction to the Midwest. In its 75-year history the firm has contributed to the city's

economy by offering its professional expertise and by utilizing the communities' varied resources.

After more than 68 years in downtown offices, Employers Reinsurance Corporation outgrew its space and in 1980 built new corporate headquarters at 5200 Metcalf in Overland Park, Kansas. Designed by a local architect and built on 26 rolling acres, the facility is recognized as being one of the nicest in the area.

While new offices have added to a pleasant working environment, Employers Reinsurance Corporation bases its success on the quality of its portfolio of accounts and a close relationship with its clientele. The skills of its professional staff and a conservative yet progressive financial policy have also generated continued growth.

"Basic to the purpose of existence of any business is the ability of an insurer to respond in the event of a catas-

*Exterior of the architecturally innovative building that houses Employers Reinsurance Corporation at 5200 Metcalf in Overland Park.*

trophe or adverse experience," explains Michael G. Fitt, chairman of the board of the firm. "Consequently, a long-standing policy of management is the maintenance of a premium-to-surplus ratio exceeding industry standards."

According to Fitt, long-term successful relationships between Employers Reinsurance Corporation and its clients is also an important advantage as in the firm's relationship with each retrocessionaire—the assuming company on a retrocession contract whereby a reinsurer cedes all or part of the reinsurance it has assumed to another reinsurer. The firm's retrocession agreements involve the world's largest pools of financial capacity.

Employers Reinsurance Corporation's treaties or contracts can be found in virtually every size company. They involve almost all lines of insurance, including property, liability, accident and health, surety, and international.

"Treaty reinsurers maintain a relatively small ratio of staff to premiums written when compared to primary insurance companies. Consequently, the quality of a reinsurance staff, both in breadth and depth, is the key to its suc-

cess," says Fitt.

The treaty staff has been developed and refined over the past 70 years. Its ingredients are high-quality general education, concentrated professional training, and hands-on experience. The outcome has been a depth of talent that has resulted in many company and industry pathfinders.

Those professionals, in turn, make sure that each reinsurance contract is individually designed to fit the needs of the client. Servicing and updating the agreement are equally important in an ever-changing and complex business environment. The dynamics of developing and maintaining a good reinsurance treaty is both an art and a science that has been developed and refined at Employers Reinsurance Corporation.

As individually underwritten lines of coverage continue to grow in importance within the firm, Employers Reinsurance Corporation has staffed its branches with area insurance professionals who have a thorough knowledge of local markets, state laws, and underwriting exposures.

The company's Special Risks Department provides both specific and aggregate excess workers' compensation coverage for employers who are self-insured. (Employers Reinsurance Corporation was the first and is the largest writer of this line of excess coverage.)

The Professional Liability Department has special expertise in the underwriting of insurance agents' and brokers' professional liability (errors and omissions) and adjusters' professional liability coverage. The firm's statistical system enables it to constantly monitor the performance of these lines to provide a fair and stable rating structure.

A domestic pioneer in libel, slander, and allied torts coverage for the communications media, Employers Reinsurance Corporation has taken advantage of the new fields of communication and technology in order to maintain its position as a leader in the development of new concepts for the media.

Anticipating the needs of clients and developing programs to fulfill

*Employees enjoy a lovely sunlit interior and look out over 26 acres of rolling grounds.*

those needs has always been the role of the company's Marketing Department. Members of the firm's legal section ensure that all negotiated contracts reflect clearly and concisely the true intent of the parties. In addition, the department provides direct assistance in specific legal areas. The Claims Department assists clients with claims processing, and the Actuarial Department evaluates loss reserves, including those that remain unreported.

Solidly based on its expertise in the reinsurance field, the company has moved forward, making some very important changes along the way. The most significant of these is its affiliation with General Electric, one of the largest corporations in America. Although now a subsidiary of General Electric, Employers Reinsurance Corporation is completely autonomous in operation.

In its 73 years of continuous operation, Employers Reinsurance Corporation has emphasized integrity, stability, service, and the pursuit of technical excellence. These cornerstones of the business are unchanged. In the coming years it will bring to the marketplace new ideas, products, and solutions for continued growth from its base in the "Heart of America."

a rocket.

Marion Laboratories, Inc., is a manufacturer of pharmaceutical products. It was founded by Ewing Kauffman in 1950. At the end of the company's first year, sales were $36,000, and a small storeroom served as the company's headquarters. Fifteen years later, the company had achieved sales of $5 million and national distribution of its products. Thirty-five years after its founding, the company's net earnings were $36 million on sales of $296 million.

The company bases its success on adherence to high quality, good service, and the declaration, "Those who produce shall share in the results." The idea seems to work. Measured in terms of sales per sales associate, the company's productivity has increased nearly 245 percent, from $57,000 in 1978 to $140,000 in 1985.

Marion's long-standing reputation as a successful marketing company is enhanced by the fact that the company has a highly trained and disciplined sales organization. Although relatively small in size when compared to other firms, the company's sales force of approximately 400 persons is highly productive, thanks to a program of extensive education and training.

Marion currently manufactures and markets over eighty different health-care products and employs about 2,000 persons, most of them in the Kansas City area. Since the mid-1970s, it has produced most of the products it sells, and in addition manufactures products on a contract basis for other pharmaceutical houses. Marion's 600,000-square-foot manufacturing facility is recognized as one of the most technologically advanced in the United States.

An unusual aspect of the company is that it does not perform primary research. Instead, Marion actively searches out compounds in other countries with a proven record of safety and efficacy.

The company prides itself on its tightly organized and highly trained sales staff, and on its highly sophisticated marketing plans. A part of this plan includes sponsorship and direct support for various educational and training programs.

"We want to continue to build on the strengths that have led to our present level of performance," said Fred W. Lyons, Jr., Marion's president and chief executive officer, who said the company's outlook for the future is exciting.

"Our people are the single most important determinant of our future success," he said. "Just as the new products we license must be the ones that are differentiated and unique, likewise our associates possess an uncommon spirit that differentiates Marion within the industry."

The "Heart of America" has a special appeal for the insurance industry, too. Close to fifty insurance companies have headquarters or major offices here, including such familiar names as Kansas City Life, Employers Reinsurance Corporation, Business Men's Assurance, and Mutual Benefit Life Insurance Company.

Mutual Benefit Life, one of the oldest and largest insurance companies in the country, celebrated its centennial in 1945 with more than $1 billion

NEW FRONTIERS FOR ENTERPRISE

in assets. Thirty years later, when the company decentralized its home office operations, Kansas City was chosen as the first expansion office. The company commissioned in Crown Center for its western home office a 28-story building designed by the Chicago architectural firm of Mies van der Rohe. A second 365,000-foot structure has since been added at the same site. Mutual Benefit began operations here serving about 400,000 policyholders in the company's western region, encompassing thirty states.

Since coming to Kansas City, the firm has been noted for its involvement in civic and cultural affairs, with emphasis on programs for inner-city young people, neighborhood rehabilitation, and support of the arts.

Mutual Benefit's emphasis on quality is a reflection of its choice of our city for its western home office. Kansas City won out over such heavy hitters as Chicago, Minneapolis, St. Louis, Denver, and Dallas on the basis of its potential for growth and its excellent labor pool.

Kansas City's belief in the work ethic is a factor often cited by service-oriented industries who come to our town. MetFirst Financial Company, a mortgage banking subsidiary of Metropolitan Life Insurance Company, is a three-year-old firm that originally was headquartered in Oklahoma City.

In its second year of operation the company had gross assets of $70 million with projected loan service of $5 billion by the end of 1987, and projected local employment in that period of about 300 persons.

In 1986, the company chose Kansas City for the relocation of its headquarters after a year-long search that included Dallas, Atlanta, and Indianapolis, among other candidates.

"We really studied the question very thoroughly," said MetFirst's president, Jerold K. Hoerner. "We didn't find any negatives.

"Kansas City is more centrally located; there's a wonderful public and private partnership with a good educational system that cooperates in employee training; great postal clearance; a good banking community; and an airline hub that gives direct routes out to other parts of the country.

"There's a great balance in Kansas City," Hoerner continued. "It's a cosmopolitan city with cultural advantages, major sports, and it's a very pleasant place to live."

As the skyscrapers grow more dense on the city's profile, some incorporate old names of now-vanished emporia like Emery, Bird, Thayer; The Palace; and Harzfeld's, once retailing giants in Kansas City. Even earlier on the scene was a little place down near the riverfront known as Eisen Mercantile Company.

Abraham Eisen, born in the Ukraine in Russia, was a boy of thirteen when he came to this country with his parents. Like so many immigrant children of his day, young Eisen took hard work for granted, and he expected to excel. He went to work for the A.J. August Distillery in St. Joseph, Missouri, and by the time Eisen was twenty-seven, he had saved $1,000 and used it to start his own distillery.

When Prohibition came, Eisen didn't complain. He sold out and started

(continued on page 180)

# H&R BLOCK, INC.
## Offering More Than 30 Years of Quality Service and Progress

Thirty-one years have passed since Henry W. Bloch and his brother, Richard, founded H&R Block as a one-office tax return preparation service in Kansas City, Missouri. Today the company prepares nearly 11 million returns per year worldwide, including nearly one in every 10 returns filed in the United States and more than one in every 11 filed in Canada.

To president and chief executive officer Henry Bloch, the end is nowhere in sight. "We still view tax return preparation as a growing business," he says. "The continuous changes in tax legislation provides expanding demand for tax preparation services and support optimism about the future of this company."

However, tax preparation accounted for only a portion of the company's $607 million in revenues in 1986. H&R Block also owns Block Management Company, founded by Joel Hyatt in 1977 to provide support to Hyatt Legal Services; CompuServe, a leading computer communications and information service; Personnel Pool of America, which provides temporary workers ranging from paralegal assistants and secretaries to food-service employees and construction workers; and Path Management Industries, the

*Henry W. Bloch, president and chief executive officer of H&R Block, Inc., founded the tax return preparation firm with his brother Richard more than 31 years ago in Kansas City.*

---

leader in business training seminars.

While tax preparation is the firm's largest and most well-known service, its CompuServe subsidiary, founded in 1969 and acquired by H&R Block in 1980, is its most high-tech. CompuServe has long offered communications and information services to some of the

---

*H&R Block, Inc., corporate headquarters at 4410 Main Street in Kansas City.*

nation's largest businesses. It is also one of the leading providers of data-processing services to *Fortune* 500 corporations. In recent years CompuServe has offered its 200,000 subscribers the opportunity to shop, conduct research, bank, and communicate electronically through telephone connections to its mainframe computers in Columbus and Dublin, Ohio.

A third H&R Block subsidiary, Personnel Pool of America, serves clients through two divisions: Medical Personnel Pool, which furnishes registered nurses and other supplemental health care personnel to nursing homes, hospitals, and residences; and Personnel Pool, which serves the temporary help needs of all other types of business and industry. In 1985 it purchased the temporary help division of Greyhound Corporation, thus expanding its support of office-skilled temporaries.

Block Management Company, another subsidiary, provides facilities and marketing and administrative services for Hyatt Legal Services, the largest personal legal services law firm in the world.

Adding to the firm's record of growth and expansion, H&R Block, in 1985, acquired Path Management Industries, believed to be the nation's largest provider of one-day business seminars.

Despite its far-flung successes, H&R Block has not forgotten its roots. The company recently showed its faith in Kansas City by building a new corporate headquarters building at 4410 Main Street in the midtown area. The firm also encourages its Kansas City employees and those worldwide to become involved in charitable and civic affairs. Through The H&R Block Foundation, the firm itself generously supports a variety of nonprofit organizations. Main donations have supported Children's Mercy Hospital, the Nelson-Atkins Museum of Art, and the Henry W. Bloch School of Business and Public Administration at UMKC. H&R Block also has adopted Southwest High School under President Ronald Reagan's Partnerships in Education Program.

# SHOOK, HARDY & BACON
## Breaking New Ground

In the 1880s Frank P. Sebree and Samuel Boyd, the original partners of Shook, Hardy & Bacon, began a law practice in offices on the town square in Marshall, Missouri. They had a practical approach to solving a client's legal problem. The guiding principles were a belief in quality legal services and a commitment to satisfying their clients' goals. When opportunities beckoned in Kansas City in 1890, the partners relocated their law offices. Today the firm of Shook, Hardy & Bacon is vastly different from that small practice on the town square, and it has grown both in prominence and in size. Yet the same principles that guided its founders remain as the foundation of this leading national law firm.

Shook, Hardy & Bacon's practice is shaped by its clients' needs for specialized business and litigation services. Whether those needs are to acquire a business, finance a new project, or defend a suit, the firm's lawyers carefully listen to each client and understand his goal prior to offering any legal advice. They then apply their high-quality legal skills, ingenuity, and insight to help

*C. Patrick McLarney (left), managing partner, and Charles L. Bacon, senior partner, looking over a model of downtown Kansas City.*

*(Left to right) Frank P. Sebree II, senior partner; C. Patrick McLarney, managing partner; and Stephen D. Aliber, partner, in the law firm of Shook, Hardy & Bacon.*

clients achieve those goals.

The firm's lawyers have a strong tradition of public service. Some years back they provided legal counsel to the corporation that acquired all the land to develop the Lake of the Ozarks. During the Pendergast Era, when Kansas City was in turmoil, Shook, Hardy & Bacon worked to establish the Kansas City Board of Police Commissioners. When the city struggled with racial unrest, the firm helped draft the civil rights plan.

Many of the firm's lawyers have distinguished themselves in positions of prominence. One served as national commander of the American Legion, another was Missouri's Assistant Attorney General, and others have served on the city council. Shook, Hardy & Bacon lawyers also serve on nonprofit boards and are leaders in bar association activities from the local to the national level.

Their successes have been recognized by their peers. Five of the firm's attorneys have been inducted into the American College of Trial Lawyers, a distinction accorded to fewer than one percent of American attorneys. Judges have been appointed to the bench while practicing law with Shook, Hardy & Bacon. Although such recognition for achievement is important, the firm's prominence comes first through client service.

Client relationships have been enduring and personal for the law firm. The first client of Shook, Hardy & Bacon is still with the firm, having received nearly a century of service. A significant portion of the firm's current revenue is from clients who have used Shook, Hardy & Bacon for 25 years or more.

As one of the area's larger businesses, Shook, Hardy & Bacon employs approximately 500 people in its Missouri and Kansas offices. Utilizing a practical management philosophy, the firm employs over 50 professionals with graduate degrees to assist with nonlegal aspects of a client's case; and thus has a vast pool of technical knowledge available to it.

As the firm begins a second century of legal service, it will occupy new offices in One Kansas City Place, Missouri's tallest building. The new location symbolizes Shook, Hardy & Bacon's commitment to Kansas City and its optimism for the future.

Outdoor dining on the Country Club Plaza provides a pleasant respite from shopping. Photo by Bruce Mathews

over again in "the big city," opening a store in what is now the River Quay area where he sold men's furnishings, ladies' ready-to-wear, and dry goods. His sons Harry and Mel worked in the store as youngsters, beginning by sweeping out at night after school and progressing to salesman and cashier.

By the time the two sons took over the business, the dry goods sector far outweighed the rest of the store's departments in popularity. "What a sweet little dress—did you make it yourself?" was no longer a snide remark, for by the 1950s, improved sewing machines, designer fabrics, and couturier patterns had created a booming business for merchants catering to fashion-minded women who wanted to save money by sewing their own clothes.

The Eisens moved with the times, and the company, now called simply EMC, converted exclusively to fabric merchandising under the name House of Fabrics. At its height it had nine fabric shops in the Kansas City area. So well-respected was the firm that sale of those three initials, EMC, was part of the deal when the brothers sold out to a national company in 1966.

Today, one of Kansas City's major ready-to-wear retailers is Dillard's. The chain of department stores, based in Little Rock, Arkansas, came onto the local scene in 1984 with the purchase of the Stix, Baer & Fuller stores which it renamed, remodeled, and bolstered with a heavy daily advertising campaign to publicize the greater number of brands the stores now carried. Less than two years later, the chain became the undisputed giant here with the purchase of the R.H. Macy & Company's Midwest division stores in Kansas City.

The Jones Store is perhaps Kansas City's oldest home-grown department store still in existence. Woolf Bros., Jack Henry, and Swanson's are long-familiar names locally known for fine ready-to-wear. More recent arrivals on the scene include Bonwit Teller, Saks Fifth Avenue, and a cosmopolitan selection of specialty merchandisers with internationally recognized names like Bally, Bennetton, and Laura Ashley. At the other end of the sophistication scale, Brookside's The Dime Store preserves from childhood's memory the red-and-gold sign, wood floors, and creatively diverse merchandise that made the original variety stores such treasure houses for kids of all ages.

Combined annual retail sales in Kansas City stand at about $10 billion. It's a number that's easy to believe when you're caught in the crush at the supermarket on the way home—particularly if you're behind a shopper like the one a local supermarket cashier waited on recently.

"They had two baskets heaped full and the tab was $482.86," the cashier recalled. "We were giving away stamps to redeem for a free set of dishes at the time, and all I can say is, they didn't have to worry about the supply of china running out before they filled up their stamp books."

Matching up the gravy boat and the serving dishes is one way to bring the customers running, but one local supermarket has thought of a different kind of matchmaking to attract shoppers: singles night.

It's the brainchild of Bob Lemons, owner of nine Bob's IGA super-

Above: Window-shoppers discover a world of fine merchandise in the city's retail stores. Photo by Bruce Mathews

Left: Visitors take advantage of one of Kansas City's favorite pastimes: a carriage tour of the famed Country Club Plaza. Photo by Bruce Mathews

# LAVENTHOL & HORWATH
## Playing a Major Role in the Rebirth of Kansas City

The history of the accounting firm of Laventhol & Horwath has two major branches that date back to the early 1900s.

Lewis J. Laventhol and I.H. Krekstein, both graduates of the Wharton School of the University of Pennsylvania, joined forces in 1923 to form Laventhol & Krekstein. About the same time, in New York City, two Hungarian immigrants, brothers Ernest B. Horwath and Edmund J. Horwath, were developing the first food cost accounting system and preparing auditing work for the restaurant, hotel, and club industries. The two brothers formed Horwath & Horwath on July 31, 1915.

These two major companies merged in 1967 to form Laventhol & Horwath. Since the early days both firms have grown through a series of mergers. With each additional company, Laventhol & Horwath has been able to expand its services to an even wider variety of businesses.

"We are proud of our past achievements and of the resourcefulness and dedication of all L&H people who have made them possible," says Stanley H. House, managing partner. "In the challenging world of business and technology, we are committed to a credo of change, growth, and excellence."

Through the years that philosophy has put Laventhol & Horwath offices on the international map. The company serves its domestic and foreign clients through its overseas organization, Hor-

wath & Horwath International. It currently has affiliated accounting and management consulting firms in more than 60 countries, with more than 200 offices.

The Laventhol & Horwath programs are structured around the entrepreneurial client. The company offers a variety of services, including tax consulting, accounting, auditing, management advisory services, and consulting.

The firm has worked with almost every phase of the business spectrum.

*The AT&T Town Pavilion under construction (below) and downtown Kansas City at dusk (above) epitomize the role Laventhol & Horwath has played in the growth and development of Kansas City.*

However, there is a special emphasis on three areas: leisure-time industries, real estate practice, and health care industries. Its client list represents apparel, appliances, retailing, distribution, transportation, textiles, electronics, manufacturing, insurance, banking, securities trading, energy, professional organizations, hospitals, motion pictures, television, lodging, restaurant, and resort industries.

In the Kansas City area, Laventhol & Horwath clients include some of the biggest names in their fields. A sampling of its special projects include the preparation of market feasibility studies for the Historic Garment District and Quality Hill redevelopment and renovation. In addition, the company provided market feasibility studies for most major hotel developments, including the Vista, Embassy Suites, the Hyatt Regency, and the Marriott. Laventhol & Horwath also did the market feasibility studies on Bartle Hall and the syndication projections on the AT&T Town Pavilion.

"We are pleased to have had the opportunity to play a fundamental role in the market and financial analyses underlying the development of many major projects now symbolic of the rebirth of the downtown Kansas City, Missouri, area," said Jeffrey K. Marvel, senior principal of Laventhol & Horwath. "We look forward to a continued role in providing advice to the development community."

# NATIONAL FIDELITY LIFE INSURANCE COMPANY
## Demonstrating an "I Care" Attitude

Kansas City became the home of National Fidelity Life Insurance Company in 1923, when its president, Ralph Rice, Sr., moved the home office from Sioux City, Iowa. Rice decided that Kansas City offered the best opportunity to launch the company on a national basis.

His decision proved correct. From its Kansas City headquarters, National Fidelity Life established a pattern of growth that has consistently marked it as a leader in its field.

As the company expanded its operations to other states, it was also pioneering new insurance coverages. In the early years, for example, it was one of the first companies to offer a juvenile policy that provided a full death benefit and double indemnity protection at an early age. It was later instrumental in the development of creditor insurance as well as accident and health coverage.

Through the years National Fidelity Life became a highly regarded writer of brokerage market products. Operating in 49 states and in most Canadian provinces, the firm now sells its products through approximately 200 general agencies and branch offices, and has in excess of 11,000 appointed brokers.

Consistent with the company's philosophy of serving needs not being adequately met elsewhere, National Fidelity Life has assumed a major marketing role in four specialties: impaired risks, super preferred risks, structured settlement annuities, and airline pilots' insurance.

The recently introduced and innovative super preferred risk insurance is for persons whose current health, lifestyles, and family health histories prove conducive to long life. Rigid requirements for coverage include such considerations as weight, physique, exercise, hereditary traits, physical examinations, and abstention from tobacco, drugs, and alcohol.

For the past 20 years National Fidelity Life has emphasized the writing of life insurance on individuals with medical impairments to whom coverage has not been available, or was available only at very high costs. This market continues to comprise a majority of its current sales.

During that same period the firm began insuring airline pilots for occupational disability, a field in which it quickly became a major carrier.

Over the past 15 years National Fidelity Life became involved with the settlement of liability claims; it began issuing annuities to provide the benefits

---

*The new administrative building of the National Fidelity Life Insurance Company at 95th and Metcalf in Overland Park, Kansas. The firm has been headquartered in Kansas City since 1923.*

awarded by the juries in these cases. The company also continues to serve the credit insurance and group insurance markets.

National Fidelity Life became a subsidiary of Great American Reserve Insurance Company (GARCO) of Dallas, Texas, in 1985. Both National Fidelity Life and GARCO are a part of the financial division of the Temple-Inland group of companies.

The company continues to maintain its close ties with Kansas City. For 52 years National Fidelity Life has occupied its own office building in the heart of downtown Kansas City, although its administrative offices are now located at 95th and Metcalf in Overland Park, Kansas.

The firm's interest in the welfare of the area is exemplified by the active involvement of its 200 local employees in such charitable fund-raising projects as the Peter Marshall Golf Classic and the United Way Campaign. That spirit of community involvement is further evidenced by participation in both the Chamber of Commerce of Greater Kansas City and Overland Park Chamber of Commerce. National Fidelity Life Insurance Company's officers and employees, at all times, are committed to demonstrating an "I Care" attitude toward their fellow workers, agents, brokers, and, above all, policyholders.

High fashion as well as a world of antiques and collectibles highlight a shopping spree in Kansas City. Photos by Bob Barrett

Opposite: Winter on the Country Club Plaza brings out shoppers who come to enjoy the sights and sounds of Christmas. Photo by Roy Inman

markets in the Kansas City area. Many news stories over the past few years have dealt with the plight of the transplanted and isolated urban-dweller who has no ready-made network of family and friends close at hand to make introductions among eligible singles.

"Go to the frozen-dinner section at the market," advise magazines for working singles. "You'll be able to see who's single from what's in the shopping basket."

Bob's, already noted locally for the upscale elegance of its stores which display antiques where others might have canned goods cutouts, took the cue and initiated a singles night in their newest supermarket. No smoke-filled bars for the single and upwardly mobile here—shoppers stroll a store adorned with an indoor fountain and potted plants, sampling free snacks while background music plays.

In a recent interview, Lemons remarked that Kansas City is the most competitive food market in the United States.

"It's a food warehouse capital of the world," he said, noting that the intense competition among merchandisers is "good for the consumer, but it's tough on the operator."

New ideas come naturally in Kansas City, a town that was founded on enterprise. It seems destined to stay that way. A recent survey of chief executives of large commercial banks showed that they saw our town as one of the ten Midwestern cities that will lead the country's economic growth in the coming years. John Naisbitt, author of the best-selling *Megatrends,* is among the futurists who predict that the Midwest, with its central location, is a hop ahead of other regions in that newest of entrepreneurial territories, the information boom.

Unexplored territory, in whatever form it takes, is the stuff of which Kansas City dreams are made.

# MORRIS, LARSON, KING & STAMPER, P.C.
## Providing Quality Legal Service at an Affordable Price

Morris, Larson, King & Stamper, P.C., is one of the youngest and fastest growing law firms in Kansas City. Since its founding in January 1962 by Harry A. Morris, the firm has expanded to cover both sides of the state line, with a total of 46 attorneys and 12 legal assistants. Since a 1973 merger with a firm headed by Roy A. Larson, the company's rapid expansion has been generated primarily through internal growth, not by mergers or other external processes.

Despite its relative youth, Morris, Larson has shown exceptional leadership and innovation in the legal field. It was, for example, the first law firm in Missouri to become a professional corporation, now the predominant form of operation for most law firms in the state. The company also has taken a leading role in the growing movement for specialty certification in the legal profession both in Missouri and nationwide.

Originally Morris, Larson's emphasis was on tax litigation, thereby establishing the basis for the company's long-standing reputation as the premiere tax firm in Kansas City and the Midwest.

Morris, once interviewed for the position of Commissioner of Internal Revenue during the Kennedy Administration, commented: "I didn't really want it because my reputation rested in successfully representing taxpayers

against the IRS. To get on the IRS' side could have tarnished that image."

The tradition of such high-level recognition has continued. Recently one of the firm's senior partners, J. Harlan Stamper, was nominated by President Ronald Reagan to become one of 17 judges of the United States Tax Court. Although that honor was graciously turned down, it demonstrated to the public the high esteem and respect in which Morris, Larson's tax practice is viewed. The company

continues to provide justification for its tax reputation by virtue of the quality of its work in that area.

However, that reputation has not served as a barrier for the firm in developing similar expertise in other areas of law. Today Morris, Larson offers services in virtually every field, including litigation, medical malpractice, corporate law, estate planning, securities law, employee benefits, antitrust law, criminal law, real estate, tax law, domestic relations law, and bankruptcy. The company is constantly making efforts to expand into new areas of legal practice while, at the same time, honing and improving existing skills and expertise in order to serve clients' needs.

For example, Morris, Larson's litigation practice involves everything from simple fender benders to complex product liability actions and antitrust suits. Its corporate law practice runs the gamut from simple incorporations to complex multiparty mergers and acquisitions.

The firm believes in providing legal services with a personal touch. According to Lynn C. Hoover, president, a very important goal at Morris, Larson is ensuring client satisfaction through quality legal service at affordable prices offered in a timely fashion.

"In keeping with this policy,

Morris, Larson maintains a practice of regularly keeping clients informed of the status of their legal matters," says Hoover. "Often this is done over a relaxing lunch in the company's own dining room or by letter or phone call."

This personal quality is matched by the desire of the firm to serve the community as well. A number of the company's members hold positions on local city councils, school boards, and the governing bodies of local hospitals and health insurers.

There is also widespread participation by Morris, Larson members in civic, bar, and numerous volunteer activities. The company has provided the Kansas City Bar Association with two presidents and the Missouri Bar Association with numerous committee chairmen, as well as continuing legal education authors and lecturers.

In addition to a sense of civic pride, Morris, Larson's commitment to community service has provided certain beneficial side effects by enabling the firm's attorneys to better render efficient personal service to clients. Especially noteworthy is the demographic makeup of the firm. All of its members hail from the Midwest, and so perhaps are better able to identify with and understand the personal problems and needs of their heartland clientele.

These factors are evident in the ability of Morris, Larson to maintain and steadily increase its varied client base. Client satisfaction and word of mouth have been major reasons for the firm's phenomenal growth and success.

Says Hoover, "While no one can look in a crystal ball and predict the future, Morris, Larson sees itself as continuing to grow in size and stature in the legal community in Kansas City and the Midwest. We expect our Kansas office to increase considerably in size over the next couple of years, mirroring the rapid economic growth in this part of Kansas City."

As Kansas City moves ahead, Morris, Larson, King & Stamper, P.C., will expand its areas of expertise and, in keeping with its policies, continue its practice of providing superior legal service on a personal basis.

# ALEXANDER & ALEXANDER
## The Day Before Tomorrow

*". . . faith is the substance of things hoped for, the evidence of things not seen."*

— *Hebrews XI: I*

It's an American success story—a classic. It's the kind that you read about or hear about from time to time.

Richard Bacon "R.B." Jones, a Kentuckian, was heading west in 1889 but never got beyond Kansas City. He lost all of his belongings in a fire. It was this devastating loss that would some day serve as the catalyst for getting Jones into the insurance business.

Meanwhile, a few hundred miles away among the rugged hills of 1890s West Virginia, two brothers named Charles and William Alexander were opening a two-room storefront insurance office on a narrow street in the town of Clarksburg.

It wasn't long until the insurance firm of R.B. Jones was established and began to prosper. In those days the

American (insurance) System of "monoline" was the trend with Jones specializing in one class of insurance, private property with special emphasis on fire protection.

By 1914 the Brothers Alexander had landed their first major account, the Baltimore & Ohio Railroad and promptly established an office in the City of Baltimore across the street from B&O headquarters. Alexander & Alexander, as they would call themselves, were on their way. In time the insurance underwriting industry would become more and more concentrated in the New York City area. This fact, together with his firm's obvious business

*William (top, left) and Charles Alexander (top, right) opened a storefront insurance office in Clarksburg, West Virginia, in the early 1890s. Inset: The four sons of Richard Bacon "R.B." Jones were instrumental in turning their father's company into an insurance brokerage giant.*

savvy, convinced William Alexander to move the company north and open A&A's first New York office in 1919.

By this time Richard Bacon Jones' four sons had joined his firm, and its first branch office was opened in Chicago in 1932. Over the ensuing years the firm of R.B. Jones grew into an insurance brokerage giant. By 1978 the company was the ninth-largest American broker with offices in 16 cities and revenues of over $30 million—and viewed by many inside and outside the insurance brokerage industry as an attractive candidate for acquisition. It was during this time that Alexander & Alexander contacted R.B. Jones—and what followed was the largest consolidation in the history of the insurance brokerage industry. R.B. Jones and Alexander & Alexander were merged on January 31, 1979.

Since the acquisition of R.B. Jones and subsequent mergers (notably with the Reed Stenhouse Companies), Alex-

ander & Alexander has grown considerably. As revenues approach the billion-dollar mark, A&A is ranked as the second-largest risk management and insurance brokerage company in the world. To illustrate, A&A is now employing 18,500 people in 110 offices in 90 U.S. cities and 60 countries worldwide.

While running the risk of sounding a bit immodest (it's been said that "too humble is half proud"), the employees of Alexander & Alexander have every reason to feel proud. The spirited entrepreneurship of the past promises great things for the future. Presently, while the company continues its worldwide expansion, A&A is the largest insurance broker in Kansas City, with the Kansas City office being the fifth largest among A&A's U.S. offices.

Alexander & Alexander's ability to attract and retain talented professionals is reflected in the outstanding personnel in its Kansas City office. The Kansas City office is staffed by professionals versed in all aspects of the insurance and risk management business. A&A offers an exceptional range of insurance, risk management, and related services. Through the Employee Benefits Division, A&A also helps protect the clients' most important asset—their employees. In seeking to earn the faith and trust of the company's clientele, the A&A team works with enthusiasm, dedication, integrity, and technical excellence.

Risk management has never been more complex. A&A experts work within the client's organization to identify risk. The first step is to gather the necessary information about the client's financial and risk management goals and objectives. To understand the client's business and financial exposures, A&A professionals visit job sites, interview personnel, and advise on potential trouble spots, moving quickly to assist in the elimination of avoidable risks and the reduction of unavoidable accidents.

Managed properly, risk can be controlled and minimized. Left alone, it can fester and threaten even the strongest business. The client knows that manag-

ing risk is Alexander & Alexander's business. From policy design to account maintenance, the A&A account executive supervises, manages, and coordinates the activity of the account with a twofold objective: to gain an adequate understanding of the client's problems from the client's point of view, and to introduce the client to all the options A&A has to offer. In providing the day-to-day problem solving often necessary as situations arise, the account executive turns to the internal staff of specialists who are directed to utilize their various expertise in areas of marketing, loss control, claims, and administration in order to ensure that the client's business operates smoothly and efficiently.

Alexander & Alexander could not have established the very special rapport which it has had with its clients through the years without an equally special relationship the company continues to have with the communities of Kansas City. The A&A Kansas City office is staffed by 240 skilled specialists and support personnel who live in and around the two-state area. A&A employees know the local scene; they are a part of it and contribute to its improvement, as they should. Aside from corporate sponsorships, A&A, culturally speaking, is a chief contributor to the Kansas City Symphony, Kansas City Ballet, Nelson-Atkins Museum of Art, Lyric Opera, and Kansas City Art Institute, to name only a few. On civic matters, A&A employees render community service to the Boy Scouts, United Way, Junior Achievement, YMCA, and Mid-America Coalition on Health Care among many others.

This giving of time as well as money deepens Alexander & Alexander's roots in the Kansas City area, roots first planted way back in 1889 by R.B. Jones. This kind of community involvment is only an indication of the many commitments made year after year by A&A to the people of this city and, in so doing, showing the unrelenting faith in the future A&A shares with its community as the company's centenary draws near.

The goal that was set for yesterday is the starting point of tomorrow—and

The secret of Alexander & Alexander's extraordinary success is not only the company's diversification but also its pioneering the development of computerized Risk Management Information Systems.

already today is yesterday's tomorrow. Yesterday, when the twentieth century began, Richard Bacon Jones and Charles and William Alexander designed what were then "innovations" in the insurance industry.

Many of the challenges for the future are here right now, with tort reform and an industrywide crisis changing traditional markets and transforming many insurance-related companies into global structures. Tomorrow will depend upon this ability to innovate—and to adapt.

Alexander & Alexander, since its founding nearly a century ago, has been changing in an ever-changing world, growing as our country has grown, reaching out to its clients to anticipate and to meet their every need—the day before tomorrow.

—Frederick Louis Richardson

189

# MISSOURI PUBLIC SERVICE
## Serving the Very Heart of the Nation's Heartland

Awakening midwestern towns were just beginning to see the benefits of electricity in 1917, when Missouri Public Service started serving its first customers from a 500-kilowatt steam power plant in Pleasant Hill. From that point on Missouri Public Service has helped foster growth.

The electrification of the Midwest not only brought comfort and convenience to its residents, but also enabled enterprise and initiative to flourish. It allowed men with vision and foresight to press forward into a new era. And Missouri Public Service helped lead the way.

It was such vision that led L.K. Green to establish the electric system to serve Pleasant Hill and the surrounding towns. Later, under the leadership of his son, Ralph J. Green, a series of acquisitions and mergers expanded the firm to its present geographic size, encompassing 28 midwestern Missouri counties. Ralph's son, the late Richard C. Green, was at the company's helm from 1958 to 1982 during its most expansive period of customer growth. William I. Owen became president in 1982.

*State-of-the-art technology at the System Operations Center enables the economic exchange of power with other utilities and provides information necessary for reliable operation of the transmission system.*

*Efficient scheduling of the work force, facilities, and materials and up-to-date customer and accounting information are available through the use of computer programs.*

Today Missouri Public Service provides electricity to nearly 35 percent of the corporate limits of Kansas City, Missouri, and about 70 percent of the Missouri-side metropolitan area. It also serves several high development areas, such as Kansas City International Airport and its surrounding office-industrial complex. In addition, it serves the suburban cities of Lee's Summit and Blue Springs, two of the fastest growing communities in the

state, as well as Grandview, Raytown, and Liberty.

In the postwar years of the 1950s growth came at a record pace with the spread of new homes, businesses, and factories to the suburbs. It was then that the area truly became greater Kansas City. Much of that growth was to the east into the area served by Missouri Public Service. In order to be nearer to that expansion, the firm moved its headquarters from Warrensburg to Raytown in 1955. Two years later it moved to its present location, a contemporary steel-and-glass building at 10700 East 350 Highway.

That same year Kansas City expanded its corporate boundaries north of the Missouri River into Platte and Clay counties. Missouri Public Service obtained a franchise with the city to serve that area, necessitating expansion of electric facilities in the Northland in order to be ready for the growth that was sure to follow.

The 1960s brought more customers wanting more electricity. To meet the growing demand, Missouri Public Service built a coal-fired generating plant on the south bank of the Missouri River at Sibley in northeastern Jackson County. It remains the company's primary power plant, with three generating units and a capacity of 445,000 kilowatts.

As Kansas City entered the 1970s, demand for electricity grew at an even

*Sibley Generating Station, a coal-fired plant on the banks of the Missouri River, serves as the company's baseload electric generating unit.*

more dynamic pace with air conditioning coming into wider use. To meet that increased demand, Missouri Public Service added several fast-starting combustion turbine generators to shoulder the summertime load. The firm also owns 8 percent (150,000 kilowatts) of the coal-fired Jeffrey Energy Center near St. Mary's, Kansas. In 1986 the company began life-extending renovation at its Sibley plant and has obtained favorable power-purchase agreements, which should meet the demands of growth into the 1990s.

Missouri Public Service is not in-

volved in nuclear power plants. Instead, it sees coal as an abundant American resource and is committed to coal-fired generation in the future.

In 1967, when the city was ready to begin construction of Kansas City

*Green Ridge Office Park, headquarters for Missouri Public Service, signifies the growth taking place throughout the company's service area.*

International Airport, Missouri Public Service had the electricity available and was ready to extend electric facilities. Along with the airport, Trans World Airlines expanded its operations and built the multimillion-dollar Overhaul Base near the airport.

More recently, within close proximity of the airport, came the development of AirWorld Center, a planned complex of offices, warehouse facilities, and distribution centers with an international look, housing such firms as Sony, Mazda, Toyota, and DeLaval. Just south of AirWorld lies the Executive Hills North development, a planned area of high-rise office buildings, commercial centers, and residential developments.

Through the years Missouri Public Service has been at the forefront of economic development efforts, working hand in hand with city, county, and state development agencies. Those efforts are not confined to the metropolitan area. The firm also helps smaller communities obtain new business and industry. In addition, the company supports its economic development program with full-time personnel assigned to area and industrial development.

Missouri Public Service continues to be a force in the metropolitan area. It came through the oil embargo and skyrocketing inflation of the 1970s in great shape, then moved into a period of stabilization. Electric rates are expected to remain fairly stable. With its major construction basically paid for, its economic health is excellent.

Missouri Public Service supplies electricity and natural gas to more than 189,000 customers in 222 western Missouri communities. Its 13,400-square-mile service area extends from Trenton in the north to Nevada in the south and eastward to Sedalia. The firm also serves such towns as Warrensburg, Clinton, Warsaw, Lexington, and Richmond. It employs nearly 1,000 persons.

A division of UtiliCorp United, Inc., Missouri Public Service is a vital cog in the future of the greater Kansas City area and western Missouri.

# UNITED MISSOURI BANK OF KANSAS CITY, N.A.
## Providing a Full Range of Financial Services

For nearly 75 years United Missouri Bank of Kansas City, n.a., has been providing individual and commercial customers with a full range of financial services. Today it is a leading financial institution in the Midwest and holds more than $1.5 billion in assets. United Missouri's 1,400 employees work hard to uphold its national reputation as a strong and stable bank.

United Missouri is the lead bank for the multibank holding company, United Missouri Bancshares, Inc., which is headquartered in Kansas City, Missouri. The holding company has 19 banks with 64 locations throughout the state of Missouri. In addition, it has entered into an agreement to purchase banks in southern Illinois and has a limited purpose trust company in New York.

In 1986 United Missouri opened its new headquarters in downtown Kansas City. Acclaimed as an architecturally significant building, the six-story structure's interior houses customer service areas for the lead bank, as well as executive and administrative offices for the holding company.

Today customers can take advantage of United Missouri's full-service array of checking and investment/savings accounts, retail and commercial loans, brokerage services, and cash management and operational services. In addition, the bank's professional advisers help individuals and corporations plan their future with regard to the complicated areas of trust, employee benefits, financial planning, and investment banking.

United Missouri serves customers not only in the Midwest but nationwide. The institution has a national reputation for its strength in such areas as employee benefits accounting, and investment services, bond trading, and securities processing.

That strength is derived from the bank's heritage, which dates back to 1913, when City Center Bank opened its doors just south of Kansas City's prosperous downtown area. During World War I W.T. Kemper purchased the institution, and within six years Kemper's oldest son, Rufus Crosby

United Missouri completed a new headquarters for its holding company and lead bank in downtown Kansas City in 1986. Located in the heart of the city's financial district, the United Missouri Bank Building houses the executive offices and major service departments of the bank.

Kemper, became the bank's president.

From the beginning R. Crosby Kemper, Sr., showed originality in his method of serving his customers and seeking new business. He developed a reputation for using basic selling techniques to aggressively pursue new business and expand the bank's customer base and its services. By the end of the decade City Center Bank had grown from a $200,000 bank offering primarily loan and deposit services to a million-dollar financial institution that provided trust and investment banking assistance as well.

Kemper also introduced the first drive-up banking facility in the Midwest. The bank opened the nation's first drive-up teller in 1931 and installed the first motor bank in America in the heart of downtown Kansas City in 1944.

The 1930s were a time of growth and expansion for the institution. It acquired Broadway Bank and Trust Company, and in 1934 it received a national charter as City National Bank and Trust Company.

In 1950 Crosby's son, R. Crosby Kemper, Jr., joined the bank, becoming president in 1959 and chairman of the board 12 years later. Under his leadership the institution continued to build a reputation for innovation. When it installed electronic data-processing equipment in 1961, City National was the first bank in the area to enter into what was then a whole new field of automation for the industry.

United Missouri began to expand across the state in the 1970s, first as Missouri Bancshares, Inc., then eventually as United Missouri Bancshares,

*One of United Missouri Bank's primary purposes is to serve its customers by meeting their needs with innovative financial services and programs.*

Inc. Banks were purchased in Boonville, Carthage, Joplin, and Warrensburg. In 1973 United Missouri chartered a bank in downtown St. Louis as its eastern anchor and expanded its presence in the St. Louis metropolitan area. It then established itself in the state capital of Jefferson City and in Springfield. By the mid-1980s United Missouri had banks in communities dotting nearly the entire state. The Kansas City area alone has six banks and 19 locations.

As the system's lead bank, United Missouri Bank of Kansas City, n.a., serves as a hub for product development and data processing for the entire affiliate group. The institution's major service divisions include credit services, business development and relationship banking, trust services, investment banking, operations, and retail banking. In addition, five wholly owned subsidiaries of the bank and holding company offer services in areas of automobile and equipment leasing, venture capital, brokerage services, mortgage banking, and administration of securities processing.

In every facet of the system, United Missouri fosters a strong commitment

*R. Crosby Kemper, Jr. (seated), chairman of the board and chief executive officer, and Malcolm M. Aslin, president of United Missouri Bancshares, Inc.*

to excellence and quality. That commitment is paramount in the company's goal to continue its strong financial performance and to maintain its high return for its shareholders. It is also exhibited in the company's concern for its people, its customers, and its community.

United Missouri Bank of Kansas City, n.a., is highly visible in its community as a corporate sponsor for various civic and charitable activities. The institution has supported such Kansas City traditions as the American Royal, the Nelson-Atkins Museum of Art, the Starlight Theater, and the Kansas City Symphony. The bank encourages its associates to actively participate in community organizations that foster a betterment in the quality of life. In addition, they are encouraged to pursue higher education and professional development in order to better serve both their customers and their community.

# 7
# THE NEW PIONEERS

At the turn of the century the city boasted an institution of higher learning known as the Kansas City College of Eclectic Medicine. In that period the height of medical technology hovered somewhere around laudanum drops and electric belts, but one of the KCCEM alumni made national headlines with transplant surgery.

By the 1930s, Dr. John Romulus Brinkley was known from coast to coast as "the goat gland doctor." He advertised his "revolutionary surgical discovery to restore failing masculinity" via the radio waves. His station, KFKB (Kansas First, Kansas Best), served up a mix of country music, sermons, and lectures interspersed with the news of miraculous cures effected at the Brinkley Clinic in Milford, Kansas.

There's a great deal less razzle-dazzle in the medical field today, but a lot more serious science going on. The University of Kansas Medical Center (KUMC), in Kansas City, Kansas, is widely renowned for its highly sophisticated testing and surgical procedures, from heart transplants to genetic evaluations. This medical center operates the Gene and Barbara Burnett Burn Center; and centers on aging, cancer, hearing, and speech disorders as well as an environmental health center. A distinguished faculty conducts research work in a wide range of biomedical fields. On KUMC's 50-acre campus is the 524-bed Bell Memorial Hospital, the teaching hospital for the university. The medical center is one of the largest employers in the Kansas City area, with a daytime population of about 10,000 employees and students. It has 222 staff physicians and a staff of medical and surgical residents chosen from among the nation's top medical graduates.

Also on the Kansas side is Providence-St. Margaret Health Center, which provides 276 staffed patient beds and 270 medical staff physicians at the service of the western sector of the metropolitan area. Services include same-day surgery, prenatal classes and family-oriented maternity care; an oncology program, and cardiac care that includes open-heart

*Opposite: The campus of William Jewell College in Liberty is beautiful any time of year, but particularly in October and November when its 2,000 students get to enjoy not only its liberal arts curriculum, but its colorful fall foliage as well. Photo by Roy Inman*

surgery. Classes include cancer and stroke support, and diabetes and stop-smoking programs. A satellite emergency care facility is operated at the Indian Springs Shopping Center.

Truman Medical Center is the teaching hospital of the School of Medicine of the University of Missouri-Kansas City (UMKC). This modern city hospital complex replaced the old General Hospital and is a Level I trauma center with 237 staffed beds and 146 staff physicians. Truman provides a low-vision clinic, high-risk pregnancy care, and oral and maxillofacial surgery.

At Truman Medical Center-East in eastern Jackson County, there is a hospital-based outpatient dental clinic, long-term care for geriatric cases, a family practice clinic and psychiatric rehabilitation programs. The hospital has 304 staffed beds and 186 staff physicians.

St. Luke's Hospital of Kansas City is the largest hospital in the area, with 570 staffed beds and 535 staff physicians. A Level I trauma center, the hospital also has the Mid-American Heart Institute, the Regional Center for High-Risk Maternity and Infant Care/Level III neonatal services, a regional neuroscience center, and a medical psychiatric unit. St. Luke's maintains centers for sexual assault treatment, renal dialysis, poison control, and cancer treatment.

Baptist Medical Center is a church-affiliated health care facility with 330 staff beds and a medical staff of 525 doctors. The hospital has the Charles F. Curry Center for Health Education, the Midwest Diabetes Referral Center, and the Eye Institute of Mid-America. The CarePsychCenter treats patients with mild to moderate stress and depression, while other hospital-based facilities serve as an alcohol rehabilitation center, an adolescent chemical dependency program site, and community-based primary health care centers. Baptist Hospital also provides coordination for the Kansas City Clinical Oncology program.

Children's Mercy Hospital at 24th and Gillham is located on what has come to be known as "Hospital Hill" because of the complex of medical services situated there. A regional pediatrics center, the hospital has 167 staffed beds and more than 300 staff physicians. Children's Mercy provides a complete range of pediatric surgical services, and maintains thirty-eight specialized outpatient clinics. Infant and pre-teen patient services include a neonatal intensive care unit, a crippled children's nursery, and cardiac, oncology, and hematology departments. The hospital also provides the services of a poison control center.

Another of the city's largest hospitals is Research Medical Center. One of the early medical centers in the city, Research was originally known as German Hospital. It has 487 staffed beds and 532 staff doctors. Special treatment centers are provided for cancer, orthopedics, and diseases of the kidney. There are special care nurseries, pain management clinics, a brain tumor institute, an arthritis rehabilitation program, and a center for neurological disorders.

Menorah Medical Center provides the community with 430 staffed patient beds and a medical staff of 405 doctors. Menorah operates the Midwest Neurological Institute, a pain management clinic, a gastroen-

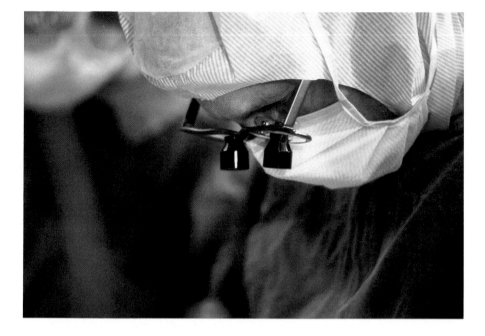

*The University of Kansas Medical Center in Kansas City, Kansas, is particularly known for its sophisticated surgical procedures. Photo by Hank Young/Young Company*

terology laboratory, an eating disorders unit, and a laser institute.

Shawnee Mission Medical Center in Merriam, Kansas, is operated by the Seventh Day Adventist Church. The center has 383 licensed beds and a medical staff of 400 physicians. It also maintains three innovative health clinics in shopping malls at Oak Park, Metcalf South, and Ward Parkway. Its community services include a Life Dynamics program, adult and adolescent mental health units, and a 24-hour emergency room.

Trinity Lutheran Hospital operates 301 staffed patient beds and has 274 doctors on its staff. Trinity's services include a psychiatric unit, diabetes control center, a wellness program, and a pain management center. In addition, there is a cardiac diagnostic center, an open-heart surgery program and extensive ophthalmology services. The Midwest Fertility Foundation is located here, as well as the Kansas City Regional Cancer Center, and the hospital has a 24-hour, on-call microsurgery limb re-attachment team.

St. Joseph Hospital is operated by the Sisters of Saint Joseph of Carondelet and has 274 patient beds with a medical staff of 456 physicians. The hospital is a Level II trauma center with a 24-hour emergency room and helicopter ambulance. Additional services include open-heart surgery, a convalescent and geriatric care facility, services for senior citizens, home care services, and family-centered maternity care.

St. Mary's Hospital has 285 staffed beds and 352 staff physicians. The hospital provides home health services, a family practice medicine center, and services for older adults.

St. Mary's of Blue Springs is a small community hospital with 74 staffed beds and a medical staff of 181 doctors. There is a full service, 24-hour emergency room, a gastrointestinal laboratory, and a rape crisis center.

Liberty Hospital north of the Missouri River is another of the several

*(continued on page 206)*

# ST. LUKE'S HOSPITAL
## A Tradition of Quality Health Care

St. Luke's Hospital has been providing quality health care to residents of the Kansas City area since 1882, when a group of determined members of St. Mary's Episcopal Church adopted as their goal "to erect a hospital which would have the comforts of a private establishment and open to all."

Toward this end they formed a nonprofit organization, the Church Charities Association. The group's dedication to the idea of a private hospital resulted in a fund-raising drive that eventually brought about the purchase of a tract of land at 1005 Campbell Street. Three years later the predecessor of St. Luke's Hospital, All Saints' Hospital, was dedicated on that site. From the beginning All Saints' Hospital functioned as an independent, nonsectarian institution, emphasizing modern facilities, high-quality care, and involvement in medical education.

In 1893 a staggering economic depression took the country by surprise and claimed All Saints' Hospital as one of its victims. However, many supporters of the institution worked to keep the dream of a private hospital alive. Leading this dedicated group was Dr. Herman B. Pearse, a well-known physician, teacher, and medical journal editor. In 1902, with the support of several prominent Episcopalians, Dr. Pearse opened the 12-bed St. Luke's Hospital in a building at Fifth and Delaware. In less than a year the growing institution moved to larger quarters at 4207 Central.

Dr. Pearse was so dedicated to the hospital that three years later he mortgaged his own home to purchase a brick mansion at 11th and Euclid to house an expanding St. Luke's Hospital. After 17 years at that address the institution was financially stable, growing, and offering dramatically improved care. In 1915 an addition to the facility doubled patient capacity and temporarily re-

*St. Luke's Hospital today is a major referral center with 500 physicians, 2,900 employees, and 500 full-time students. In 1985 the hospital provided over 165,000 days of care in more than 30 medical subspecialties.*

*Student nurses pose at St. Luke's Hospital, 11th and Euclid, circa 1906. Today the institution's School of Nursing offers diploma and continuing B.S.N. education programs. The hospital also supports 38 other educational, residency, and fellowship programs.*

lieved a pressing need for more space.

In 1923 St. Luke's Hospital moved to its present location at 44th Street and Wornall Road, where its facilities initially included 150 beds and such innovations as a solarium on each floor and an outpatient department. Additions

were undertaken almost immediately, and the institution has been involved in expansion and renovation ever since, continually representing the state of the art in hospital care and treatment.

Today St. Luke's Hospital is a 686-bed major nonprofit health care complex with 500 physicians on its medical staff. The institution, which ranks among the top one percent in size of the more than 4,700 private hospitals in the United States, serves the greater Kansas City metropolitan area and a surrounding six-state region, affording a

*The hospital's Mid America Heart Institute is world renowned for excellence in the diagnosis and treatment of heart disease. It features patient rooms, state-of-the-art surgical suites, and diagnostic facilities.*

wide variety of acute and primary care services.

St. Luke's Hospital furnishes comprehensive world-recognized cardiac treatment in its Mid America Heart Institute. It also features a Level I Trauma Center and Level III neonatal nursery, both supported by *The Spirit of Kansas City-Life Flight* emergency helicopter service, a joint program of St. Luke's Hospital and Saint Joseph Hospital. A fixed-wing aircraft air ambulance service is also available.

The regional St. Luke's Perinatal Center, a joint enterprise with Children's Mercy Hospital, serves high-risk mothers and infants. Outpatient surgery is performed at St. Luke's Ambulatory Surgery Center. The hospital's Oncology Center features an extensive array of diagnostic, treatment, and support services. An Outpatient Center, currently under construction, will house a wide variety of outpatient services for cancer victims and patients requiring rehabilitation therapy and other specialized services.

St. Luke's Hospital also has a

number of specialty programs, including a medical/psychiatric unit, a state-designated Arthritis Treatment Center and Arthritis/Rehabilitation Unit, a developmental preschool program, a Regional Neuroscience Center, a kidney dialysis/transplantation program, and a team-oriented heart transplant program. Acquisition of innovative medical technology, such as magnetic resonance imaging (MRI) equipment, helps to keep St. Luke's Hospital at the forefront of advances that enhance patient diagnosis and care.

The institution's School of Nursing offers a diploma program and opportunities for continuing B.S.N. education. The hospital also maintains medical education affiliations with the University of Missouri-Kansas City School of Medicine and the University of Kansas School of Medicine.

The hospital's Lifewise program makes available comprehensive wellness and corporate health programs to the community. Services include programs on stress reduction, weight loss, and healthy life-styles. The Lifewise at the Vista corporate health and fitness facility offers exercise plans and health information to the business community.

Throughout its long history St. Luke's Hospital has remained resistant to the "factory" concept of medicine

and the depersonalization of hospital care. The Right Reverend Arthur A. Vogel, bishop of the Episcopal Diocese of West Missouri and chairman of the hospital's board of directors, has disavowed this concept as inconsistent with the traditions of St. Luke's Hospital and contrary to its patients' desires, and has adopted "The Presence of Care" as the hospital's motto.

The St. Luke's Hospital Foundation generates philanthropic support for the institution, and under the leadership of its president, David H. Hughes, provides significant funding for the hospital's charitable and educational programs.

Guided by Edward T. Matheny, Jr., president of the hospital and foundation chairman, and by Charles C. Lindstrom, the hospital's executive vice-president and chief executive officer, St. Luke's Hospital of Kansas City continues to provide excellent health care services, facilities, and programs, with an accompanying commitment to medical education and research.

*More than 11,000 surgeries are performed at St. Luke's Hospital each year. In 1985 patient admissions totaled 23,500, with more than 850,500 laboratory and 100,500 radiology procedures performed, and 129,700 patients seen in the hospital's outpatient clinics.*

# BLUE CROSS AND BLUE SHIELD OF KANSAS CITY
## Offering Unique Services to the Community

It started with a contract between Dallas schoolteachers and Baylor University. For a prepayment of 50 cents per month, the teachers could receive medical treatment at the university's hospital. Soon other employee groups in Dallas had enrolled in the plan, and within 10 years there were more than three million members in what had become known as Blue Cross plans.

Physicians, observing the success of Blue Cross plans, recognized the need for patients to budget in advance for medical expenses.

In 1938 the American Medical Association's House of Delegates endorsed the principle of voluntary health insurance, and a decade later the Blue Shield symbol and name were chosen to represent prepaid physician services.

To most people, Blue Cross means hospital coverage, while Blue Shield is synonymous with medical coverage. The two consolidated in 1978, forming the Blue Cross and Blue Shield Association.

Today Blue Cross and Blue Shield is the nation's largest third-party payer. Though each plan is an autonomous, not-for-profit corporation that operates within a designated geographic area, all are members of the Blue Cross and Blue Shield Association located in Chicago.

Blue Cross and Blue Shield plans protect more than 80 million people,

---

*The cross and shield are symbols that represent high-quality health care protection. A customer service center is located in the lobby of Blue Cross and Blue Shield's office at 3637 Broadway in midtown Kansas City.*

and nearly one-third of the population of the United States has Blue Cross and Blue Shield coverage. There are currently 79 plans in the United States, Puerto Rico, Canada, and Jamaica. One of those plans is Blue Cross and Blue Shield of Kansas City.

The Kansas City Blue Cross plan got its start in 1938 with seven member hospitals and two employees. The first group of employees to sign an agreement with Blue Cross of Kansas City was from Fred Wolferman, Inc. After one year the Blue Cross plan had 10 member hospitals, 8 employees, and nearly 14,000 members.

Kansas City Blue Shield was established in 1943, with initial working capital supplied by several of the nearly 400 doctors who had signed contracts to participate in the program. The Palace Clothing Company was the first Blue Shield group, and after a year more than 300 businesses from 19 Missouri counties had signed up with Blue Shield of Kansas City.

In 1982 the Blue Cross and Blue Shield plans merged, creating Blue Cross and Blue Shield of Kansas City. Today the Kansas City plan serves a territory that encompasses 30 counties in western Missouri, as well as Johnson and Wyandotte counties in Kansas. Over 850,000 people are served by the Kansas City plan.

"The basic objective of the Blue Cross and Blue Shield plans has always been to make high-quality, effective, and economical health care services available to people," says Richard P. Krecker, president and chief executive officer of Blue Cross and Blue Shield of Kansas City. "And this philosophy prevails at the Kansas City plan."

According to the organization's Mission Statement: "Blue Cross and Blue Shield of Kansas City is committed to offer health care coverage and other related services to business, labor, government, and individual subscribers. It is an organization which is focused on and directed by the community it serves and shall operate in a prudent and financially sound manner. In a broader sense of purpose, Blue Cross and Blue Shield of Kansas City

*Blue Cross and Blue Shield of Kansas City is committed to hiring outstanding people and providing them with a positive work environment. Customer service representatives, for example, receive telephone skills training, and have access to a state-of-the-art computer system when answering inquiries.*

shall use its experience, cooperative provider agreements, and administrative capabilities to offer products at the best value possible and shall encourage healthy life-styles."

Policy direction and corporate governance for Blue Cross and Blue Shield of Kansas City is provided by a board of directors. In addition to the president of the organization, the board consists of 17 individuals, representing all segments of the public, and seven physicians. "We are extremely fortunate to have a board of directors who are so dedicated and conscientious," Krecker notes. "Their wise guidance is a valuable asset to our company and to the community."

Blue Cross and Blue Shield of Kansas City has contractual agreements with hospitals and physicians to offer services to Blue Cross and Blue Shield subscribers. The plan also offers a variety of health care products. "The wide range of coverages available, combined with the discounts we receive from participating hospitals and doctors, has added to our marketability and enrollment growth," says Krecker.

These products include Comprehensive Major Medical, a traditional type of coverage with a deductible and coinsurance; Preferred-Care, a preferred provider organization that offers incentives to use the services of providers who have agreed to discount the cost of their services (available to individuals as well as groups); Preferred-Care Dental, a dental preferred provider organization; Total Health Care, Missouri's largest federally qualified independent practice association health maintenance organization; Pharmaceutical Card System, Inc., a prescription drug program that provides prescription drugs to subscribers for only a two-dollar or four-dollar copayment; third-party administration, for groups that choose to self-insure, offered through LaHood & Associates, a wholly owned subsidiary; life insurance, offered through the Missouri Valley Insurance Agency, a wholly owned subsidiary; and Total Health Care 65, Tie-In-Plan, and Senior-Care, all products for Medicare-eligible citizens.

The company's financial performance, enrollment growth, and product diversification have been outstanding. Revenues for 1985 were $11.5 million, and the most significant achievement for the year was in enrollment, with 32,000 new members added.

"The progress we've made," Krecker emphasizes, "can be traced to our employees. We are committed to hiring outstanding people and providing them with a positive and caring work environment. We want to offer a top-notch place to work with significant challenges that afford opportunities for growth."

As part of an ongoing evaluation that keeps Blue Cross and Blue Shield of Kansas City ahead of its competition, the management staff, in 1985, defined corporate values that are goals for all employees. This corporate culture—to be service oriented and market sensitive, to improve efficiency in cost and performance, to be less bureaucratic, and to effectively use buying power—stresses the importance Blue Cross and Blue Shield places on its integrity and reputation.

"Our long-standing tradition in the market gives credence to our advertising slogan," Krecker says. "Blue Cross and Blue Shield: The most trusted health care protection in history."

# SAINT JOSEPH HEALTH CENTER
## Innovation, Expansion, and Cooperation Characterize its Commitment to the Community

The history of Saint Joseph Health Center dates back to seventeenth-century France, when the Sisters of St. Joseph of Carondelet first founded their religious community dedicated to serving the needy. Eventually, the Sisters crossed the ocean to come to America, ultimately venturing to Kansas City where, in 1874, they opened the city's first private hospital at Seventh and Pennsylvania to serve Kansas City's 35,000 residents.

In the 1880s, after the discoveries of France's Louis Pasteur and England's Lord Lister, Saint Joseph Hospital pioneered the use of special sterilization procedures, curtailing deaths from postoperative infections. The hospital was also the first institution west of the Mississippi to use X-ray equipment.

By 1910 the city's population was over a quarter-million, and the Sisters decided it was time to expand their quarters. A new 250-bed hospital was opened in March 1917 at Linwood and Prospect. In 1935 the hospital's auxiliary was formed, and that organization's early efforts provided the money to institute the Pediatrics Department at a time when polio victims were long-term patients.

As the first private hospital in Kansas City, Saint Joseph kept up with the times. In the early 1970s the city's boundaries moved south, and a decision was made to purchase a 46-acre tract of land at I-435 and State Line.

The third Saint Joseph Hospital opened its doors in January 1977, providing a 300-bed institution and adjacent medical office building. In addition, the satellite facilities in Grandview and Lee's Summit were opened to provide major and minor

*For 60 years Saint Joseph Hospital was located at Linwood and Prospect. In this X-shaped building, which was hailed as the latest in architectural design, the hospital's physicians and staff pioneered many "firsts" in health care for Kansas Citians.*

emergency care for those rapidly growing communities. A Life Flight emergency rescue helicopter program was added in 1978, the fifth such program in the nation. In 1986 the hospital changed its name to Saint Joseph Health Center to more accurately reflect the broad scope of services it provides. And, in 1987, the health center launched a major expansion project, including another medical office building, expanded outpatient facilities, and an innovative

women's and children's unit.

Inbred with the pioneer spirit, Saint Joseph Health Center has always worked with others to achieve a common goal. And those partnerships have benefited both the institution and the Kansas City community.

More than 450 physicians are on the medical staff of Saint Joseph Health Center, working in partnership with the institution to provide contemporary health services, including 24-hour emergency care, family-centered maternity care, pediatrics, state-of-the-art cardiovascular and radiology procedures, a full range of outpatient services that include day surgery and a preadmission clinic, and a number of community outreach programs. These, along with the many other services that the

*In 1978, shortly after the institution's relocation to I-435 and State Line, Saint Joseph Hospital became the fifth hospital in the nation to operate an emergency rescue helicopter, Life Flight. After nine years of operation, this life-saving program has transported more than 7,000 patients and has flown more than 700,000 accident-free miles.*

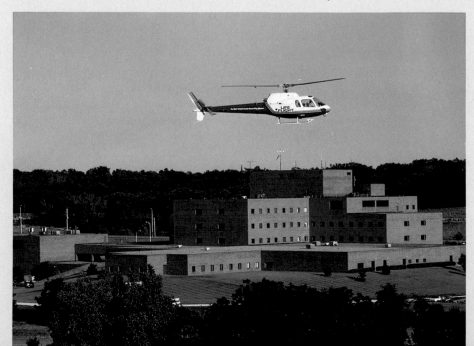

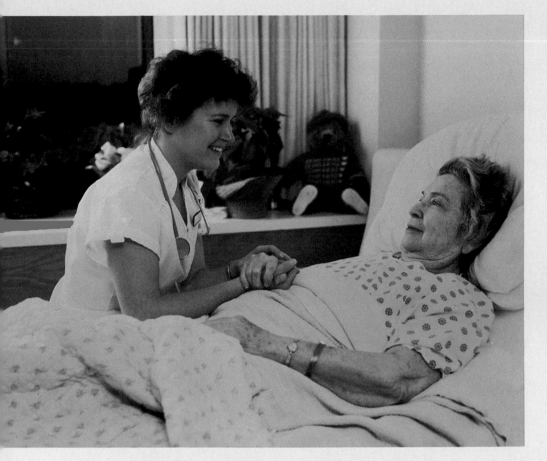

*Saint Joseph Health Center prides itself in the special kind of care that its staff provides to patients. Concern and respect for each individual are part of its mission in the community, which began more than a century ago in 1874.*

health center provides, are designed to offer high-quality, cost-effective health care, supported by the latest technology.

In 1985 Saint Joseph Health Center opened Carondelet Manor, a convalescent and geriatric facility on the health center's campus. The 180-bed center is a joint venture between Saint Joseph Health Center and Dominic

Tutera, M.D. Open-air courtyards, shops, a chapel, and natural lighting create a unique homelike atmosphere for the residents, while physicians and staff from the health center provide comprehensive medical care. To complement this service, the health center established Carondelet Home Care Services, Inc., which provides a wide range of nursing, therapeutic, and counseling services, all delivered in the home.

Also in 1985 two major Kansas City hospitals established partnerships with Saint Joseph Health Center to provide unique health care services to the area.

That year Saint Joseph Health Center invited St. Luke's Hospital to join in the life-saving Life Flight heli

copter emergency rescue program. "The interest in a partnership came from a desire to expand the community service that Life Flight was already providing and to improve the cost effectiveness of the program," says Sister Mary Frances Johnson, chairperson of the board of directors of Saint Joseph Health Center.

In addition to another landing base that will increase the program's responsiveness, the Life Flight partnership allows Saint Joseph to share in the cost of operation, which includes the 24-hour, state-of-the-art dispatch center located at Saint Joseph Health Center. *The Spirit of Kansas City* Life Flight helicopter has logged more than 700,000 accident-free miles and transported more than 7,000 patients during its eight years of operation. The service is staffed by critical care professionals and operates within a 150-mile radius, 24 hours a day.

The second partnership was formed with Baptist Medical Center to share the costs of a revolutionary new diagnostic procedure called Magnetic Resonance Imaging (MRI). This highly sensitive and safe diagnostic imaging technique uses magnetic and radio frequency fields to "take a picture" of body tissue. MRI is effective in diagnosing soft tissue abnormalities and can detect such diseases as multiple sclerosis. The service is housed in a mobile unit that travels between the two institutions on a regular basis.

Through developments such as these, Saint Joseph Health Center continues its mission that began 113 years ago—providing quality health care for any person in need of its services, and offering it in a manner that respects the dignity of each individual. That special kind of care has become a hallmark of Saint Joseph Health Center, one that continues to guide its service to the Kansas City community.

*Residents and visitors experience a homelike atmosphere at Carondelet Manor, a special geriatric and convalescent facility on the Saint Joseph Health Center campus. The facility is owned by Dominic Tutera, M.D., and managed by Saint Joseph Health Center.*

# INDEPENDENCE REGIONAL HEALTH CENTER
## At the Forefront of Health Care

The history of Independence Regional Health Center is a history rich with people—physicians, employees, volunteers, and board members who, for the past 77 years, have come together with the common goal of providing excellent health care to the people of the community.

The mission of service began in 1909 when Joseph Smith III, president of the Reorganized Church of Jesus Christ of Latter-Day Saints, along with his fellow church leaders, promoted the construction of a convalescent home in Independence, Missouri. The 3-story, 26-bed, and 11-staff-member nursing home was initially intended to be a place of "refuge and help for the sick and afflicted of the church." But during the first week of operation, a railroad accident necessitated the amputation of a man's leg. He became the first patient in what is now a thriving health care complex of 367 beds, providing multiple services and a continuity of care for persons of all ages. As the third-largest employer in Independence, Independence Regional Health Center currently has 1,100 employees, 200 medical staff members, and 1,000 volunteers. A full-service hospital accredited by the Joint Commission on Accreditation of Hospitals and other professional associations,

*In 1930 the cornerstone for the north tower complex was laid.*

Independence Regional Health Center is a not-for-profit institution.

"We've worked very hard in the past 25 years to bring to eastern Jackson County the medical specialties people need," says hospital president Joseph Lammers. And in so doing Independence Regional Health Center has in-

*In 1986, to better convey the comprehensive list of specialties that are offered to the people of eastern Jackson County, the name of the hospital was changed to Independence Regional Health Center.*

stituted and continues to build upon highly technical procedures. These include open-heart surgery, cardiac catheterization, laser surgery, gastroenterology, plastic surgery, and digital subtraction angiography (DSA), an X-ray procedure that allows visualization of the arterial system by an intravenous or interarterial injection.

Other services offered by Independence Regional include pain manage-

*People who care for people at Independence Regional Health Center.*

ment, The Senior Network, a diabetic resource center, oncology services, sleep disorders, and pediatric developmental health, as well as 24-, 48-, and 72-hour maternity care programs that offer greater options to mothers in managing their own birthings. The Extended Care Unit provides short-term skilled or rehabilitative care after a hospital stay.

The hospital's 24-hour Emergency Room includes a Trauma and Rape Crisis Center. The One Day Surgery Center was designed for patients who require surgery too complex to be performed in a physician's office, but not requiring overnight hospitalization.

Anyone who has been diagnosed as having heart disease is a candidate for participation in the Phase II Cardiac Rehabilitation Program. Participants in the program learn to evaluate and adjust their life-styles so that they can enjoy themselves to the fullest—physically and emotionally. A support group made up of participants and their families is also part of the program.

HealthLine, Independence Regional's Wellness Division, offers a variety of programs to promote good health for individuals and employers. Through discussion and personal attention, HealthLine provides a practical approach to fitness and positive living.

"A hospital's challenge and responsibility is to respond to the changing health needs of the people it serves. Two specialized services, psychiatric services and care for the elderly, are at the forefront," says Lammers. "We saw an

*Independence Regional Health Center gives patients access to highly skilled medical specialists and state-of-the-art equipment.*

increased need for mental health services because of stress, alcohol, and drug-related problems—especially in adolescent psychiatric services."

A parallel growth pattern is projected for geriatric care. A $1.5-million grant in 1975 from the Homer McWilliams Trust was earmarked to address the health care needs of older persons. Consequently, this laid the foundation for the development of a combination of programs. These include home health care, homemaker services, adult day health care, transportation, and hospice services.

The adult day health care service is an alternative to institutional care and can provide relief to the family caregiver from one to five days per week. It also provides a place for activities, companionship, supervised care, and nutritious meals and snacks.

Hospice care at Independence Regional Health Center serves people who choose to remain at home during the final stages of life. It is medically directed, but also includes psychological, pastoral, social service, and bereavement support to the terminally ill patient and the family.

Undoubtedly, the health care industry and Independence Regional Health Center have experienced changes in the past 77 years. The hospital's history of a strong foundation of care and service will continue to be built upon to meet the changing needs of the people of the region.

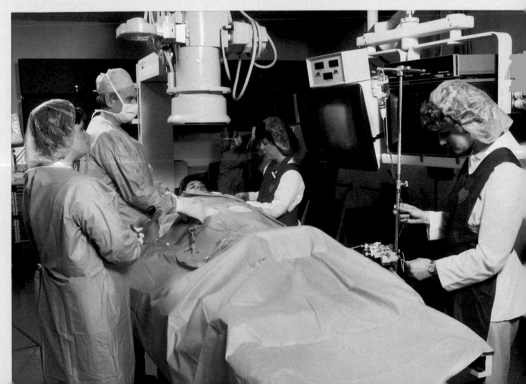

small community hospitals in the metropolitan area. It has 140 staffed beds and 160 staff physicians. This institution offers an outpatient surgery program, intensive care, a sleep laboratory, a skilled nursing facility, a non-invasive vascular laboratory, and a wide range of community education programs.

Olathe Community Hospital has 100 patient beds and 61 staff physicians in this suburban Johnson County hospital. The institution provides short-stay maternity care, a pediatrics unit, pregnancy and post-partum workout classes, poison prevention, and lifestyle correction programs.

Lee's Summit Community Hospital is located in the heart of John Knox Village, the nation's largest retirement center. It maintains 114 staffed patient care beds and has a medical staff of 137 doctors. The hospital provides Lifeline communication services for area residents, a drug and alcohol abuse referral program, cardiac rehabilitation, and a number of community health programs.

Medical Center of Independence is a Level II trauma center and designated rape crisis center for the eastern metropolitan area. It has 210 staffed beds with a medical staff of 197 physicians. An unusual feature offered at this hospital is a series of free prenatal and sibling classes.

North Kansas City Hospital is a Level II trauma center. It has 325 patient beds and 225 staff doctors. Among its broad range of services are cardiac catheterization and rehabilitation, a mental health center, a neonatal intensive care facility, laser surgery, and an alcohol and drug rehabilitation unit.

Humana Hospital in Overland Park has approximately 200 doctors on staff. Hand rehabilitation is a specialty at Humana, along with cardiac care and open heart surgery. The hospital also has a women's center.

Veterans Administration Medical Center provides care to eligible veterans. The hospital has 472 patient beds and a medical staff of 80 doctors.

Osteopathic centers include University of Health Sciences Lakeside Hospital and Park Lane Medical Center. Perhaps the most visible of the three is University of Health Sciences Hospital, the teaching hospital for University of Health Sciences, a school of osteopathy. It has 150 staffed beds and has 145 doctors. The hospital operates a mobile critical care unit, three satellite family practice centers, and a drug and alcohol abuse program.

Lakeside Hospital has 167 beds and 125 staff doctors, with a full range of traditional hospital services, a full-service emergency room, and a one-day surgery program for some cases. The third osteopathic center, Park Lane Medical Center, is a 110-bed hospital with expanded surgical services and a 24-hour, physician-staffed emergency room.

With the sound body well cared for, we turn to the sound mind and find that there are nearly three score schools in the metro area with courses leading to degrees ranging from a two-year associate certificate to doctorates in medicine, dentistry, education, and biological sciences. There are two major schools of medicine, eight institutions offering baccalaureate degrees, five colleges providing masters' programs, and twelve colleges offering associate degrees.

*Children's Mercy Hospital is located on "Hospital Hill," so named because of the number of health-care facilities situated there. Photo by Bruce Mathews*

The presence of so many urban campuses has resulted in increasing attention to the "commuter student," the full-time homemaker or other worker, who carries out a program of study while holding down a full-time job.

The University of Missouri-Kansas City, founded in 1933 as the University of Kansas City, is one of four campuses in the University of Missouri (UM) system. The school was established as the University of Kansas City, one of the major beneficiaries of the philanthropist William Volker (for whom Volker Park is named). Taken into the UM system in the 1960s, the institution has expanded to encompass the Kansas City Conservatory and the Kansas City School of Medicine. A total of ten schools make up the Kansas City campus, including the College of Arts and Sciences and several professional schools. The university is the home of a nationally top-ranking National Public Radio affiliate, KCUR-FM, on the air with founding Broadcast Director Sam Scott since 1957. Known for media excellence, UMKC also has the Marr Media Library, a collection of audio and video archives considered second only to that of the National Vocarium in Washington, D.C. There are approximately 6,000 full-time students and over 5,000 part-time students. The university also has an active continuing education program and hosts the free community access Communiversity series. The prestigious Carolyn Benton Cockefair program annually presents a notable guest lecture series. The school's new Center for the Performing Arts is home to the Missouri Repertory Theater, founded by Professor Emeritus Patricia McIlrath. The Linda Hall Library of Science and Technology, and his-

# HUMANA HOSPITAL-OVERLAND PARK
## In Pursuit of Medical Excellence

Humana Hospital-Overland Park, located at 10500 Quivira Road, is a fully modern 400-bed general medical and surgical hospital serving the Johnson County community. Since 1978 it has addressed both the family and business health needs of this rapidly expanding area with an integrated system of conventional acute care and specialty services.

Humana, the only proprietary hospital in Kansas City, is part of an international company that owns and operates 87 acute-care facilities in 23 states as well as England and Switzerland. At the end of fiscal year 1985 Humana's 87 hospitals contained 17,706 beds and employed more than 43,800 people.

As part of the vast Humana system, the Overland Park facility is able to achieve productivity and efficiency through cost-effective methods of buying and managing. Close attention is also given to staffing, budget control, and training.

Although hospital costs are of concern to patients, it is the quality of services and the environment of care encompassing those services that are most important. Humana Hospital-Overland Park responds to those needs with skilled, empathetic employees and excellent facility design.

Its 24-hour emergency department, for example, provides the incoming patient with immediate medical assessment and close proximity to support services. A recently expanded maternal and newborn care wing offers a

Family-centered obstetrics has been a strength of the hospital since it opened and paved the way for a center devoted to meeting the special needs and concerns of women's health issues.

higher level of service to newborns with significant medical problems, in many cases, allowing mother and sick baby to remain in the same hospital close to home.

Physicians and surgeons on the medical staff work with the most technologically advanced equipment and the latest medical and surgical treatments. The surgical department is equipped for open-heart surgery and neurosurgery, as well as other major and minor procedures.

The institution's Cardiac Rehabili-

Humana Hospital-Overland Park.

tation Program is designed to serve the individual who has heart disease, elevated risk factors, or who has had heart surgery. The programs offered can help patients improve cardiovascular function and reduce coronary risk factors. They also provide information and education so that individuals can make wise choices to maintain and improve their health.

A new cardiac catheterization laboratory with state-of-the art equipment opened in 1986. In addition, specialty services at the hospital include the Women's Center, which was designed by women to address the private nature of their health concerns. Through its outreach programs the hospital initiated the first physician information service in the area for newcomers and developed an extensive Community Health Education Department to provide seminars and classes for the community on a variety of health-related topics.

As a proprietary institution Humana Hospital-Overland Park is able to give additional support to the community in the form of state and local income tax, property tax, and sales tax. More than 600 people from the area are employed by the hospital and are able to increase their skills with continuing education and training.

Whether it is through its comprehensive hospital services or its community health projects, Humana Hospital-Overland Park is responsive to the health needs of the thriving Kansas City community in which it does business.

The University of Missouri-Kansas City is one of four campuses in the University of Missouri (UM) system. Photo by Michael A. Mihalevich

toric Pierce Street row houses are also on the campus.

Kansas City Art Institute near the Country Club Plaza is a venerable institution which began life nearly a century ago as the Kansas City Sketch Club. An independent private college considered to be one of the finest art schools in the nation, the school offers undergraduate degrees in art and design and has a full-time enrollment of about 500 students. Missouri's beloved Thomas Hart Benton was once chairman of the school's painting department. The internationally known sculptor Dale Eldred is chairman of the sculpture department. Ken Ferguson, equally famous for his ceramics, is chairman of that department at the Art Institute. A Bachelor of Fine Arts degree is earned by graduates successfully completing a course of study in fields including painting, printmaking, sculpture, photography, ceramics, textiles, and design. High tuition costs

An independent private college considered to be one of the best art schools in the nation, The Kansas City Art Institute offers undergraduate degrees in art and design to its 500 students. Photo by Michael A. Mihalevich

are offset by a strong financial aid program. The annual Renaissance Festival is its best known fund-raiser.

Avila College is a Catholic, four-year liberal arts college with an enrollment of about 1,800. Advanced degrees available include master of business administration and master of science in education and psychology. The school has an extensive nursing education program and a respected department of performing and visual arts. Enrollment currently stands at about 1,800, and part-time study programs are available. Avila also annually hosts one of the best of the many good writers' workshops in the area.

Rockhurst College is a Jesuit-founded, Catholic liberal arts college with a strong reputation as a pre-professional and business administration school. In addition to the traditional daytime classes, there are weekend and night classes in both undergraduate and graduate curricula. The college has a daytime enrollment of about 1,800 students, and another 600 attend evening classes. The Rockhurst graduate business program annually attracts a large enrollment.

William Jewell College in Liberty is a Baptist liberal arts college with a total enrollment of about 2,000. It is one of the few colleges offering the Oxbridge Alternative Tutorial Program, modeled after curricula followed at Oxford and Cambridge universities in England. The school has an exceptionally active overseas study program and is widely known for its annual Fine Arts Concert Series programs. (Italian tenor Luciano Pavarotti's first American recital was given in a Fine Arts concert, a coup which was repeated at his tenth anniversary recital.)

Community colleges, the successors to the junior colleges of an earlier era, have attained a high level of acceptance in Kansas City. There are seven of these two-year institutions, offering an impressive number of courses leading to associate degrees, as well as a number of practical and eclectic courses. Located in virtually every sector of the metro area, the community colleges are particularly popular as an efficient and economical way to fulfill basic academic requirements close to home.

Donnelly College in Kansas City, Kansas, is a two-year Catholic college offering both associate of arts and associate of science degrees. There is an excellent English as a Second Language program, a day-care program, and both day and evening classes. Donnelly's total enrollment is around 1,000 students.

Also on the Kansas Side is Johnson County Community College in Overland Park. This two-year school enrolls about 8,000 degree-seeking students each semester, and another 20,000 non-credit students. The school is noted for its particularly fine electronic media department.

Kansas City Kansas Community College is a two-year college offering several special programs in the field of adult education. These special curricula make it possible for an adult to attend college full time while holding full-time employment. In this program, students attend one classroom session per week, view one televised course each week, and attend one weekend semester each month. The programs cover social sciences, humanities, and natural sciences.

Metropolitan Community Colleges is a consortium of four two-year colleges on the Missouri side of the metropolitan area. The easternmost of the four is Longview Community College in Lee's Summit. Located near the historic country residence of lumber baron R.A. Long, the school also has a satellite campus in Blue Springs. Longview offers a liberal arts curriculum with science, business, and data processing among the fields covered.

The northernmost of the four is Maple Wood Community College north of the Missouri River. Maple Wood features vocational and trans-

The Kansas City Art Institute's ceramics courses teach excellence in the craft of pottery-designing with classes offered by internationally-known sculptors such as Dale Eldred and Ken Ferguson. Photo by Michael A. Mihalevich

(continued on page 220)

# RESEARCH MEDICAL CENTER
## Celebrating 100 Years of Community Service

Research Medical Center, a 536-bed acute care health provider located at 2316 East Meyer Boulevard, is dedicated to community service and encouraging illness prevention. Photo by Chuck Kneyse

More than 100 hundred years ago a group of concerned civic leaders in Kansas City saw a need for a private hospital to serve people in the Midwest. Dedicated to serving a "suffering humanity," German Hospital opened its doors in 1886. What began in a six-room house at 23rd Street and Holmes eventually grew to become Research Medical Center, a major health care facility.

In 1955 Research Medical Center broke ground for its new 65-acre home at 2316 East Meyer Boulevard. Eight years later the hospital opened its doors with a total capacity of more than 500 beds, offering state-of-the-art equipment and technology. In 1980 a new north wing, Rehabilitation and Rheumatology Unit, and a 32-bed Intensive Care Unit were added. Six years later the 536-bed Research Medical Center celebrated its centennial year as an active, vital member of the community.

"Community service, along with providing quality medical care and encouraging illness prevention is a stated value of Research Medical Center,"

says Richard W. Brown, president of the facility. "We're an institution that operates in the public interest, and community service is part of our mission."

More than 500 staff physicians, 2,600 employees, 450 volunteers, and 50 members of various boards of directors make up the Research Medical Center team. The vast complex also includes doctors' office buildings, student residences, staff apartments, and a Child Development Center for employees. In 1984 the 100-bed Research Psychiatric Center was added to the campus, representing a joint venture between Research Medical Center and Hospital Corporation of America.

However, the institution's growth has not been limited to its Meyer Boule-

vard campus. A smaller version of Research Medical Center, Research Belton Hospital, holds 75 beds. It provides wide-ranging health services to residents of southeast Kansas City. Research's HealthPlus center at I-435 and Roe Avenue in Overland Park offers a new approach to fitness and health management with a comprehensive wellness program. The medical center extended its physical coverage to the entire community in 1985, when the Research Eagle air ambulance began operating.

Recognizing the need for highly specialized programs to treat the critically ill, Research Medical Center has selected four clinical areas, designating them as centers of excellence. They include The Center for Cardiovascular and Pulmonary Diseases, which treats diseases of the lungs and heart; The Center for Neurological, Orthopedic, and Rheumatoid Diseases, which deals with patients suffering from diseases and injuries of the nervous and skeletal systems; The Center for Neoplastic Diseases, which administers to those who suffer from cancer; and The Center for Renal Diseases, which offers a full range of services to patients with chronic kidney disease.

Recognizing the need for highly specialized programs to treat the critically ill, Research Medical Center selected four clinical areas, designating them centers of excellence. They are The Center for Cardiovascular and Pulmonary Diseases; The Center for Neurological, Orthopedic, and Rheumatoid Diseases; The Center for Neoplastic Diseases; and The Center for Renal Diseases. Photo by Chuck Kneyse

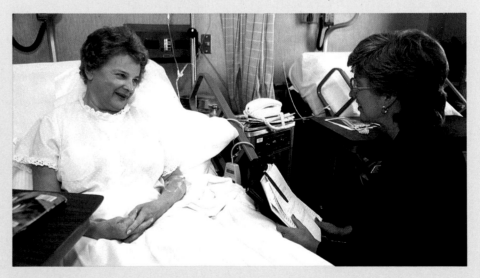

# TRINITY LUTHERAN HOSPITAL
## A Commitment to Provide Superior Health Care

Swedish Hospital opened its doors on October 28, 1906, in a renovated three-story building in downtown Kansas City, Missouri. According to the institution's first annual report, 225 patients were treated during the year, but 150 were turned away because of insufficient room capacity.

However, all that changed as the hospital grew along with Kansas City. Throughout the years the facility maintained close ties with the Lutheran Church. In 1921 its name was changed to Trinity Lutheran Hospital, and in 1962 it became an institution of the Central States Synod of the Lutheran Church.

Today Trinity Lutheran Hospital, located at 3030 Baltimore, holds 360 beds and stands on the city's highest elevation overlooking Penn Valley Park. The institution employs 850 people, with 280 physicians on the medical staff. Its annual operating budget of $40 million makes Trinity Lutheran more than a landmark in the traditional sense—it's a vital force in the city's economy.

"The mission of Trinity Lutheran Hospital is to provide superior health care to residents of all ages in Kansas City and its surrounding region through development and maintenance of strong specialty programs," said the late George W. Dickinson, former chief executive officer of Trinity Lutheran.

"The hospital is also committed to its location at the central city core where it provides those services."

Over the years the institution has earned regional recognition in several specialty programs, including cancer treatment, cardiology/cardiovascular surgery, eye surgery, and pulmonary medicine. These areas of specialization provide strength and stability for the hospital, and it is in these fields that Trinity Lutheran has widely respected and well-known medical specialists along with the latest in technology and equipment.

Earning a reputation for medical leadership, Trinity Lutheran pioneered several firsts, including the first open-heart surgery in the early 1960s, the opening of the city's first Intensive Care Unit (1962), the founding of the area's first private Oncology Unit for the treatment and care of cancer patients (1974), and the establishment of the first limb reattachment team in the region prepared to handle round-the-clock emergencies (1979).

Early in 1984 Trinity Lutheran Hospital and neighboring St. Mary's Hospital combined their cancer out-

*In order to keep up with the demands of advanced technology and a growing patient base, Trinity Lutheran Hospital built this new facility. The lobby, surgery, laboratory, radiology, pharmacy, and physical and occupational therapy areas are housed there.*

patient programs by establishing the Kansas City Regional Cancer Center, which provides the area's largest number of hospital beds used solely for cancer victims. An outpatient clinic, specialized dental care, pain clinic, hostel facility, and state-of-the-art laboratory facilities provide outstanding care for cancer patients.

"Our staffs are trained exclusively for care of the cancer patient," said Dickinson. "Our program encourages outpatient care. That helps reduce the cost without sacrificing the excellence of our program."

With a recently opened Speas Center for Women, a new cardiac diagnostic center, a modern data-processing center, and expanded outpatient surgery facilities, Trinity Lutheran Hospital is going forward with its mission of continual development of new programs that will enable the institution to achieve its objectives and fulfill its future goals.

# ST. MARY'S HOSPITAL
## At the Heart of Health Care

St. Mary's Hospital's service to Kansas City began in 1909 when the city's 193,000 residents had a need for additional organized health care. The Sisters of St. Mary met that need and opened St. Mary's Hospital of Kansas City.

Since then St. Mary's has grown from a four-story, 150-bed facility to a 370-bed, full-service, acute care hospital. As a member of the SSM Health Care System, a St. Louis-based, multi-hospital corporation, St. Mary's is part of the largest health care system in Missouri.

Located at 2800 Main Street, the hospital is in the easily accessible mid-town area, just minutes from all parts of the city. With more than 1,000 health care professionals and nearly 400 physicians, St. Mary's provides quality care in a variety of areas, with a special focus on the family.

"St. Mary's Hospital's comprehensive programs and services are designed not only to meet the needs of our patients, but also of their families," says William P. Thompson, executive director. "Our family orientation challenges us daily to provide not only high-quality technical care, but the human touch as well."

The St. Mary's Hospital Family Medicine Center, located at 2900 Baltimore, is staffed by family practice

*Patient education is of prime importance at the St. Mary's Hospital Family Medicine Center. There patients are instructed in all aspects of health and wellness. The center also houses a library that contains more than 100,000 pieces of patient education materials.*

*St. Mary's Hospital, located at 2800 Main Street, is a full-service institution with a special focus on the family.*

physicians who treat patients and their families and educate them in all aspects of health and wellness. In addition, the center provides a valuable link to other primary care physicians and specialists.

The hospital's family-centered obstetrics program gives parents the option of a traditional labor and delivery facility or a comfortably furnished birthing room. The entire program is designed to make childbirth a family affair. St. Mary's is also well known for helping problem teenagers with Life-Start, a comprehensive adolescent mental health and substance abuse program.

When cancer strikes, the victim's family is involved. St. Mary's oncology program includes an inpatient unit designed exclusively to meet the physical, emotional, and spiritual needs of cancer patients and their families. A full-service radiology department houses state-of-the-art equipment used in the diagnosis and treatment of cancer. In addition, St. Mary's has special services to identify cardiac problems, offer inpatient care, and provide successful

cardiac rehabilitation.

The hospital also realizes that older adults are a vital part of the extended American family. In response to a growing need, St. Mary's offers services and educational programs to meet the special considerations of older adults. This includes a skilled nursing unit, which provides nursing and rehabilitative services to patients who are not ready to return home, but who do not need the full services of an acute care hospital. An extension of this program is the St. Mary's Hospital Home Health Agency, which delivers care to homebound patients.

St. Mary's Hospital's services also extend to the Kansas City business community. CONCERN, the hospital's employee assistance program, offers short-term counseling to employees of more than 25 Kansas City-area organizations. Industrial and occupational medicine services are also available, as St. Mary's continues to develop additional programs for business and industry in Kansas City.

By combining the efforts of dedicated health care professionals with state-of-the-art technology, St. Mary's Hospital continues its tradition of offering family-centered health care to Kansas City residents.

# UNIVERSITY OF MISSOURI-KANSAS CITY
## Joining the Community on the Path to Excellence

The University of Missouri-Kansas City was first conceived out of a community concern to have a center of learning for a growing city. That community interest has not diminished as the institution takes its place as Kansas City's leading source of professional and advanced graduate study.

The Kansas City Chamber of Commerce and local church leaders pooled their resources and influence in 1929 to create what was then called the University of Kansas City. In 1963 the institution became part of the University of Missouri system and was renamed the University of Missouri-Kansas City.

Today UMKC has a growing reputation among the nation's urban universities for teaching, research, and service to the community through its academic units. They include the College of Arts and Sciences; the schools of Basic Life Sciences, Business and Public Administration, Dentistry, Education, Law, Medicine, Nursing, and Pharmacy; the Conservatory of Music; and programs in engineering and computer science/telecommunications.

George A. Russell, the institution's chancellor, has expanded community interest in a center of learning for Kansas City into a full partnership between UMKC and the community.

To help the Kansas City area build quality public school programs, UMKC organized the successful Metropolitan Area Schools Project. One of

*UMKC is Kansas City's only comprehensive university dedicated to research, education, and service to the community. It offers graduate and professional education and undergraduate programs to nearly 12,000 students.*

*Scofield Hall, UMKC's main administrative building, was formerly owned by Walter S. Dickey, an early Kansas City entrepreneur.*

the project's outstanding programs is the Mathematics and Physics Institute for students with above-average aptitude in math and physics.

To help the city answer its need for computer technology, UMKC and United Telecommunications, Inc., together developed a strong research-based academic program in computer science and telecommunications. The first of its kind in this field, the program provides for research support from United Telecom for UMKC faculty and graduate students.

Kansas City also is rapidly developing into a regional health center. To assist that growth UMKC has established, with the support of local businesses, a unique School of Basic Life Sciences, which is drawing researchers

and national resources to the area for scientific research in academic fields ranging from genetics and molecular biology to biophysics.

To enhance area economic development, the university has entered into an agreement with private developers to build the UMKC North Campus Development, a 50-acre research and development park that will house offices and laboratories of private companies and government agencies, as well as facilities for faculty and student researchers.

"The university is a key ingredient for innovation in Kansas City's economy," says Russell. "As a center for teaching and research, UMKC is an incubator for scientists, doctors, engineers, economists, teachers, and government officials who will respond to the social and economic problems that affect our future."

As broad in scope as UMKC's partnerships are, they are still only part of what the institution is doing to reach the standards of excellence set for it in the long-range plans of the University of Missouri system.

Says Russell, "This means UMKC is committed to capitalizing on its strengths in the sciences, in the visual and performing arts, and in urban affairs. The university will also continue to develop academic programs that support the social and economic needs of the Kansas City metropolitan area and the State of Missouri."

# WESTERN MISSOURI MENTAL HEALTH CENTER AND THE GREATER KANSAS CITY MENTAL HEALTH FOUNDATION
## A Community Concern

Western Missouri Mental Health Center's (Center) public-supported system of psychiatric health care has had a 20-year history in Kansas City. Owned and operated by the State of Missouri, the Center's mission is to provide continuing psychiatric care to Kansas Citians.

Services provided include prevention, treatment, and rehabilitation. Individuals move easily from one treatment mode to the next as their condition changes. Comprehensive services extend into the community through outpatient and residential care, and through professional support to area agencies.

"Throughout our history Western Missouri has maintained its devotion to service," says Dr. Morty Lebedun, the Center's superintendent. "Everything that is available in the field of mental health is offered here."

Approximately 2,700 inpatients and 1,500 outpatients are treated annually in the three buildings clustered around Truman Medical Center. The Center employs 700 workers, including a professional staff of 225 persons.

The story of the Center began in 1950, when the city-supported Psychiatric Receiving Center (which later became a part of the Center) was established to meet the mental health needs of the community. A fledgling Kansas City Association of Trusts and Foundations, private citizens, and a responsive city government were all brought together by a common concern for those people with limited funds who suffered from mental illness. Through the creative efforts of public and private entities, a new, nonprofit corporation was founded as the parent body of PRC, the Greater Kansas City Mental Health Foundation (Foundation).

The Foundation, now 36 years old, has, according to its executive director, Dr. Charles Wilkinson, a continuing commitment to its objectives: mental health service, training, and research. It has been the catalyst for the high quality of mental health expertise and services currently provided for the public sector of Kansas City. The recipient of many awards, the Foundation was named one of the eight most successful community mental health centers in the nation in 1963. It has also conducted research in drug abuse, family studies, disasters, and violence.

The Center serves as the clinical base for the training of graduate and undergraduate students in several men-

*Services provided by the Center include prevention, treatment, and rehabilitation.*

*Center and South buildings, two of three clustered around the Truman Medical Center, treat 2,700 inpatients and 1,500 outpatients annually with a professional staff of 225.*

tal health disciplines. The Foundation, through a contractual arrangement with the state, supplies all of the psychiatric staff for the Center. The Foundation/Center amalgam serves as the Department of Psychiatry for the School of Medicine, University of Missouri-Kansas City. It not only provides psychiatric education to medical students but also operates the largest psychiatric training program in the state.

In both spirit and application, the Center continues to endorse the concept of public-private cooperation initiated by the Foundation. Area residents serve on planning and advisory boards, ensuring citizen participation in the planning and delivery of mental health services. Their participation also helps to create a climate of public support for those who have received professional treatment.

According to Dr. Lebedun, Western Missouri Mental Health Center is moving to decentralize services by creating supervised group homes. "This would not have been possible 30 years ago," he says. "The State of Missouri has wisely moved cautiously in reducing the number of people in hospital beds and increasing community placement. Cooperative support and resources have made this possible."

# WILLIAM JEWELL COLLEGE
## Strong Leadership Expands Horizons

Founded in 1849 by the Baptists of Missouri, William Jewell College in Liberty began as a men's college on a frontier outpost. It was a small center for learning and culture in a rough-and-tumble wilderness. At the town square, thousands of immigrants gathered for wagon trains heading west along the Santa Fe and Oregon trails.

The institution was named for Columbia physician Dr. William Jewell, who gave $10,000 for the establishment of a Baptist college in Missouri. Colonel Alexander Doniphan, a prominent attorney, civil rights advocate, and military leader, also played an important role in the college's early history.

During the Civil War Jewell Hall, the oldest building on campus, was used by the Union Army as a stable for horses and as an infirmary for wounded soldiers. A line of rifle pits extended across the hilltop campus. It was said Liberty was "Union by day and Confederate by night."

The institution became coeducational in 1921 and managed to grow despite economic depression and wars.

From the beginning William Jewell College had strong leadership. Its earliest faculties were made up of men

*William Jewell College.*

with academic degrees from American and European universities. Under the presidencies of Dr. John Priest Greene, Dr. John Herget, and Dr. Walter Pope Binns, the institution won a national reputation—not only for academic excellence but also for moral and inspirational impact upon its students. Its current president is Dr. James Gordon Kingsley, a respected educator and speaker.

Today the undergraduate college continues its reputation for excellence in the liberal arts. It has been cited in several prestigious surveys in such publications as *U.S. News and World Report*, the *New York Times'* "Best Buys in a College Education," and guides by Barron's and Peterson's.

Solid in the liberal arts with some professional sequences, the college features two innovative academic programs. The Oxbridge Alternative al-

*Founded as a men's college in 1849 with a grant of $10,000 from Dr. William Jewell, the institution became coeducational in 1921.*

lows students to pursue a major in the tutorial mode, patterned after the educational styles of Oxford and Cambridge universities. The Foundations Program is an alternative to the traditional distribution of requirements and consists of a series of six interdisciplinary core courses.

William Jewell College also sponsors several overseas study programs. They include course offerings at Oxford University, Cambridge University, and Harlaxton College in England; Seinan Gakuin University in Japan; and at institutions in Austria, Germany, France, and Spain.

The college is renowned for its Fine Arts Program, which brings famous and rising performers to the area. Luciano Pavarotti gave his first professional recital on the stage of Gano Chapel and has returned to appear on the program three times. Quality, variety, and discovery are the themes of the program, which features performances in dance, music, and theater.

Today, as in the past, William Jewell College represents an exceptional educational value, offering strong academic programs in a top-quality setting.

# NORTH KANSAS CITY HOSPITAL
## There's No Better Place to Get Better

North Kansas City Hospital is *the* major hospital in the Northland, conveniently located near Interstate 35 and Highway 210 East, just 10 minutes north of downtown Kansas City, Missouri.

North Kansas City Hospital is one of the area's most modern acute care facilities, with 360 licensed beds and a full range of medical services. More than 250 physicians representing 32 medical specialties comprise the medical staff. The hospital employs nearly 1,200 people, making it one of the Northland's major employers and contributing significantly to the local economy.

Some of the many medical services the hospital offers include: general medical/surgical care; a Level II Trauma Center (Emergency Department); modern maternity unit and neonatal intensive care nursery; outpatient surgery and testing; cardiac care unit, cardiac catheterization laboratory, and cardiac rehabilitation program; intensive care unit; laser surgery; osteoporosis screening; self-referral breast screening; cancer treatment unit; physical and occupational therapy services; comprehensive radiology and laboratory services; inpatient and outpatient alcohol and drug abuse treatment programs; mental health center; and community education programs.

### Maternity Care

More and more expectant couples are choosing North Kansas City Hospital for maternity care. The modern unit offers some of the best facilities and programs in the Kansas City area for the expectant couple, the newborn, and even grandparents and siblings.

Skilled physicians and a professional nursing staff work with families to provide a pleasant birthing experience. With agreement of their physician, couples may choose from a variety of options, including use of birthing rooms, 24-hour delivery, a more traditional birthing setting, rooming in, family-centered delivery, unlimited visitation for the father, and special visitation privileges for grandparents and siblings.

North Kansas City Hospital is a 360-licensed-bed, acute care facility located at I-35 and Armour Road East.

Prenatal classes provide couples who choose to deliver at North Kansas City Hospital with information on the latest in birthing techniques and care of the newborn. Classes are also available to help siblings adjust to the new family addition, and grandparenting classes teach grandparents-to-be about new methods of infant care. The infant car seat loaner program is also popular with new parents leaving the hospital.

Newborns receive expert care in the infant nursery. And for those who require specialized medical attention, the neonatal intensive care nursery is staffed with physicians from Children's Mercy Hospital who specialize in the field of neonatology.

*A variety of educational classes are available for expectant parents both before and after delivery.*

## Cardiac Care

People who need care for heart disease or other heart-related problems find an array of services at North Kansas City Hospital. The Cardiac Care Unit houses 22 private critical care rooms with the latest in monitoring and emergency equipment.

These patients are aided in their return to a normal, active life as soon as possible with the help of the hospital's three-stage cardiac rehabilitation program. Exercise, reconditioning of the heart muscles, and modifying habits that put them at risk are components of the program.

North Kansas City Hospital also provides a cardiac catheterization laboratory, the first in the Northland area. The laboratory is under the direction of skilled physicians who provide testing to permit a much earlier diagnosis of heart conditions. A timely diagnosis enables a patient's physician to develop a more complete treatment program. People suffering a heart attack can be brought to the catheterization laboratory to receive the most current medication available, which can significantly reduce the amount of damage done to the heart muscle.

## Laser Surgery

One of the more recent developments in the health care field involves the use of lasers. Laser surgery can be

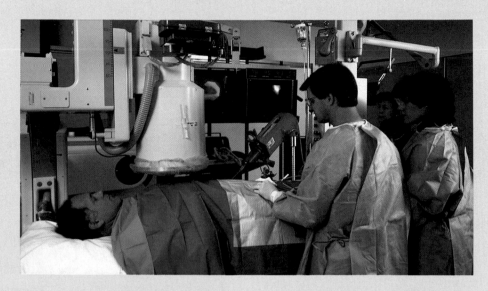

*Cardiac catheterization is a procedure that helps in the early diagnosis and treatment of heart conditions.*

performed for a variety of medical problems and can be done with little, if any, discomfort to the patient, and often on an outpatient basis.

North Kansas City Hospital has three types of lasers for surgical proce-

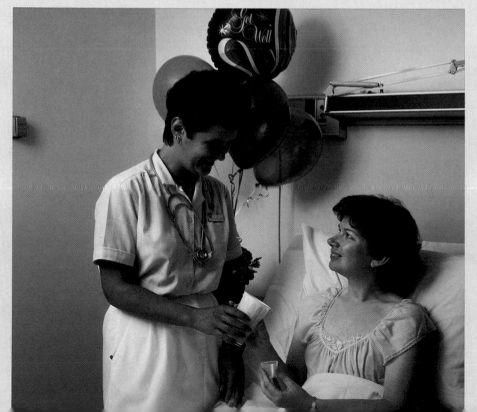

*North Kansas City Hospital offers a full complement of medical services and cares for patients with some of the most advanced techniques and state-of-the-art equipment available in the Kansas City area.*

dures. The Yttrium Aluminum Garnet (YAG) laser is used primarily in the microsurgical treatment of detached retinas, glaucoma, cataracts, and diabetic eye disease. The Argon laser removes skin discolorations, birthmarks, and tattoos. The third type, a carbon dioxide laser, is particularly effective with surgeries of the throat and cervix.

## Drug and Alcohol Treatment

North Kansas City Hospital offers hope for the alcohol and drug abuser through The Recovery Program. In addition to detoxification, inpatient, and outpatient programs, The Recovery Program offers a treatment option which allows patients to attend sessions during the day and spend evenings at work or with family.

The Recovery Program is staffed with professionals who teach patients the addictive disease process, stress management, and the warning signs of relapse. Both group and individual therapy are provided.

## Mental Health Center

A division of North Kansas City Hospital, Tri-County Mental Health Center provides inpatient psychiatric care, a treatment option offering daytime care, outpatient counseling for adults and children, programs for the elderly, an eating disorders treatment program, and an employee assistance program. Tri-County is the largest non-state-operated mental health center in Missouri.

fer courses for students planning to continue their education at a four-year school.

The MCC midtown campus is Penn Valley Community College, which has an enrollment of about 2,000 full-time students and more than 3,000 enrolled in part-time studies. One of the first area campuses to offer intensive coverage of black studies, Penn Valley also specializes in allied health programs and has an especially strong data processing department. The school is home to the Kansas City Community Opera, a high-caliber amateur troupe which annually presents several complete operas in their original languages.

Pioneer Community College is the fourth and smallest of the MCC cluster. This facility specializes in business and office skills training with some on-site programs offered through local businesses. An unusual enrollment system permits students to begin classes at any time during the year.

One of the earliest area colleges, Park College, began as a pioneer effort on the Missouri river front in Parkville. The college was founded as a Presbyterian school. It is now affiliated with the Reorganized Church of Jesus Christ of Latter Day Saints and has a very large extension program. A masters' program is offered in such fields as religion, public affairs, and equine studies. A unique feature of this picturesque, woodland campus is the extensive underground limestone mining operation with which the school adds to its revenues.

Ottawa University at Kansas City, which has a campus in Overland Park, is a part of a four-year bachelor of arts institution with its main campus in Ottawa, Kansas. A Baptist school, Ottawa pioneered in participatory curriculum structuring. Students attending the Kansas City classes earn credits toward degrees through independent study and in

Built on a hillside over-
looking the town of
Parkville, Missouri, Park
College draws many
Kansas Citians to its beau-
tiful campus. Photo by
William W. Westerman

classes arranged to accommodate a full-time work schedule.

Four universities outside the metropolitan area offer special programs in Kansas City. In addition to K.U. Medical Center, there is the University of Kansas Regents Center in Overland Park. The Regents Center provides graduate and upper-level undergraduate courses during evening hours. Non-credit courses include a well-respected series of courses in Chinese, usually taught by native speakers of the language.

Baker University, a United Methodist Church school in Baldwin, Kansas, has established facilities in Overland Park. Its programs are designed with employed adults in mind, and a master's degree in liberal arts can be earned here. Principal study areas are management and human relations, technology and society, and communications.

Webster University in St. Louis also has a branch in Kansas City. The school offers a master of arts degree in business and management and is designed for the employed adult with evening and Saturday classes.

In addition to institutions of higher learning, the Greater Kansas City metropolitan area contains more than forty public school districts. There are ten on the Kansas side of the state line, and several of these are consistently rated in the academic top ten nationally. Special education programs are provided for the learning disabled, mentally retarded, visually impaired, severely handicapped, health-impaired, and physically handicapped. There is also an emphasis on special programs for gifted and talented students. All districts offer staff counselors, physical and occupational therapists, and audiologists. (Kansas law requires schools to offer adaptive physical education classes.)

In addition to the public schools, there are a total of twenty-five parochial and non-sectarian schools on the Kansas side of the metro area, and fifty-one on the Missouri side.

# BAPTIST MEDICAL CENTER
## A Leader in Health Care

"The 1980s have brought a virtual explosion of activity for the medical center," says Dan H. Anderson, Baptist Medical Center's president. "Changes in technology, increased labor costs, and general inflation combined to put greater emphasis on providing quality health care in a cost-effective manner. Many of the new programs created at Baptist Medical Center were in response to these new pressures and needs of the community."

Anderson, who took the reins as president in 1980, steered the hospital toward corporate reorganization. With the restructuring came the formation of the parent company, Baptist Health Systems. Baptist Medical Center is its largest subsidiary, and Anderson is president of both corporations.

*Baptist Medical Center, located in south-central Kansas City, Missouri, has experienced much growth throughout its 26-year history. The expansion includes the medical office building connected to the medical center by a skywalk.*

*Family practice is a primary emphasis at Baptist. The Goppert Family Care Center provides a convenient physicians' office, located within the medical center. The center also includes an 18-member medical residency training program.*

"After considerable discussion and planning with our board of trustees, we decided to reorganize. We developed a multidimensional plan that would put us in a position to be more responsive to the changes that were occurring in the health care environment," Anderson explains.

In response to many changes, Baptist Medical Center began to develop alternative care facilities and programs. In 1981 the Midwest Diabetes Care Center opened to provide outpatient diabetic services. Two years later an inpatient diabetic unit was added. During that time an alcohol and drug dependency unit was created to provide inpatient rehabilitation programs for adults. An Adolescent CareUnit and the Outpatient Care Clinic followed in 1984.

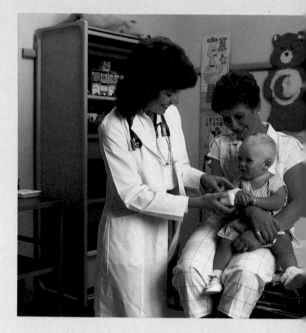

As the health care industry placed more emphasis on alternatives beyond traditional acute hospital care, Baptist began to expand its projects outside the medical center. In 1983 the third of five Primary Care Centers opened, offering

convenient medical care to patients in close proximity to those locations.

The Wellness Services program also was launched in 1983. It administers tailor-made programs to businesses that want to keep their employees healthier. Two years later the program was made available to the community at large.

"In our country there is a growing awareness of life-style and how it affects people's health, and that we are ultimately responsible for our own health and well-being," says Ronald D. Keel, vice-president of corporate development. "According to the classic marketing model, we defined the consumer needs and responded to them."

To meet the other needs of the community, Baptist Medical Center formed Kansas City's first Preferred Provider Organization (PPO) in 1983. Composed of hundreds of Kansas City physicians and 13 area hospitals, Preferred Health Professionals (PHP) offers lower health care costs to the employees of business and industry.

When the government no longer reimbursed costs for patients who remained hospitalized indefinitely, Baptist responded by offering service alternatives both within the hospital and at home. Long Term Care was formed in 1984 and provided extended hospital stays to patients who had stable medical signs but still required skilled care.

HomeCare and Private Care Plus were created that same year to furnish skilled nursing and intermittent or personal care for homebound patients. Associated Medical Equipment (AME) was formed in 1985, and the three services work together in a one-stop-shopping format known as Baptist Home Services.

"The home is a logical extension of alternative care systems," says Keel. "Coupled with the cost concern is the awareness that people don't want to be institutionalized if they can be provided for in their home in a safe and caring manner."

In 1985 Baptist continued to expand its internal and external services. That year saw the completion of the

Personalized nursing care is one of the keys to Baptist's past and future success.

Rockhill Medical Plaza North, which is connected to the medical center by a skywalk. The Center for Eye Surgery, a unique, self-contained outpatient center devoted exclusively to diseases of the eye, and the Center for Radiation Ther-

The Baptist Triathlon was launched in 1983 to link endurance athletes with the wellness concept. More than 500 athletes compete in swimming, biking, and running each fall.

apy, which treats cancerous diseases with radiation, moved into the building within a few months of its opening.

Today Baptist Medical Center is a vital and exciting organization with 1,200 employees and 508 members on its permanent medical staff. "We're seeing many changes in health care, with a greater emphasis on outpatient services and a changing relationship between physicians and hospitals," says Anderson. "We've taken our potential and molded it into the organization that is Baptist Medical Center. We've maximized that potential, and I believe we have become a leader in health care."

# UNIVERSITY OF KANSAS MEDICAL CENTER
## Excellence in Patient Care, Teaching, and Research

Over the years the University of Kansas Medical Center has had an impact on the lives of many area residents, providing the necessary expertise in patient care, teaching, and research to help people lead full, healthy lives.

Classes in medicine were first held on the University of Kansas' Lawrence campus in 1889. The University of Kansas School of Medicine, forerunner of the medical center, found its first Kansas City home in 1905 in the original Bell Memorial Hospital in Rosedale. As the school and hospital grew along with the city, a larger site was needed. In 1924 the University of Kansas School of Medicine and Bell Memorial Hospital moved to new quarters at 39th and Rainbow Boulevard, about one mile south of the original site.

Since then the medical center has grown into a 50-acre campus with more than 50 buildings, including a modern hospital addition that was completed in 1979 and dedicated once more as Bell Memorial Hospital. With 5,500 area employees, the medical center has also branched out to the Wichita campus of the University of Kansas School of Medicine, where third- and fourth-year medical students may complete their studies.

The educational pursuits of the medical center have grown and broadened as well. In addition to the School of Medicine, the University of Kansas Medical Center now includes schools of nursing, allied health, and graduate studies. More than 2,500 students on campus are challenged not only to learn the latest health care techniques, but also to become acquainted with modern health care issues, such as providing care for an aging population, ethical concerns in the health care field, and how to offer quality, affordable health services in the future.

The University of Kansas Medical Center faculty numbers nearly 700 persons, who share their background with health care providers in communities across Kansas, through continuing education and outreach activities.

In addition, the 220 full-time medical staff members represent the full spectrum of modern, specialized care.

*University of Kansas Medical Center students have access to the exceptional collection of rare historical manuscripts housed in the Clendening History of Medicine Library. The late Dr. Logan Clendening, physician and KU faculty member, donated the core of the collection.*

There is also an excellent hospital staff, an example of which is the nursing service, with many of the nurses trained in specialty areas.

The 500-bed facility provides general and specialty inpatient service for more than 17,000 area residents annu-

ally. An additional 320,000 visits are made to the medical center's outpatient clinics each year.

"The students we teach in the patient care setting challenge the staff with their questions about diagnoses and treatment plans," notes Gene Budig, university chancellor. "The patient benefits from the inquiring environment the students foster."

The University of Kansas Medical Center was the first Kansas City hospital to perform a heart transplant. From July 1984 to February 1987, 18 heart transplants were performed at the institution. Kidney, cornea, and bone marrow transplants are also performed at the medical center.

The teaching hospital serves as a regional resource for health problems such as cancer; aging-related illnesses; infertility; gynecological, kidney, and musculoskeletal disorders; gastrointestinal illnesses; diabetes; hearing and speech disorders; blood and infectious diseases; inherited disorders; neurologi-

*KU's laminar air flow rooms provide sterile living units for leukemia patients undergoing bone marrow transplants, and other immune-suppressed patients. Routine care is provided through a curtain to protect the patient's germ-free environment.*

*Research is an important part of KU's mission. In addition to laboratory research, the KU staff researches and tests many new medicines and therapies. Patients benefit from the availability of these state-of-the-art treatments.*

cal problems; handicapping conditions in children and adults; and childhood diseases and trauma.

To handle many of these special areas, the University of Kansas Medical Center has armed itself with the latest state-of-the-art technology and equipment. It boasts a dynamic diagnostic radiology department, equipped with the best technology and personnel available, enabling the design of new equipment and procedures by the department itself. A magnetic resonance imager provides the best diagnostic imaging possible. In addition, precise radiation therapy is administered to cancer patients through the Hospital Department of Radiation Oncology. This unit also boasts of the latest in equipment and technology.

The medical center also has a lithotripter, which shatters kidney stones with shock waves, offering a revolutionary alternative to major surgery. Sixteen area hospitals have made arrangements to use the institution's lithotripter to maximize efficiency.

Special features of the medical center include The Gene and Barbara Burnett Burn Center, a special 10-bed unit for victims of severe burns; The Sutherland Microsurgical Center, which allows plastic surgeons to perform delicate operations; The Neonatal Intensive Care Unit, a special area for the care of premature and sick infants; and the use of Yag and Argon lasers for gynecological, eye, ear, nose, throat, gastrointestinal surgery, and other surgery.

*The original Eleanor Taylor Bell Memorial Hospital on "Goat Hill," circa 1910. The medical center campus today consists of 50 buildings on a 50-acre campus, including a new hospital facility completed in 1979.*

Research has long been an integral part of the University of Kansas Medical Center's mission. Past achievements include being one of the first institutions in the nation to test insulin for diabetic patients, discovering the importance of blood platelets in the clotting of blood, and finding the need for a balance between water and salt in the body, known as electrolyte balance.

One of the most ambitious areas of exploration under way at the medical center involves the fight against cancer. Scientists at the hospital are developing and testing cancer drugs, designing the best treatment plans for radiation therapy, and determining how different cancer cells work. They are also working to devise new extra-low-dose diagnostic equipment to detect breast cancer.

Inquiry into how the various components of the body function is complemented by research on specific diseases such as diabetes, infertility, cardiovascular and kidney disorders, and neuromuscular ailments. The latter includes Amyotrophic Lateral Sclerosis (ALS), Muscular Dystrophy, and eye disease. In addition, experts at the University of Kansas Medical Center are studying causes and solutions to environmental occupational hazards. As one faculty member concluded: "There's a lot of research going on here, and that helps to keep us on the front line."

# THE KANSAS INSTITUTE
## A Model for Successful Innovative Psychiatric Health Services

Kansas Psychiatric Institutes, Inc., was founded in 1983 when it purchased a freestanding psychiatric hospital in Olathe. The acquisition of this hospital, now The Kansas Institute, was the cornerstone of a comprehensive mental health delivery system that is serving and rapidly impacting the greater Kansas City area.

The Kansas Institute in Olathe is the forerunner of the company's expanding mental health programs offered to Kansas City. These programs include emergency psychiatric services and management agreements for psychiatric units in medical-surgical hospitals.

The amplified delivery of comprehensive mental health services to the area includes an increase in freestanding psychiatric hospitals. In 1986 the Olathe facility was enlarged and renovated to house its clinical program in a modernized 50-bed setting. In addition, the company has acquired land at College and Nall boulevards in Overland Park for a second freestanding facility scheduled for completion in 1987. It also has a certificate of public need for a 40-bed psychiatric hospital and a 20-bed residential treatment center in Liberty, Missouri.

*The facility utilizes a multidisciplinary team for intensive and individualized treatment from admission to discharge. Photo by Steven R. Attig, Olathe*

In Kansas City and throughout the nation, freestanding psychiatric hospitals fill a specific purpose in mental health care. Because they offer more intensified services in a programmatic approach, they will complement the psychiatric services of medical-surgical hospitals, which usually provide shorter term crisis intervention.

"The philosophy of Kansas Psychiatric Institutes, Inc., is to provide a full continuum of comprehensive inpatient and outpatient services to the Kansas City population," says Bryan W. Lett, vice-president and chief operating officer. "Its goal is to create a network of mental health services accessible to the greater Kansas City area through location, design, and placement."

As the first of such hospitals in the area, The Kansas Institute in Olathe is a model for successful and innovative health services that promote mental wellness and remediate mental illness. Its comprehensive inpatient programs serve children, adolescents, and adults.

Through the integrated efforts of experienced managers and mental health professionals, the facility utilizes a multidisciplinary team for intensive and individualized treatment from admission to discharge for patients ranging in age from six years old to senior citizens. The team includes a psychiatrist, social worker, expressive therapist, registered nurse, team coordinator, educational teachers, and

other mental health professionals. The Kansas Institute provides an open medical staff comprised of 15 psychiatrists in Olathe for admission and psychiatric treatment purposes. The Kansas Institute, through its integrated teamwork, maintains a staff-to-patient ratio of better than 2.5 to one.

The program begins with a careful and complete evaluation, including a physical examination and laboratory work-up. The hospital utilizes the esoteric laboratory services for state-of-the-art diagnostics and treatment of psychiatric illnesses. Under the coordination of a medical director, the treatment for each patient is a comprehensive and intensive 24-hour process on both a one-to-one basis and through group therapy.

The intensive approach to patient treatment is structured to understand and respond to the needs of the individual, including physical, emotional, social, vocational, and academic needs. This approach prompts the emergence of a healthier person, better prepared to cope with the realities of life and to better integrate with family and community. The expressive therapies (art, music, occupational, and recreational) used in treatment allow for the exploration of new and creative ways to express thoughts and feelings in a nonverbal manner.

According to the directors of The Kansas Institute, children consistently

have the most need for the facility's psychiatric services, followed by the adolescent and adult population.

Both children and adolescents are provided with a full education program through the services of three full-time teachers. Family members are also involved in the treatment program through therapy and support groups.

Several unique programs are incorporated into The Kansas Institute's delivery of health care. The programs enrich its services and are considered by the staff to have genuine merit in promoting mental health.

One such program is the hospital's sexual abuse component, the first comprehensive inpatient service of its kind in the Midwest to be included within the

*Comfortable surroundings carry out the tradition of quality patient care. Photo by Steven R. Attig, Olathe*

*The Kansas Institute's contemporary, cheerful atmosphere enhances the comprehensive psychiatric treatment programs for children, adolescents, and adults. Photo by Steven R. Attig, Olathe*

framework of a treatment program for children, adolescents, and adults. The service was prompted by the high percentage of psychiatric patients who have sexual abuse in their histories.

Wilderness Therapy is another innovative program established at The Kansas Institute. Adventure Education, which is part of the program, is a nontraditional approach to treating adolescents. Week-long backpack trips allow direct opportunity for adolescent patients to master difficult problems that require new skills and mutual cooperation. The youngsters are taught to deal with their problems by learning self-sufficiency and a more realistic perspective of themselves and their en-

vironment.

Another first for the metropolitan area is the Emergency Psychiatric Service, which operates 24 hours a day and is a subsidiary program to other hospital services. As part of this program a clinical team provides psychiatric consultation upon request to hospital emergency departments, inpatient services, individual practitioners' offices, clinics, schools, the clergy, and business and industry.

The clinicians evaluate individuals and their families in emotional or psychiatric crisis, defining the nature and extent of the problems, then providing helpful intervention and recommending appropriate referrals in conjunction with the referring professional. Under the auspices of a psychiatrist and four clinical specialists, the service also offers help to individuals and families in short-term, crisis-oriented psychotherapy and provides counseling when appropriate.

The Kansas Institute is committed to respond to the mental health needs of the Kansas City community through crisis intervention and treatment. It is also dedicated to promoting mental health awareness through education and information programs. With this objective in mind, The Kansas Institute offers free monthly community education programs. It also provides a free speakers' bureau of specialized staff members, including psychiatrists, social workers, and clinicians, who speak on a variety of topics to groups and organizations throughout the city.

According to Monica Bazan, director of marketing management for the Kansas Psychiatric Institutes, Inc., "By providing information and increasing the awareness about mental health and mental illness, the stigma associated with psychiatric hospitals decreases and individuals in need of help will be more inclined to utilize available resources.

Through the continual innovations introduced at The Kansas Institute, new programs will be expanded into the greater Kansas City area to meet the challenge of providing quality mental health care to the community.

# THE UNIVERSITY OF HEALTH SCIENCES
## The Osteopathic Medical Center of Kansas City

Few metropolitan areas have the availability of osteopathic medicine to the extent provided by The University of Health Sciences/Health Care System. This expanding network of osteopathic health care now includes two full-service hospitals, three satellite clinics, and a 500-unit retirement facility with its own medical pavilion. The epicenter of this system is the university's College of Osteopathic Medicine.

This broad spectrum of osteopathic health care is an outgrowth of the institution's 70-year history of medical practice. Its growth is based on a philosophy of fundamental concern for the whole person, and its orientation is family medicine.

The presence of the college, located at Independence Boulevard and Woodland Avenue, complements the range of educational opportunities that are offered in Kansas City and contributes substantially to the city's economy through its yearly influx of students from all 50 states. More than 5,000 physicians have been trained at Kansas City's College of Osteopathic Medicine. Its 139 graduates in 1986 were members of the institution's 100th graduating class.

The college is accredited by the Bureau of Education of the American Osteopathic Association and is approved by the State Board of Education. Although applications continue to increase, acceptance into the rigorous four-year academic program is not easy. Applicants must have received a four-year baccalaureate degree from an accredited college, must demonstrate superior academic achievement, and must possess a solid foundation in the biological and physical sciences.

Both University Hospital, adjacent to the college, and Lakeside Hospital, at 8701 Troost Avenue, serve as teaching facilities where physicians, upon graduation, may complete their internships and residencies. The hospital also ful-

*One of the latest additions to The University of Health Sciences/Health Care System's diagnostic tools is the CT scanner mobile unit, which can be moved for use at other facilities.*

fills an important mission by providing the people of Kansas City with comprehensive medical programs and personalized, quality health care.

Particularly accessible to downtown and the northeast section of the city, University Hospital has a staff of 137 physicians who combine their skills with the most modern and advanced equipment available.

The osteopathic physician brings an added dimension to general medical practice by using a personalized patient-oriented philosophy of medical practice.

Comprehensive health care at University Hospital includes expanded outpatient services, 24-hour emergency care, a Security Blanket Club for expectant parents, a one-day surgery program, and a Mobile Critical Care Unit that offers support care for an area within a 100-mile radius of the hospital.

Lakeside Hospital provides community health education, home health care, and childbirth classes as part of its community outreach program. Strong emphasis is placed on its drug and alcohol rehabilitation services.

Sick Bay, a program for children with minor illnesses whose parents are unable to care for them at home, is a special service of both hospitals. The control and management of pain and the elimination of its causes are the objective of the pain clinics provided by both hospitals. Lakeside Hospital's 24-hour, 48-hour, and 72-hour maternity care programs are popular and safe alternatives to traditional maternity care. Other special services at both hospitals include arthroscopy, state-of-the-art orthopedic surgery that offers small cosmetic incisions, short hospitalization, and rapid recovery; and endoscopic examinations, gastroenterological medical services using the latest in miniaturized TV technology and flexible tubing.

To augment the health care offered by both hospitals and to increase their availability to families in the larger geographic community, three satellite clinics are now in operation in southwest Kansas City, Kansas City-North, and the Independence-Raytown district. Family practice, obstetrics/gynecol-

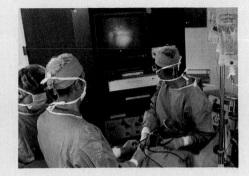

*Arthroscopy, enhanced by miniaturized technology, is one of the latest technologies to assist the orthopedic surgeon.*

ogy, pediatrics, radiology, laboratory, and minor surgery services are provided at the clinics, as is osteopathic manipulative therapy—manual medicine.

The University of Health Sciences/ Health Care System also addresses the complex health needs of the elderly. University Towers, located at 700 East Eighth Street, provides safe, convenient living units for the active, older person. Recreational activities, a swimming pool, shops, and optional meal choices are provided at this residential facility. Residents may also purchase a health care package that entitles them to 60 free days in the facility's medical pavilion and continuity of care through the resources of University Hospital.

The widespread acceptance of these health care programs indicates a bright future for osteopathic medicine in Kansas City, which has fostered a climate for the education and training of osteopathic physicians since 1916.

"As Kansas City families continue to respond to the personal and professional medical care provided by osteopathic medicine, The University of Health Sciences and its Health Care System will continue to offer the kind of medical care that provides an added dimension to general medical practice," says Leonard Mennen, D.O., Dean for Academic Affairs.

As to the future, more satellite clinics are planned for the convenience of Kansas Citians in outlying areas. More attention will also be given to senior citizens as The University of Health Sciences/Health Care System continues with its commitment to provide osteopathic medical care to Kansas Citians from birth to old age.

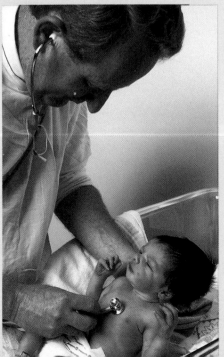

*Osteopathic physicians use current methods of preventing, diagnosing, and treating illnesses but also adhere to a personalized patient-oriented philosophy of medical practice.*

# 8
# KANSAS CITY LIFE: A STYLE ALL ITS OWN

Kansas City pulses and glows with a sparkle all its own. It's a city that has always loved a performance or a parade. By 1858, two auditoriums, Frank's Hall and Long's Hall, hosted concerts, chautauquas, and dramatic presentations. Five years after the Civil War ended, the Coates Opera House opened a thirty-year run of dramas, concerts, and operas. The opulent Gilliss Theater, complete with newfangled electrical lighting and palatial furnishings, saw its first season in 1883. Famed actor Edwin Booth starred on opening night at the Warder Grand Opera House in 1887.

Almost from the city's beginnings, there was a common urge for the finer things. Cultural pursuits flourished on all sides, but it was jazz that put Kansas City on the map in a big way. Jazz has been a major part of the city's music scene since the Depression days when musicians flocked to the city. Andy Kirk, leader of the Clouds of Joy band, recalled those hard times in a 1959 *Jazz Review* article:

"They had a great many [theater] houses around the Southwest but nobody had any money to get into the theaters with . . . We gave a final concert in Memphis . . . and just did get back to Kansas City. When we got back home, there was no Depression. The town was jumping!"

The great jazz pianist Mary Lou Williams recalled Kansas City in Prohibition days as "a heavenly city—music everywhere . . . and fifty or more cabarets rocking on Twelfth and Eighteenth Streets."

During the staid fifties and psychedelic sixties the sound of jazz was muted, but by the mid-seventies, it not only enjoyed a resurgence but came back with a cachet and social significance that had eluded earlier generations. In 1982 the Kansas City Jazz Commission was established to keep the music playing, and the 18th & Vine Heritage Celebration

*Opposite: Worlds of Fun, a popular family amusement park in the north part of town, appeals to young people who love balloons, special rides, and plenty of fun. Photo by Bruce Mathews*

*Next page: Crown Center's free summer concerts on the square draw thousands of music lovers from around the city. Photo by Michael A. Mihalevich*

*Above: The late great Count Basie was a familiar face at Crown Center's free outdoor summer concerts. Photo by Michael A. Mihalevich*

*Above, right: Local clubs jump to the sound of jazz that has made Kansas City famous. Photo by Bob Barrett*

*Right: Sax player Herman Walters shows off his musical prowess at a local night spot. Photo by Bob Barrett*

*Opposite, top: The Kansas City Jazz Festival in Volker Park draws thousands of music lovers. Photo by Michael A. Mihalevich*

Above: Budding artists are invited to express their talent in chalk on the grounds of the Nelson Gallery. Photo by Bob Barrett

Right: Some prefer to bring their own music to the 18th & Vine Heritage Celebration. Photo by Michael A. Mihalevich

Starlight Theater, the beautiful theater under the stars in Swope Park, hosts concerts and musical plays with top national performers. Photo by Bruce Mathews

each fall features jazz, pop, gospel, and reggae.

Jazz is more than music in Kansas City—it's a heritage and a cultural landmark. Modern audiences enjoy the best of the masters' styles and the evolving sounds of new artists on the scene.

Year 'round, local clubs jump to the sound of jazz, and each summer our town celebrates with the Kansas City Jazz Festival. The playbill is different every year, with new acts, old favorites, local artists, and nationally famous names like the Count Basie Orchestra, Jay McShann, Ida MacBeth, Joe Williams, and the Duke Ellington Orchestra.

A night on the town in Kansas City can run the gamut from experimental drama at the Unicorn Theater, a professional Equity house, to classical opera at the famed Lyric Opera. The Missouri Repertory Theater presents everything from Shakespeare to Stoppard, and the Kansas City Theater League brings first-run Broadway plays to the Midland Theater, originally a magnificent old movie palace. Starlight Theater, the beautiful theater under the stars in Swope Park, presents concerts and musical plays. An Equity house, Theater for Young Americans, awakens a taste for the performing arts in the younger generation. Theater Under the Stars is open-air theater on the campus of Penn Valley Community College, featuring local performers in musical plays.

One of Kansas City's great cultural coups came about through a cooperative effort of the city, the black community, and the resident ballet company. Since 1984, the New York-based Alvin Ailey dance company has come to Kansas City, their officially-declared "second home," for a series of performances at the historic Folly Theater. The group also performs and does workshops in schools across the city.

Above: The renowned State Ballet of Missouri performs its charming version of the "Nutcracker," part of the troupe's repertoire of both modern and classical works. Photo by Bruce Mathews

Left: The Lyric Theater, a showcase for many cultural and artistic presentations, is the home of Kansas City's famed Lyric Opera, where professionals appear in operas sung in English. Photo by Bob Barrett

The Kansas City Symphony, seen here performing at the Radio Day Concert, is making inroads on the cultural scene. Photo by Michael A. Mihalevich

Headed by artistic director Todd Bolender, the resident State Ballet of Missouri, formerly the Kansas City Ballet, has broadened its outreach across the state to St. Louis. Performing at the Lyric Theater, the troupe presents both modern and classical works, and guest artists like Mikhail Baryshnikov and the American Ballet Theater have performed here under its aegis. The Westport Ballet Theater, a talented group of local dancers, performs at the historic restored Folly Theater downtown.

The Lyric Opera of Kansas City is one of the city's most beloved cultural institutions. Guest artists and local professionals appear in operas sung in English. An all-local company of talented amateurs, Kansas City Community Opera, presents operas in their original languages at Penn Valley Community College. Several long-established amateur companies provide full seasons of performances in settings as diverse as barns and shopping centers.

Two dinner theaters, Waldo Astoria and Tiffany's Attic, provide a proving ground for young hopeful performers and a continuing parade of well-known stars in frothy comedies. Music in the Park brings free concerts to parks throughout the city every week during the summer, and the Kansas City Symphony Orchestra presents classical concerts and

At the annual fall Renaissance Festival held in Bonner Springs, Kansas, hundreds of costumed actors and musicians entertain thousands of visitors who come to step into the past when Merry Old England reigned supreme. Photo, above, by Bruce Mathews. Photo, above left, by Michael A. Mihalevich

takes its show on the road to schools and civic events like the Spirit Festival.

The Kansas City Spirit Festival, held annually during the Fourth of July weekend, is an extravaganza of music, entertainment and fireworks that starts at the Liberty Memorial and lights up the whole city with fun.

The Renaissance Festival, a benefit for the Kansas City Art Institute, is a trip into the past for six autumn weekends each year when hundreds of costumed actors and thousands of spectators mingle in the rush-strewn streets of a village near Bonner Springs, Kansas.

Pioneer days come alive at Lake Jacomo's Missouri Town 1855 Fall Festival. Santa-Cali-Gon Days in Independence celebrate the three pioneer trails that helped establish the area. Old Shawnee Days festival in spring also celebrates the pioneer era, as does the River Days celebration at the reconstructed 1808 Fort Osage near Sibley, Missouri. Harry's Heyday in Grandview celebrates President Harry S. Truman.

One of the top national rodeos, the Abdullah Shrine Rodeo, takes place once a year with racing, steer wrestling, bulldogging, clowns, and an equestrienne queen. Benjamin's Trail Town is the site of an annual

Fourth of July rodeo and appearance by the Heart of America Indian Club's native dancers. Guadalupe Center, heart of Kansas City's old Mexican community, presents La Fiesta Mexicana every year, complete with mariachis. La Festa Italiana celebrates the city's Italian heritage yearly. St. Dionysios Greek Orthodox Church and the Greek Orthodox Church of the Annunciation each present an annual festival, and our town is now home of one of the nation's biggest St. Patrick's Day parades and celebrations.

Kansas City's urban parks are popular sites for summer cultural events. The Asian Festival honors the city's growing Oriental population, and the Ethnic Enrichment Festival is another chance to see all these groups and more, like the nationally-famous Strawberry Hill Tamburitzen Dancers; the St. Andrew's Society's fife, drum, and bagpipe corps; and Irish step-dancers. More bagpipes play and local Highland dancers, internationally honored, perform as they toss the caber and hurling stones during the annual Highland Games.

Undoubtedly the most famous annual event of all is the American Royal Livestock, Horse Show and Rodeo, the largest combined livestock,

*Above: Kansas City is home of one of the nation's biggest St. Patrick's Day parades and celebrations. Photo by Bob Barrett*

*Above, left: The city's growing Asian population celebrates its heritage annually, hosting the Chinese New Year Celebration. Photo by Bob Barrett*

*Opposite: These young dancers celebrate their heritage outdoors performing as part of a celebration of Hispanic culture at Barney Allis Plaza. Photo by Michael A. Mihalevich*

horse show, and rodeo in the nation. The Royal, held in the fall, tradition-
ally opens with one of the city's biggest and liveliest parades.

Over a thousand artists and performers take part in Arts Fest, a three-
day extravaganza of dance, drama, and music that is part of the Crown
Center Arts Festival, a juried exhibition. The Plaza Fine Arts Fair brings
artists and art lovers to the streets of the Country Club Plaza each year,
with music provided by students from the Conservatory of Music at the
University of Missouri-Kansas City. Art in the Woods is an annual juried
art show held in Corporate Woods Office Park, and Art Westport is a
lively outdoor exhibition of juried fine arts held in the heart of fun-loving
Westport. Mid-Four, sponsored by the Kansas City Junior League, is
one of the city's oldest juried art exhibitions.

The Nelson Museum (William Rockhill Nelson Gallery of Art and
Atkins Museum) is the city's greatest single treasure house of art. The
Burnap English pottery collection makes it a center for scholars. Its
famed Oriental collection, founded in the 1930s by Laurence Sickman
(now director emeritus), is internationally recognized as one of the finest
in the world. Major works by Caravaggio, Degas, Guercino, Church,
Monet, and Pisarro are but a few of the more than 50,000 works of art
owned by the museum, which recently celebrated its fiftieth anniversary
with a fund-raising drive that brought it nearly $60 million. The Nelson's
Friends of Art and Contempory Art Society are longtime supporters of
and contributors toward the purchase of contemporary works of art for
the museum's permanent collection.

242

Equally beloved is the Kansas City Museum, a living album of the
city's past, housed in lumber baron R.A. Long's palatial mansion atop
Cliff Drive. In Independence, the museum to see is the Harry S. Truman
Library and Museum, a mecca for Truman historians. The Liberty Memorial Museum, near Pershing Square, exhibits a touching collection
of World War I memorabilia. Tureman House, on the UMKC campus,
houses the Toy and Miniature Museum of Kansas City, a delight for
dollhouse lovers. Langer Automotive Museum in midtown exhibits a fine
collection of cars and even an airplane or two. Throughout the metropolitan area, local historical societies preserve little slices of life from earlier
times in house museums. The Alexander Majors House Museum near
Ward Parkway shopping center is a tribute to this city's early years as
a transportation center, and to the dedication of Majors' granddaughter
Eliza Johnston, who preserved the estate for posterity. Just south of the
plaza the John Wornall House Museum, a Civil War-era house, is open
for tours.

The Ben Ferrel-Platte County Museum in Platte City is a literal
copy—from the same plans—of the 1882 Governor's Mansion in Jefferson City, scaled down from three stories to two. Weston, home of the
McCormick Distillery, is a history-conscious antebellum river town
which contains twenty-two square blocks which are on the National Register of Historic Places.

Liberty, in Clay County, is Jesse James country. The bank he robbed
there is now a historic site, and his birthplace, a farm near Kearney, is

*Right: Northland play-grounds Worlds of Fun and adjacent Oceans of Fun are Disney-style theme parks that attract thousands of visitors each season. Photo by Hank Young/Young Company*

*Below: The "Cotton Blossom" excursion boat, beautifully lit at night, is just one of the many highlights of Worlds of Fun. Photo by Hank Young/Young Company*

a museum where a drama about his life is staged annually. Also in Clay County is the restored Watkins Woolen Mill, a completely equipped nineteenth-century mill that is now a National Historic Landmark.

Near Sibley, just northeast of Independence, is Fort Osage. Built, abandoned, and plundered of its dressed logs and stones in the early 1800s, the restored trading post is a favorite for parents and children on an outing. And of course, the playground that tops them all is up north in Worlds of Fun and Oceans of Fun, Disney-style theme parks that attract thousands of visitors each season.

When it comes to play, few spectacles can match the sight of the 1985 world champion Kansas City Royals baseball team, at home in Royals Stadium at the Truman Sports Complex. In the other half of the complex, Arrowhead Stadium, the Kansas City Chiefs are the hometown football heroes. Across town at Kemper Arena, the Kansas City Comets play soccer. There's also the annual Big Eight Conference Basketball Tournament, and the yearly NAIA National Basketball Tournament, both held at the Kemper. Wrestling aficionados can see the bruisers battle at Kemper Arena or at the Kansas City, Kansas Memorial Hall, where the grunt-and-groaners are a tradition of fifty-plus years.

Kansas City is one of the best shopping towns around, and many families from as far as 200 miles away make a shopping "trip to town" once a month or so. Crown Center is an event in itself, with fine hotels, exciting restaurants, and some of the most unusual small shops around. The Country Club Plaza is the world's first shopping center. Now over fifty

*Next page: The Royals Stadium, the other half of the Truman Sports Complex which also houses Arrowhead Stadium, hosts thousands of fans who come to see the Kansas City Royals play a home game. Photo by Bruce Mathews*

*Below: The world champs in 1985, the Kansas City Royals are the city's hottest summertime attraction. Photo by Hank Young/Young Company*

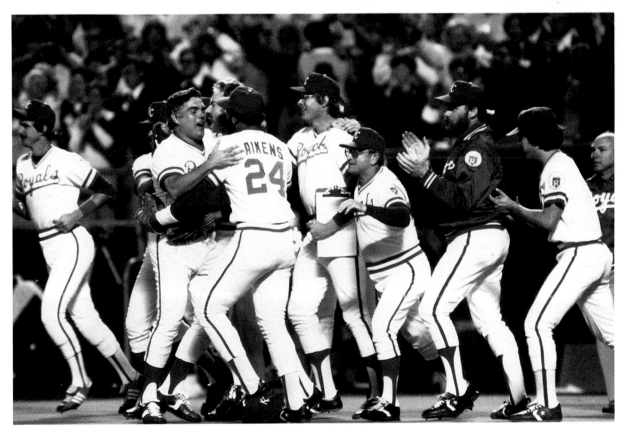

years old, it's filled with upscale shops and entertainment from strolling
mimes to street concerts and art fairs. At Christmas time, its miles of
colored lights make a fairytale village of its spires and towers. Westport
is the place to go for the offbeat and arty; on weekends it's a thronging
singles scene. For serious, all-round shopping, most folks head for one
of the dozen or so huge suburban shopping centers in the suburban areas.

Nearly 1,100 congregations represent the scores of religious faiths and
denominations in the city, from Baptist to Baha'i, Methodist to Menno-
nite, Jewish to Jehovah's Witnesses, Presbyterian to Pentecostal. As their
downtown locations suggest, some of the city's earliest congregations
were Catholic. The gleaming gold dome of the Cathedral of the Immacu-
late Conception has been a landmark for many years, as have the stately
stones of St. Paul's Episcopal Church in midtown and the stark white
walls of Community Christian Church in the Plaza, designed by Frank
Lloyd Wright. Seminaries located here include Calvary Bible College,
Midwestern Baptist Theological Seminary, Nazarene Theological Seminary, St. Paul School of Theology/Methodist, University of Central
America, and Western Bible College. Parochial education is provided
through the Catholic Diocese of Kansas City-St. Joseph, Episcopal Dio-

# CHAMBER OF COMMERCE OF GREATER KANSAS CITY
## Works for Community Growth

For 100 years the Chamber of Commerce of Greater Kansas City has been at the forefront of economic development. Originating as the Commercial Club in 1887, the organization officially became the Chamber of Commerce of Greater Kansas City in 1916. In 1987 the nonprofit association's membership included 4,000 area firms—a 42-percent increase from seven years ago.

The organizations that belong to the chamber represent a broad cross section of the business and professional community in the seven-county metropolitan area. Throughout its history the chamber has spearheaded the development of business interests that have helped diversify the economic base of the city. Garnering support for major bond issues is one of its functions; supporting responsible local taxation for the funding of capital improvements is another. In addition, the organization is a community leader in successful efforts to secure a fair share of funds from Missouri's recent $600-million bond issue.

Bob MacGregor, president of the Chamber of Commerce of Greater Kansas City, puts it this way: "As the area's primary voice of business, the chamber plays a major leadership role in fulfilling Kansas City's potential, but the real test of success comes in coping with new and increasing demands on our community's resources."

So far the chamber has risen to meet the challenge. A broad base of volunteer and financial support provides the organization with a matrix from which major economic development structures continue to evolve. For example, in 1976 members of the chamber founded the Kansas City Area Eco-

*Among the Chamber of Commerce of Greater Kansas City's current concerns is the revitalization of downtown. The chamber conceived and organized the Downtown Council.*

nomic Development Council to attract new businesses to the community and market Kansas City's assets to the rest of the nation. Today the chamber remains the council's primary source of funding. In addition, the chamber contributes to the Kansas City Corporation for Industrial Development (KCCID), an agency that helps in the retention and financing of businesses. The chamber also established the Downtown Council, another key component in the metropolitan development picture.

Chamber volunteers and professional staff members are engaged in a wide variety of programs designed to enhance the area's ability to both retain and attract commercial and industrial investments. These programs include agribusiness development and small business assistance. In addition, the chamber's Transportation/Environment/Energy Department works closely with the Governmental Affairs Department to ensure the establishment of the most effective laws and regulations in these areas. Other concerns include minority economic development and a program to support the arts through a cultural affairs committee.

Directly related to all its programs is the organization's commitment to strong governmental relations. The chamber is charged with the responsibility of working with the local, state, and national levels of government in developing measures and actions favorable to a strong economic climate. In addition to its activities in Missouri, the chamber has joined with the Kansas Chamber of Commerce and Industry to monitor actions on the state level. On the local level a program was recently launched whereby the chamber is working closely with Kansas City's city council to help ensure that future growth will not be hindered by restrictive laws and regulations.

In the wake of a building boom, Kansas City's progress is visible and exciting, and the Chamber of Commerce of Greater Kansas City is responding in many ways, bringing the organization to the forefront of a host of pressing issues that will mark the outcome of the city's growth.

*These golfers take advantage of the fine green offered at Mission Hills Country Club. Photo by Bruce Mathews*

cese of West Missouri, Jewish Federation and Council of Greater Kansas City, International Headquarters of the Church of the Nazarene, Lutheran Education, and Unity School of Christianity.

Nationally-affiliated service clubs, lodges, fraternities, professional organizations, and civic improvement associations exist by the score in our town, along with such uniquely Kansas City organizations as the Greater Kansas City Chinese Club where Chinese language and customs are celebrated, and the Heart of America Indian Center, which provides services, information, and social activities for Native Americans of all tribal backgrounds.

There are more than sixty public libraries in the city, with special collections like the Linda Hall Library of Science and Technology, the largest privately endowed library of its kind in the nation. The Clendenning Memorial Library at KU Medical Center is the largest biomedical library in the area. The downtown headquarters of the Kansas City Public Library houses the Missouri Valley Room and its extensive collection of regional historical records. Genealogists from all over the country trace their family trees through the records of the Reorganized Church of Latter Day Saints Library, and historians seek out the wealth of federal archival information available in the National Archives Records Administration offices here. Midwest Research Institute, near the Country Club Plaza, is a long-established and nationally respected "think tank."

# CONVENTION AND VISITORS BUREAU OF GREATER KANSAS CITY
## In the Business of Selling the City

The visitor industry has long been a vital part of the Kansas City economy and currently ranks as the third-largest industry in the metropolitan area. The city's first convention hall was built in 1899, and in 1918 the first convention and visitors' bureau was formed as an arm of the chamber of commerce. It was in 1966 that the Convention and Visitors Bureau of Greater Kansas City incorporated as a not-for-profit organization and achieved independent status with an annual budget of $244,000 and a limited staff.

Today the bureau has an annual operating budget of more than two million

*The visitor information booth at Bartle Hall serves the information needs of conventioneers while representing the interests of bureau members. Dining reservations can be made and information on area attractions is available at the booth.*

dollars and 30 full-time employees. It consists of three divisions: Administration, Convention Sales, and Tourism, with several departments functioning within that structure.

As a nonprofit association, the bureau is governed by a 30-member board of directors. The day-to-day activities are the responsibility of the president, who serves as chief executive officer.

Each of the divisions has a director who reports to the president.

The bureau is a membership-based organization representing virtually every type of business in the Kansas City area. Local businesses benefit from membership in the association through programs designed to assist them in promoting their services or products to visitors to the area.

On a daily basis the bureau operates just as any other marketing firm or organization. Both the Convention Sales and the Tourism divisions conduct aggressive advertising and promotional campaigns in national and regional markets. The bureau has received numerous awards over the past several years recognizing its advertising campaigns and group tour marketing programs.

"All the activities of the staff of the bureau are designed to accomplish one goal—bring more convention delegates and tourists to the area," explains bureau president Jim Hutchinson. "The Convention and Visitors Bureau of Greater Kansas City exists for one purpose—it is in the business of selling Kansas City."

*The bureau aggressively sells Kansas City as a destination for meetings and leisure. Here a television commercial is filmed to attract summer visitors from Des Moines, Omaha, and Wichita.*

Above, left: This miniature train takes visitors on an excursion through Swope Park which is, at 1,769 acres, the country's second largest urban park. Photo by Bruce Mathews

Above: One of the more photogenic residents of the popular Kansas City Zoo in Swope Park pauses to have a picture taken. Photo by Michael A. Mihalevich

Next page: The Bartle Hall convention center at Barney Allis Plaza hosts thousands of visitors each year. Photo by Bruce Mathews

Kansas City is the home of Swope Park, at 1,769 acres the nation's second largest urban park, as well as Loose Park, a former Civil War battleground; and scores of city, county, and state-administered parks and recreation areas, including Lake Jacomo, Longview Lake, Prairie Lee Lake, Shawnee Mission Lake, Smithville Lake, and Wyandotte County Lake.

The fastest-growing cities in the metropolitan area are Lenexa and Olathe, both in Johnson County. In Jackson County, Blue Springs and Lee's Summit show the most rapid growth.

Of the metropolis' nearly 1.5 million persons, approximately 30,000 are foreign-born, with most of those coming from Europe, Asia, North and Central America. Racial distribution is about 85 percent white and 13 percent black, with a little over 2 percent comprised of other racial populations.

Nearly 1,000 conventions are held in Kansas City annually, bringing more than 625,000 visitors from across the nation and making a positive economic impact on the city each year of about $1 billion.

People who come to visit Kansas City remember it as one of the friendliest and most hospitable cities in the world. Many of them return again and again, some to make it their home, recognizing the truth of the claim it makes: Kansas City is one of the most livable cities in the nation.

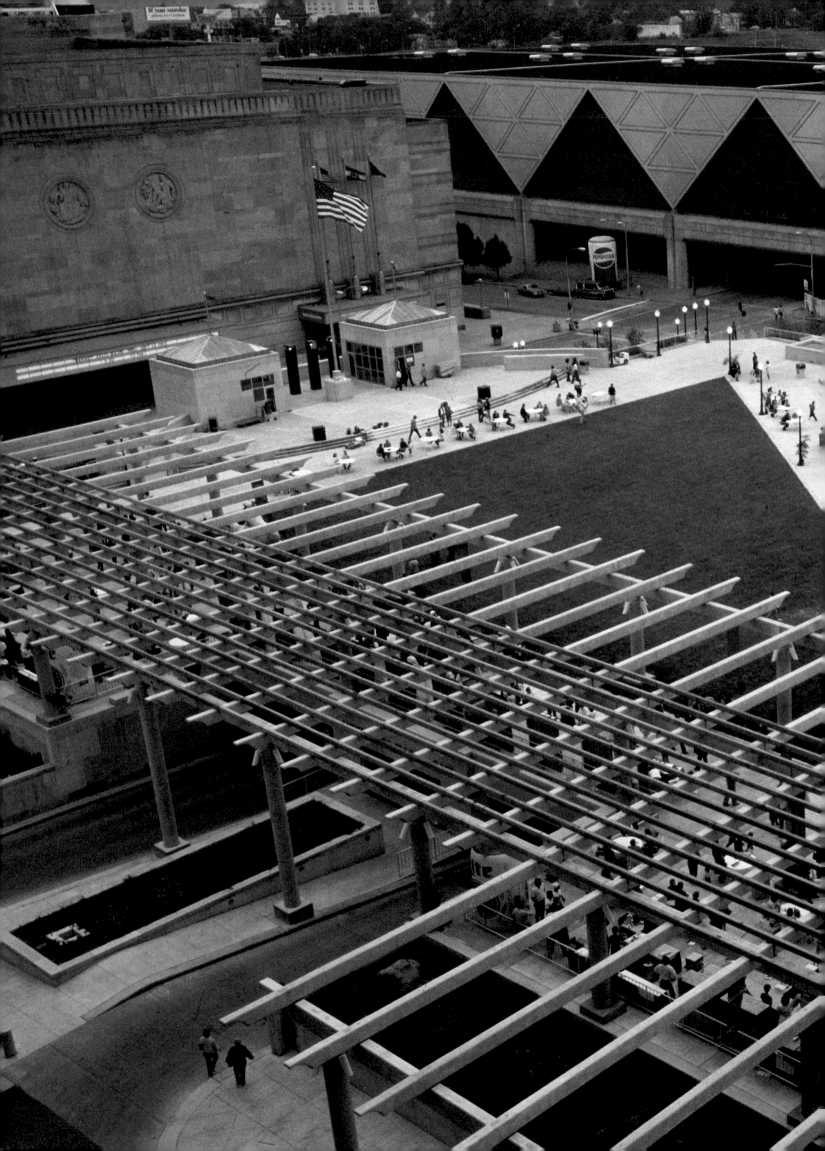

Above: Football is the
name of the game when
the Kansas City Chiefs battle other National Football
League teams at Arrow-
head Stadium. Photo
by Hank Young/Young
Company

Opposite: Many Kansas
Citians take to the skies as
the heady sport of hot-air
ballooning increases in
popularity each year.
Photo by Bruce Mathews

# EPILOGUE: THE KANSAS CITY SPIRIT

Fireworks and bands, crowds and celebrations—the Spirit Festival—come to mind these days when people talk about the Kansas City spirit. There was a time, though, when the phrase recalled not fireworks but fire—raging flames that threatened to destroy the city's greatest promise.

The building that stood at Thirteenth and Central in 1900 is long gone, but its story will live as long as the city does. Henry C. Haskell and Richard B. Fowler told it best in *City of the Future* as they recounted the opening of Kansas City's Convention Hall in 1899 and the city fathers' coup in luring the July 4, 1900, Democratic national convention here.

"The men of this town among the clay banks had the unblushing nerve to make their bid for one of the two biggest political events in the country. They sang the praises of their new hall before the paint was dry, pulled political wires and beat their drums in competition with such established cities as Chicago, Cincinnati, and Milwaukee . . . it worked. Raw, sprawling Kansas City took the promise of the convention out from under the noses of its rivals just as it had grabbed the railroads in other years . . . Because of [the Convention Hall] Kansas City was to make itself a center of events in the West and a city to be recognized by the nation."

Just ninety days before the Democratic national convention was due to open, on April 4, 1900, a fire broke out in Convention Hall. The fire bells rang at 1 p.m.; by 1:15 p.m., the conflagration was so intense that the onlooking crowd saw the hall's steel girders curl up and collapse in the flames. Two years' work had just gone up in smoke. It took a year to raise the money for the structure and another year to build it.

It was time for the city's hopes to roll over and die—except that this was Kansas City. Circulating among the crowd were the city boosters who had labored so hard to bring the town to national notice. They were quietly taking pledges for subscriptions to rebuild the hall in ninety days.

*Opposite: A dazzling fireworks display is the grand climax of Kansas City's Spirit Festival, held annually on the Fourth of July. Photo by Keith Kreeger/Mathews Communications*

That evening, *The Kansas City Star* carried the news that the new Convention Hall had been destroyed . . . and that nearly 100 donors had already pledged money to rebuild it.

"The 90-day building job was a triumph of inspired human effort," Haskell and Fowler wrote. "Kansas Citians went directly to the heads of the steel and lumber companies. They went to the presidents of the railroads to make sure of fast transportation. Guards rode with shipments of steel to break through any delays. Normally easygoing workmen set themselves a terrific pace. And the job moved ahead twenty-four hours a day, seven days a week.

The night of July 3 the workmen moved out and the next morning the bunting and flags were in place. For visiting newspapermen the Kansas City comeback was a more exciting story than the expected nomination of William Jennings Bryan.

"'Kansas City spirit' was more than a boasting phrase. Tested by fire Kansas City was ready to celebrate the new century . . . None of [the] . . . civic leaders doubted that it was to be Kansas City's own personal century."

In the nearly ninety years that have passed since that Fourth of July, the Kansas City spirit has been tested by almost every element of nature and invention of mankind. It has weathered floods and tornadoes, economic depressions and political upheavals. Each time it has emerged stronger than ever.

It began more than a century ago, when Kansas City was a few frame buildings on a couple of muddy roads by the river. When the present downtown was timberland, Crown Center was a rocky bluff, the Country Club Plaza was a swampy bottoms, and College Boulevard was buffalo

*Above: The inimitable blues singer Ida McBeth performs onstage during the annual Kansas City Spirit Festival. Photo by Hank Young/Young Company*

*Above, left: The Kansas City Spirit is alive and well every Fourth of July when the entire community takes part in the event that has become a tradition. Photo by Bruce Mathews*

*Opposite: Fireworks, food, bands, entertainment and more brings Kansas Citians together to celebrate the Kansas City Spirit Festival. Photo by Bruce Mathews*

*This page and opposite: Youngsters know a good time is in order when they help join in the fun at the Spirit Festival, held annually on the grounds of the Liberty Memorial. Photos by Bruce Mathews*

prairie, Kansas City's greatest futurist, Charles Carroll Spalding, made this promise:

"Sometime, perhaps in fifty years or less, this nation will be numbering one hundred million people. One-fourth of this population will then be living east of the Mississippi, and three-fourths of them west of it, and this side of the Rocky Mountains. Kansas City will then occupy the commercial and geographical centre of that immense population. . . . Kansas City, with her river commerce, her railway system, her interior commerce, her mineral wealth, her climate, her empire of soil, producing grain, staples, fruits, vines . . . and finally, with her geography, making her the commercial centre of the Rocky Mountain and Mississippi Empire, may we not with some degree of assurance say, that it is her destiny to become the extreme western and central commercial emporium of mountain, prairie, and river commerce."

In this century, famed illustrator Norman Rockwell portrayed the spirit of Kansas City as a vigorous man rolling up his shirtsleeves, ready to get to work. He holds the plans for the city's future in his hands, and his eyes seem fixed on a distant horizon. Over the years, the vision changes, but the spirit remains the same. The people of Kansas City have always believed in the city's promise, and the promise—no matter how big, no matter how seemingly impossible—has always come true.

# PATRONS

The following individuals, companies, and organizations have made a valuable commitment to the quality of this publication. Windsor Publications and the Chamber of Commerce of Greater Kansas City, the Convention and Visitors Bureau of Greater Kansas City, the Kansas City Area Economic Development Council, and the Kansas City Corporation for Industrial Development gratefully acknowledge their participation in *Kansas City: The Spirit, The People, The Promise.*

Alexander & Alexander*
AT&T
Baird, Kurtz & Dobson*
Baptist Medical Center*
Better Business Bureau of Greater
  Kansas City
Black & Veatch*
Blackwell Sanders Matheny Weary and
  Lombardi*
Blue Cross and Blue Shield of Kansas
  City*
Boylan & Company*
Bucher, Willis & Ratliff*
Builders Block Co.
Burns & McDonnell*
George Butler Associates, Inc.*
Charter American Mortgage Company
Clarkson Construction Company*
Consolidated Freightways*
Cook Paint and Varnish Company*
Doubletree Hotel*
ECB
Employers Reinsurance Corporation*
Executive Hills Inc.*
Faultless Starch/Bon Ami Company*
Fleming Companies, Inc.*
James C. French Agency
  Equitable Financial Companies
Gann Enterprises
H&R Block, Inc.*
Howard Needles Tammen & Bergendoff*
Humana Hospital-Overland Park*
Independence Regional Health Center*
William Jewell College*
The Kansas Institute*
Laventhol & Horwath*
Linscott, Haylett, Wimmer & Wheat,
  P.C.*
Evelyn Maes
Mid-America Car, Inc.*
Missouri Public Service*

Mobay Corporation*
Morris, Larson, King & Stamper, P.C.*
National Fidelity Life Insurance
  Company*
N.C.S. Precision Manufacturing
J.C. Nichols Company*
North Kansas City Hospital*
Patty Berkebile Nelson Immenschuh
  Architects*
Peat Marwick Main & Co.*
JCPenney
Pfizer Inc.
Reimer and Koger Associates, Inc.
Reorganized Church of Jesus Christ of
  Latter Day Saints*
Research Medical Center*
Russell Stover® Candies*
Safeway Stores, Incorporated/Super
  Food Barn*
Saint Joseph Hospital*
St. Luke's Hospital*
St. Mary's Hospital*
Shook, Hardy & Bacon*
Stinson, Mag & Fizzell*
Stratco, Inc.*
J.A. Tobin Construction Company*
Trinity Lutheran Hospital*
TWA Credit Union
United Missouri Bank of Kansas City,
  n.a.*
United Telecommunications, Inc.*
The University of Health Sciences*
University of Kansas Medical Center*
University of Missouri-Kansas City*
Via Express Delivery Systems, Incorporated of Greater Kansas City
Western Missouri Mental Health Center
  and the Greater Kansas City Mental
  Health Foundation*
Yellow Freight System, Inc.*
The Zimmer Companies*

*Corporate profiles of *Kansas City: The Spirit, The People, The Promise.* The histories of these companies and organizations appear throughout the book.

# SELECTED BIBLIOGRAPHY

## BOOKS

Bodine, Walt, and Thomas, Tracy. *Right Here in River City.* Garden City: Doubleday Publishing Co., 1976.

Brown, A. Theodore, and Dorsett, Lyle W. *K.C.: A History of Kansas City.* Boulder: Pruett Publishing Company, 1978.

Bryant, Keith L., Jr. *Arthur E. Stilwell.* Nashville: Vanderbilt University Press, 1971.

Dorsett, Lyle W. *The Pendergast Machine.* New York: Oxford University Press, 1972.

Garreau, Joel. *The Nine Nations of North America.* New York: Avon Books, 1982.

Garwood, Darrell. *Crossroads of America.* New York: W.W. Norton, 1948.

Hagen, Harry M. *The Complete Missouri Travel Guide.* Missouri Publishing Co., 1984.

Haskell, Henry C. Jr. and Richard B. Fowler. *City of the Future.* Kansas City: Frank Glenn Publishing Co., Inc., 1950.

Landmarks Commission of Kansas City, Missouri. *Kansas City—A Place in Time.* Kansas City: 1977.

Miller, Patricia Cleary. *Westport.* Kansas City: Lowell Press, 1983.

Reddig, William M. *Tom's Town.* Philadelphia and New York: J.B. Lippincott Company, 1947.

Russell, Ross. *Jazz Style in Kansas City and the Southwest.* Berkeley and Los Angeles: University of California Press, 1973.

Sandy, Wilda. *Here Lies Kansas City.* Kansas City: Bennett Schneider, Inc., 1984.

Schirmer, Sherry Lamb and Richard D. McKinzie. *At the River's Bend.* Woodland Hills, CA: Windsor Publications, 1982.

Spalding, C.C. *Annals of the City of Kansas and the Great Western Plains.* Kansas City: Van Horn & Abeel's Printing House, 1850, facsimile edition Frank Glenn Publishing Company, 1950.

## OTHER SOURCES

Board of Trade of Kansas City, Mo., Inc.
The Chamber of Commerce of Greater Kansas City
*City Magazine*
Convention and Visitors Bureau of Kansas City, Inc.
Corporate Report/Kansas City
Kansas City Area Economic Development Council
*Kansas City Business Journal*
*The Kansas City Star*
*The Kansas City Times*
Missouri Valley Room (vertical files) - Kansas City Public Library
National Geographic Society

*The Harry S. Truman Library and Museum, the first institution of its kind in the country, is home to thousands of important documents of the Truman era. Photo by Bob Barrett*

# INDEX

Annunciation, 241
Green, Jeffrey, *170*
Green, L.K., 190
Green, Ralph J., 190
Green, Richard C., 190
Green Ridge Office Park, *191*
Greene, Dr. John Priest, 217
Guadalupe Center, 241

**H**
Hale, Steve, 154
Hall, Donald, 57, 164
Hall, Joyce C., 53
Hall Library of Science and Technology,
  Linda, 11, 251
Hallmark Cards, Inc., 11, 51, *51*, 53, 57
Hallmark Technology and Innovation
  Center, 63
H&R Block, Inc., 178, *178*
Hanson, Duane, 46
Harrell, A.J., 44
Harry's Heyday, 239
Hatfield, David 39
Hatfield, Mike, 39
Hatfield, Randolph, 39
Haylett, Ward H., Jr., 112, *112*
Heart of American Indian Center, 251
Heeter, James A., 49
*Helicon Nine,* 154
Hemingway, Ernest, 153
Hempy, Theodore, *170*
Henry, Dan, 154
Henson, Paul, 146-147
Herget, John, 217
Highland Games, 241
Hilton International Company, 143
Historic preservation, 69, 71, 74-75, 77,
  101
Hoerner, Jerold K., 177
"Hong Kong," 159
Hoover, Lynn C., 186-187
Horwath, Edmund J., 182
Horwath, Ernest B., 182
Hosler, Daniel M., 106
Hospitals, 176, 195-199, *198, 199,* 202-
  206, *202, 203, 204, 205, 207,* 208, *208,*
  212-214, *212, 213, 214,* 216, 218-219,
  *218, 219,* 222-223, *222,* 226-227, *226,*
  *227*
Hot-air ballooning, *257*
Hotels, 53, 57, 63, 71, 88, *88,* 93
House of Fabrics, 180
House, Stanley II., 102
Howard Needles Tammen & Bergendoff,
  80-81
Hughes, David H., 199
Humana Hospital-Overland Park, 206,
  208, *208*
Hung, Alice, 159
Hung, Jimmy, 159
Hunt Midwest Enterprises, Inc., 93, 145

Hutchinson, Jim, 252
Hyatt Regency Hotel, *35, 57*

**I**
Immenschuh, David, 90
Immigrants, 11, 159, 163
Independence, Missouri, 16, 28-29, 101
Independence Regional Health Center,
  204-205, *204, 205*
*Independent Magazine, The,* 154
Indians, 13, *16*
Industrial parks, 77, 79, *79,* 86, *86,* 93,
  107
Info Master, 145
Inland Storage and Distribution, 145
Insurance, 174-177, 183, *183,* 188-189,
  200-201, *200*
International Headquarters of the
  Church of the Nazarene, 251
International Transit and Storage, 145
Interstate highways, 91, 139

**J**
Jack Henry, 180
Jackson County Courthouse, *28*
James, Frank, 23
James, Jesse, 23, 26, 243, 245
James, Leland, 152
James Street Viaduct, *94*
Janus Capital Corporation, 34
Jazz, 11, 28, 231, *234, 235,* 236
Jensen-Salsbury Laboratories, 127
Jessee, Randall, 154
Jewell, William, 217
Jewell College, William, *194,* 211, 217,
  *217*
Jewish Federation and Council of
  Greater Kansas City, 251
"Job Fair," 155
Johnson, Sister Mary Frances, 203
Johnson County Community College, 79,
  211
Johnston, Eliza, 243
Johnston, Louisa, 19
Jonas, Matthew G., 167
Jones, Richard Bacon, 188, 189; sons of,
  *188*
Jones Store, 180
Judd, James B., 170, *170,* 171

**K**
Kaleidoscope, *53,* 57
Kansas City Area Economic Development
  Council, 164
Kansas City Art Institute, 28, 209, *210,*
  *211*
Kansas City Bolt and Nut Company, 28,
  39
*Kansas City Business Journal,* 153
*Kansas City Call, The,* 154
Kansas City Chiefs, 245, *256*

Kansas City College of Eclectic Medicine,
  195
Kansas City Comets, 245
Kansas City Community College, 211
Kansas City Community Opera, 238
Kansas City Corporation for Industrial
  Development, 36
Kansas City Downtown Airport, 28, *144*
Kansas City, Galveston & Lake Superior
  Railroad, 24
Kansas City International Airport, *80,*
  143, *106, 145*
Kansas City Jazz Commission, 231
Kansas City Jazz Festival, *235,* 236
Kansas City, Kansas, Memorial Hall,
  245
Kansas City Life, 176
Kansas City Museum, 243
Kansas City Public Library, 251
Kansas City Royals, 155, 245, *245*
Kansas City Southern Industries, Inc.,
  34, 37
Kansas City Southern Railway Company,
  34
"Kansas City Spirit" (Rockwell illustra-
  tion), *264*
*Kansas City Star, The,* 26, 154
*Kansas City Star and Times,* 153
Kansas City Stockyards Company, 25,
  125, 126
Kansas City Suburban Belt Railroad, 34
Kansas City Symphony Orchestra,
  238-239, *238*
Kansas City Theater League, 236
Kansas City Think Tank, 157
*Kansas City Times, The,* 26
Kansas City Youth for Christ Church,
  157
Kansas City Zoo, 11, *243*
Kansas Institute, The, 226-227, *226, 227*
Kansas Town Company, 17
Kauffman, Ewing, 176
Kaw River, *16*
KCPT, 157
KCTV, 155
KCUR-FM, 157
Keel, Ronald D., 223
Kemper, William T., 34, 192
Kemper, Rufus Crosby, Jr., 193, *193*
Kemper, Rufus Crosby, Sr., 192-193
Kemper Memorial Arena, Crosby, 128,
  *129,* 245
Kessler, George, 81
KFKB, 195
Kimball, Charles, 164
King, Edward J., Jr., 37
King Radio Corporation, 37, 39
Kingsley, Dr. James Gordon, 217
Kingston Construction Company, 101
Kirk, Andy, 231
KMBC, 155, 157